Play
Poker
Like the
Pros

Play Poker Like the Pros

Phil Hellmuth, Jr.

HarperResource

An Imprint of HarperCollins*Publishers*

For my parents, Lynn and Phil, who helped me believe I could do anything and who supported me even after they freaked out over my newfound occupation.

To Grandma Aggie, who loved a good game of cards.

Photograph on page 395 © ultimatebet.com

HarperCollins books may be purchased for educational, business, or sales promotional use. For information please write: Special Markets Department, HarperCollins Publishers Inc., 10 East 53rd Street, New York, NY 10022.

FIRST EDITION

Designed by William Ruoto

Library of Congress Cataloging-in-Publication Data has been applied for.

ISBN 0-06-000572-6

07 WBC/RRD 36 35 34

Contents

Acknowledgments

Thanks to my amazing wife, Kathy, for supporting me as I travel around the world playing poker for a living. Thanks to my children, Phillip III and Nick, for putting up with Daddy's line, "Don't talk to me while I write my book." Thanks to Andy Glazer, who was the single biggest help to me in writing and editing this book. Andy gave me two weeks of full-time help with this book and made it much better—and much more readable. In fact, Andy's fingerprints are all over this book. Thanks to Jason Karl for the illustrations and charts that he created. Thanks to Annie Duke for reading and editing Chapter 14. Thanks to Jon Karl for smoothing out Chapter 15. Thanks to University Coffee Cafe in Palo Alto for putting up with me while I wrote for six hours a day for two months. A special thanks to my agent Sheree Bykofsky and my editor Matthew Benjamin for having faith in me and believing that I could finish this book.

Introduction: How to Learn to Play Poker

By Andrew N. S. Glazer

Professional Poker Player, *Card Player Magazine*
Tournament Poker Editor and weekly gambling
columnist for the *Detroit Free Press*

Phil Hellmuth, Jr., a seven-time winner of the World Series of Poker, has put together a powerhouse of a book—the culmination of more than 17 years of tournament play. *Play Poker Like the Pros* will teach you how to play and win the most popular casino and family poker games.

Phil begins by laying out how to set up and play each game and then moves on to explain basic and advanced strategy for each game. Phil teaches exactly which hands to play, when to bluff, when to call a bluff, when to raise, and when to fold. He demonstrates how to play against a mouse (a timid player), a jackal (a crazy player), and an elephant (a player who always calls). In addition, Phil provides priceless strategies for reading other players and being patient and cool under pressure.

Depending on how good you already are, how much poker you play or want to play, and how high the stakes are that you play for or want to play for, this book could help win you thousands of dollars.

How to Read *Play Poker Like the Pros*

In order to use any poker book effectively, even this one, and before risking lots of hard-earned dollars at the tables, the reader probably should understand the following:

1. Your reading process should be active, not passive. By "active," I mean that you shouldn't read the book the way you might read a novel, hurrying on through because the book excites you so much that you want to get to what promises to be a dazzling conclusion. If you read or skim *Play Poker Like the Pros*, the lessons may make sense as you're reading them, but you're extremely unlikely to remember them; and even if you remember them, you're unlikely to be able to apply them successfully at the tables, because every hand is different, and subtle changes in circumstances can easily change the correct approach to a situation.

Instead, as you read *Play Poker Like the Pros*, you should move more slowly than you'd probably prefer, and you should ask yourself questions about what you've just read. Could you explain it to someone else? If the situation changed slightly, what effect might that have on the advice? What if the stakes were higher or lower, your opponents were stronger or weaker, you were tired or sharp, your table image of tight or loose had changed because of the way you'd played some recent hands, you did or didn't have any knowledge of how your opponents played (or vice versa)? The list is almost endless. In poker, context is king, and you need to take the time to consider various contexts.

Although Phil offers numerous examples and demo hands throughout the book, if you can stop and try to think of another hand while you're reading, and discern how the advice you've just read might affect how you play that hand, you will learn a great deal from *Play Poker Like the Pros*.

2. Don't try to do too much at once. Although you might enjoy *Play Poker Like the Pros* so much that you want to read it cover to cover from the first moment you pick it up, you'll be asking too much of yourself, unless you plan to go back and reread individual sections carefully. Phil covers a lot of territory in this book, and it's just not possible to absorb it all in one sitting, even if that sitting is an "active" one.

Just how you break the book down is up to you and your current level of understanding poker. You might want to read all the hold'em material in one day, or you might move much more slowly. You're the one who knows your capabilities. Trust your judgment.

3. Don't assume that an introductory section or chapter is "beneath" you, just because you're an experienced poker player. You might be surprised at some of the matters Phil Hellmuth considers introductory. If you're already a hotshot, you can probably move through introductory sections pretty quickly, but you're doing yourself a disservice if you just skip them.

4. If possible, try to integrate your "book learning" (as the old pros disdainfully call it) into your game by alternating active reading with playing. Until you take what you read here and try to apply it in a real game with money at stake, you can't really be sure that you've learned what you think you've learned.

It wouldn't hurt that integration process one bit if you applied a bit of scientific method to your poker experiments. By this I mean that using a control base in your experiments will allow you to understand what sort of effect your experiments are having on your results. Perhaps the best control base you can use is integration of new concepts one at a time. For example, suppose that in reading the intermediate hold'em chapter, you come across seven fairly major new ways of thinking about the game. If you try to apply them to your game all at once, it's going to be difficult for you to understand which of these new approaches is helping you (or for that matter, which of them you even understand). If you add one at a time, it will be easier for you to see how that one change affects your results.

You shouldn't carry this piece of advice too far, however, because it's likely that you will encounter hundreds of new concepts in *Play Poker Like the Pros*, and if your plan is to integrate one new concept for each playing session, you will be investing too much money in too many poker games without enough weapons in your bag of tricks. You can try something new for half an hour, or if the changes are relatively minor, you can probably try several new ones simultaneously. Just don't change everything about the way you play all at once, or you won't have any idea of what changes are working, or why.

Incorporating seven major changes in your game simultaneously might well improve your results, but it could be that five of the changes are helping and two are hurting, because you aren't applying them correctly. If that happened, your results would improve, but not as much as if you could figure out which changes are helping and which aren't. If a change isn't helping, you might want to reread the section, or you might simply decide that this is one case where what works for Phil doesn't work for you.

5.   Try to focus on one particular game, especially at first. While there's nothing wrong (and indeed there is much right) with reading *Play Poker Like the Pros* from cover to cover, you will probably find it much easier to improve your play if you decide (or if the supply of local games decides for you) to specialize in one game before you try to master all of them. Most people have a finite amount of time they can invest in studying poker, and you'll probably find that it's easier to try to master games one at a time. There's nothing wrong with playing other games occasionally (and if you're a home game, "dealer's choice" player, you won't be able to approach the learning process any other way), but focusing your study on one game will make it much easier to learn and remember subtle nuances of that game.

Ultimately, though, you will probably need to learn more than one game. Kitchen poker is usually dealer's choice, and the higher-stakes side games tend to involve rotation from one game to another. There is also a bit of cross-training advantage to playing multiple games. You might easily achieve an epiphany about hold'em while playing seven-card stud, as the difference between the two games teaches you an important lesson.

6.   Don't make this the only poker book you ever read. I have a certain natural bias about the value of *Play Poker Like the Pros*, but unless you're a Hellmuth-type savant, there's other reading

you should be doing. It's impossible to cover everything you need to know about poker in one book, and there are a number of other superb books available to you. By the time you've read and absorbed *Play Poker Like the Pros*, you'll know enough about poker to be able to recognize the difference between a good poker book and a bad one, and unfortunately—in large part owing to the large number of self-published books on the market—there are a lot of bad ones out there. Don't automatically reject a self-published book just because it's self-published, because some of them are excellent, but it can be a red flag.

7.   Pick the right stake level for your practice games. If you're a millionaire and want to learn poker so that you can eventually play high-stakes poker against your millionaire buddies, it probably doesn't make much sense to play $2 to $4 poker while you're learning. Low-stakes and high-stakes poker games tend to create very different impressions about what kind of hand it takes to win: in low-stakes games, it's common, though not universal, for large numbers of players to remain in a hand for a long period of time, meaning that it will usually take a fairly strong hand to win the pot.

If you are not a millionaire but plan to play for medium stakes eventually, it just makes good economic sense to play in lower-stakes games when you are starting out, so that you can begin to develop a feel for the ebb and flow of the game and how certain hands tend to develop into other kinds of hands. You'll also lose less during the learning process.

8.   Don't beat yourself up for mistakes you make while you're learning. Almost as important, don't let other players intimidate

you with sharp criticism of your play. There's an immense difference between the combination of education and experience and one's intelligence. An inexperienced player is not an idiot. Everyone has to start somewhere. If you let either self-criticism or other players' criticism destroy your self-confidence, you're probably doomed as a poker player, because confidence is a key to success. Remain open to constructive criticism, and remain open to learning, but don't let yourself or anyone else destroy your potential with sharp words.

9.   Rereading is not a sign of weakness or a low IQ! As you start integrating what you read in *Play Poker Like the Pros* (or, for that matter, any other good poker book) with actual practice with money on the line, it makes excellent sense to return to your source material and reread a section, a chapter, or even the entire book.

There are numerous poker books I have read several times, and I almost always find that I spot or learn things on the second, third, or fourth reading that I didn't get the first time around, sometimes because I didn't have the experience base to understand what the author was trying to teach me, and sometimes because my own game had grown so much in the interim that advice that was good for me at one stage of my career was not good for me at a later stage.

If you do find yourself eventually surpassing your teachers (and good luck trying to surpass Phil!), congratulations, and don't forget the immortal words of Sir Isaac Newton: *"If I have seen further than others, it is because I have stood on the shoulders of Giants."* Phil Hellmuth is indeed a poker giant, and that leads me to my last point about how to use this or indeed any poker book.

10. In the end, you have to find your own style. Phil Hellmuth is one of the greatest poker players who has ever lived, but a lot of what makes him great simply cannot be taught. He can play hands that other players, even other great players, cannot, because he has an ability to "read" how strong or weak his opponents are. We spend a lot of time trying to teach you about how to read opponents in the book, but at Phil's level, some of what he can do borders on a sixth sense. Learn what you can from *Play Poker Like the Pros*, but in the final analysis, you will have to understand yourself, your strengths, your weaknesses, your motivations for playing, and just how serious you want to be about what is, after all, a game, albeit one that can be highly profitable (or costly).

Phil has given you a very useful tool in *Play Poker Like the Pros*, but when it comes time to push the chips into the pot, *you're* the artist, and unless you play a style that you're comfortable with, you won't win. Use the tool he's given you wisely, and you can become your own kind of master craftsman. To me, that sounds a lot more fulfilling than trying to be an imitator, and it's far more likely to be successful, too.

A Note to Beginners

Although the table of contents lists what you will be able to find in *Play Poker Like the Pros*, you may not yet be advanced enough in your studies to understand what the chapter headings mean. What Phil has done is break down the most important, most commonly played games in the modern poker world, and then offer information about each of them. While beginners will learn more than intermediate or advanced players, simply because they have much more to learn, every poker player alive will find something useful in this book. Even if you're a superior professional player, you'll learn more about Phil's game, and if you want to win titles at the World Series, the road to those titles often must pass through Hellmuth.

Beginners can help themselves by taking advantage of the material in the appendixes, particularly Appendix 1, and the Glossary. When an author is assembling a book for players at various levels of experience, it's awkward to stop and define every phrase or term. The more experienced players don't want that kind of format, and by the time you reread *Play Poker Like the Pros* (and I think you'll find yourself doing so every few years) you won't want it either. Nonetheless, the basic definitions and rankings are here, for those of you who need them.

One thing you may notice is that there is a relatively large amount of material about Texas Hold'em, usually referred to just as "Hold'em." There are two reasons for this. First, Hold'em has become far and away the most popular casino and card-room form of poker. That's where most of the games are, and this means that's where most of the money is. Second, many poker concepts apply across the board, from one game to another, but need to be explained in the context of a specific game. Because Hold'em is the most popular game, Phil chose to explain many of these general principles within the sections on Hold'em.

The other games covered in detail are Omaha and Seven-Card Stud. These are the next two most popular games, and you can find them in many variations. Many home games are based on Seven-Card Stud, and learning the general principles here will help you adapt to the incalculable number of bizarre "dealer's choice" games found in basements and at kitchen tables around the world.

The Universe Conspired to Help

The man had a dream
He knew what he wanted, it seems

Once he was sure in his heart this was it
He vowed someday that he would achieve it

He wasn't quite ready to do his thing
But he felt fairly certain what the
future would bring

When one day the time was right
When he was ready to fight the good fight

He conquered all his excuses and set forth
To take the risk-fraught first step
without any remorse

Once he took the first step down the line
The universe conspired to help make sure
he was fine

He never dreamed he would accomplish so much
That the universe would give him such
incredible luck

Now older and wiser he understood the hardest part
Was convincing himself that it was time to start.

—Phil Hellmuth

Chapter 1

Skill versus Luck
in Poker

Most people today misunderstand poker. Let's be frank: most people know poker from the low-stakes games they now play (or grew up playing) with their family and friends. In these low-stakes home games, luck often plays a much bigger role than skill.

The money to be gained or lost in a home tends to mean next to nothing, and everyone at the table plays almost every hand to the end. The dealer's choice games are often nonstandard, even bizarre variations (often fun) where, for example, deuces, black kings, or one-eyed jacks (or all of them) are wild. In this type of poker game, people just put their money in the middle (in the "pot") and hope to make the best hand. Often, there doesn't seem to be much strategy or thought involved. When the evening winds up, everyone seems to agree that "Johnny sure was hot tonight!" You don't hear anyone saying, "Boy, did Johnny play great tonight. I sure am afraid of *him* at the poker table."

One reason why luck has such a big role in home-style poker games is that many of the skills we use in pro-style games just don't come into play in a home game. For example, three of the more important skills that we use are being patient in determining which starting hands to play, bluffing, and reading people. Patience, like discipline, is a virtue in many areas of life, and poker is no exception. It is in the nature of professional or tough high-stakes poker games that it is mathematically correct to fold a lot of hands right away. If you are playing too many hands (which equates to too many *bad* hands) in a tough poker game, you will often find yourself "drawing mighty thin," that is, trying to win by catching particular cards that are in short supply.

The plain fact is that if you play too many hands in a pro-level poker game, you just cannot win, certainly not in the long run and probably not even on just one given night, no matter how lucky you are. But if you're playing a lot of hands in a home poker game, you may be in good shape anyway, because the sheer size of the pot will wind up offering you odds sufficient to draw to an inside straight (add a nine, for example, to your 7-8-10-J hand) or another "unlikely to hit" hand. You'll usually lose, but when you do manage to hit the card you need, you're going to win a huge pot.

Further, the number of cards that can complete what you need in the late rounds of a hand in a home game is often larger than one sees in the pro game, because the dealer has designated various wild cards or rules that allow you extra draws or give you chances to buy another card or replace a card.

Because you don't see these big pots and people paying you off with weak hands in a pro poker game, patience is crucial there. In the traditional home-style poker games, patience not only is not as important but may actually clash with the "spirit" of the game—that "We're all here just to have fun and gamble." Playing a more technically informed style may win you more money in a home game, but it might also mean that you're not invited back the next time the game is held! In a casino poker game or an online poker game, of course, you don't need to be concerned that you might not be invited back.

Another key difference between home poker games and the games that the pros play is that bluffing actually succeeds in the pro-style games! In a home game, it's extremely hard to pull off a bluff, because you usually can't bet enough money on the last bet to get your opponents to fold. For 25 cents, someone who is convinced he is beaten is nonetheless willing to throw the two bits into the pot, just to see what you have, and, oops, there goes your attempted bluff. In fact, in most situations in these home games where there is a "bet on the end" (in the last round of action in a given hand), someone is always egging someone else on to be the "sheriff." "Bill, you call that boy and be the sheriff this hand! We can't let him bluff us!"

In the pro game, bluffing is a sound strategy, because in the late stages of a hand there aren't many people who haven't folded. If you've been playing very few hands (that is, patiently), and have seldom been *caught* bluffing during a day of play, then when you *do* bluff, it's hard for those remaining in the hand to "call you down" through the last bet. Long live the bluff! Bluffing well is an art form, and I will be addressing it at various points throughout this book. The bluff is one of the poker craftsman's tools that is seldom available to players in wild, friendly, low-stakes games.

Another important element in pro poker games is reading

your opponents. Are they riding on "hot air" or the real thing? In a lot of home games, there is just so much money in the pot, relative to the size of the final bet, that it makes sense to call that bet. (What do you have to lose?) In pro poker, there is enough money involved, and enough actual thought processes are being utilized, that many situations come up where you can take advantage of a good read—which might arise either from your ability to detect weakness or strength in body language or from your ability to assess the implications of the betting pattern on the hand—and make either a good call or a good fold. But it's hard to read someone who hasn't really been thinking about the hand and can't possibly be nervous about losing $1.75! The skill factor in poker is much higher in the pro game. There is just too much at stake for anyone to rely solely on luck.

Let's take a quick glimpse at the high-stakes poker world, an enterprise that yields several of my friends over a million dollars a year! At this level, too, luck is a factor on any given day, week, or month, but what's different is that if you play better poker than your opponents do, pretty consistently, you'll find that over almost any *two*-month period your winnings have exceeded your losses. Furthermore, if you play better poker than your opponents over a *six*-month period, your results will have moved very solidly in the winning direction. Making a few well-timed bluffs each day will add up to a lot of money each year!

In fact, if an inexperienced poker player were to sit down for a few hours with a group of world-class poker players, he would have virtually no chance to win over even an eight-hour period. This very fact is why five or six top pros might be willing to sit down in the same game with this fellow and each other: the money that even one amateur is likely to contribute makes it worth their while to do battle with so many respected opponents.

This is why so many of the top poker players today drive fine cars and live in palatial homes. Right now, as you're reading this book, there is a $600–$1,200-limit poker game at the Bellagio Casino in Las Vegas and a $400–$800-limit poker game at the Commerce Casino in Los Angeles. There is a $200–$400-limit poker game in Tunica, Mississippi; a $100–$200-limit game at the Taj Mahal in Atlantic City; and a $200–$400-limit game somewhere in New York City. They're playing no-limit poker in San Francisco at the Lucky Chances Casino and high-stakes pot-limit poker in London at the Grosvenor Victoria ("The Vic") and in Paris at the Aviation Club de France. In Vienna, at the Concorde Card Casino, they're playing $75–$150 Seven-Card Stud. (I'll have more to say about these two-figure games in Chapter 2.)

If that's not enough action for you, four nights a week in Los Angeles, there is a $2,000–$4,000-limit Seven-Card Stud game at Larry Flynt's Hustler Club Casino, with Larry himself often playing. In the $400–$800-limit poker game it's easy to take a $25,000 swing in one hour. In the $2,000–$4,000-limit game, where movie stars, former governors, and billionaires play, it's not uncommon for someone to win or lose $250,000 in one night. In these "nosebleed" poker games (the term refers to the altitude of the stakes), strategy, discipline, calculation of the odds, and practiced observation contribute to a game that involves much more skill. Better play wins more hands in the long run.

Imagine yourself facing down Larry Flynt in the $2,000–$4,000 Seven-Card Stud game at the Hustler Club Casino.

You're sitting there trying to figure out if he has a strong hand or is full of hot air (bluffing). If you decide right, you will win $25,000, but if you're wrong, it will cost you $25,000. What do you do? You make a good read—of the situation, of the odds, of your opponent—and make an educated guess, rather than a plain old boldfaced guess! The chief difference between your home poker game and the games of the big players is the preponderance of luck in the one and the preponderance of skill in the other. In a game (the Flynt game) where winning just one $4,000 bet a night would mean an income of $16,000 per week (this game runs four days a week), one carefully earned bet can make a great deal of difference.

That's the way things look into the high-stakes "side game" world at large, but there is even more evidence that skill is present and important in high-stakes poker tournaments today. (When I say "side-game" world, I mean the nontournament poker world.) Why do the same people, by and large, keep winning poker tournaments year after year? They win because they apply finely honed strategies and tactics, calculate and recalculate the odds, read their opponents well, avoid becoming predictable, and know how and when to make a good bluff.

Some of the most famous poker players in the world today have made their names in poker tournaments. Doyle "Texas Dolly" Brunson has eight bracelets (titles) from the World Series of Poker (WSOP) at age 66. I have seven, and so does Johnny "The Oriental Express" Chan. "Amarillo Slim" Preston—whose name is known even to the general public—has four or five WSOP titles, depending, as Slim himself would say, on "who does the telling."

I'm proud to say that I was the all-time leading money

winner in WSOP history in 2001, having won more than $2,800,000. (Unfortunately for me, Johnny Chan and T. J. Cloutier both passed me in 2002. But there is no one within $600,000 of the three of us.) As I write this in 2002, only six people have won more than $2 million in their WSOP "careers" (that is, on the all-time list); and Johnny Chan just crossed the $3 million mark in 2002. (He beat me there! But I'll win the race to $7 million!) Although the same people don't win *all* the poker tournaments, by the time year's end rolls around, the same people always seem to end up having won several tournaments, year in and year out. This is one of the appealing aspects of poker tournaments: the record is out there for everyone to see; some players are consistently successful, and others are not. (The side games, though very lucrative, keep no records.)

If serious poker were a game where luck predominated, this would not and could not happen. Everyone involved would win about the same number of tournaments as everyone else (as tends to happen in slot tournaments or craps tournaments), and no one would make (or lose) any serious money. But that's not what years and years of proven, recorded results show.

One last note: Beware of playing in the small stakes poker games in Las Vegas or other casinos. No matter how good you are it is very hard to beat the "rake" (the money that is taken out of every pot each hand). It's best to avoid the $2-$4 limit games and below, and watch the rake--if it seems like it's too much, then play with shorter money in a higher limit game that is beatable.

Chapter 2

Texas Hold'em:
Setup and Basic Play

This chapter will introduce you to Texas Hold'em, commonly referred to as "Hold'em," the most popular poker game in the world today. The chapter should teach you enough to allow you to sit down and play the game without needing to ask your fellow players a lot of what feel like embarrassing questions. (Beginners, by the way, shouldn't feel embarrassed about asking questions; everyone has to start somewhere.) Later chapters will guide you through the subtleties of beginning, intermediate, and advanced strategy.

Learning the basic structure, or format, of Texas Hold'em (Hold'em) is easy. This doesn't mean, though, that there isn't a great deal of strategy involved: there is. But the way the game is constructed is fairly simple, compared with a game like chess, where you must learn how to move many different pieces, or even compared with many wild home poker games, where the rules for a game often take way too long to explain. ("Seven-

Card Stud, threes and nines are wild, but if you catch a three face up you must match the size of the pot to keep the card or else fold. You can buy an extra card on the end for $20 or replace a card on the end for $10, and if you catch a four face up you get an extra card free.")

If you were to walk into a card room or a friend's house to play Texas Hold'em, and hadn't seen Hold'em before, you would want some explanation. But once you understand the pattern of the deal, whose turn it is to bet, how much that player can bet, and what all of the options are (*checking, calling, betting, raising,* and *folding*) during the play of a hand, then you'll have a solid foundation for understanding the basic strategy tips you'll find in the later chapters. After reading (and absorbing) this chapter, you'll be able to introduce Hold'em into your own Saturday night poker game, although I wouldn't recommend playing it for much money until you've learned some strategy!

The Role of the Dealer

In most poker games, including Texas Hold'em, the deal rotates clockwise. When you're playing at home, you simply change dealers after each hand, moving the deal around the table clockwise, one player to the next, but in a casino there is a professional dealer at the table who deals every hand. The dealer will shuffle, deal, keep the bets right, and help control the tempo of the game. A good dealer will keep things moving, both by dealing quickly and reliably and by diplomatically encouraging action from the slower players.

The Role of the Button: Whose Deal Is It?

In "casino-style" Hold'em, the dealer uses a white plastic puck roughly 2 inches in diameter, called the *button*, to indicate who the dealer would be if the game were being played without a professional dealer. Usually, the puck has the word "dealer" printed on each side. Instead of simply passing the deck one player to the left after each hand, as you do in home poker games, you sit still while the professional dealer moves the button one spot to the left after each hand, and then deals. Why bother with this step? For one thing, no one has to wonder, or ask, whose deal it is. More important, the "dealer" (the player sitting behind the button) acts last in Hold'em in each round of betting and thus has a significant positional advantage, because (among other things) that player has more information available to him when it's his turn to bet than the players who had to act first. The use of the button ensures that each player—though never actually dealing the cards—gets a chance to enjoy that advantageous position once in each round of hands. And of course with eight or more players at the table, next-to-last is a pretty good spot to be in too.

The button also enables us to determine the order of play for each hand. The player seated to the left of the button acts first (except on the very first betting round), and the player who owns the button acts last (with that same first-round exception). We turn to those exceptions next. By the way, I recommend that you use a button even when you're playing Hold'em in your home poker game, and dealers are truly dealing. It helps remind people who dealt, and whose turn it is to deal next, and I think it also makes for an easier transition to casino Hold'em.

The Two "Blinds" to the Left of the Button

Before the first round of betting, and before any cards are dealt, those first two players, directly to the left of the button, post (place in front of them) what we call the *blinds*. We call these the "blind" bets because those two players must invest them in the pot, in preset amounts, before they can look at any cards. Immediately after the button, we have the *small blind*, which is usually, but not always, set at half the size of the next blind, which is called the *big blind*.

    The size of the blinds is determined by the size of the game. The small blind is usually half a small bet, and the big blind is usually a full small bet. In a hypothetical $2–$4 game, the small blind would be $1 and the big blind $2. Limit Hold'em games are thus defined by their bet sizes. For example, you might play $2–$4 Hold'em, or $10–$20 Hold'em, or whatever. In the $2–$4 game, all bets and raises during the first two betting rounds are made in $2 increments, and all bets and raises during the final two betting rounds (the third and fourth rounds) are made in $4 increments (you can't bet, say, 50 cents, or $3 on any round). As you might expect, in the $10–$20 game all bets and raises during the first two betting rounds are made in $10 increments, and all bets and raises during the final two betting rounds are made in $20 increments. In Las Vegas, the maximum number of bets is five, unless there are two players left in the pot—they can then raise and reraise until the money in front of one of them is gone.

Hold'em Setup

Two Cards Are Dealt, Facedown

Once the blinds are posted in the pot (directly in front of the players), the dealer deals two cards facedown to each player, one card at a time. The position of the button and the two blinds determines whose turn it is to act first during a hand of Texas Hold'em. (The illustration shows a poker table with players sitting around it, the blinds posted and two down cards in front of each player.) The cards that have been dealt are your own "private" cards, often called *hole cards*; take care not to let your neighbors see them. They belong to you and you only for the duration of one hand, and as soon as you see them, you should begin assessing the strength of your hand. Later on in the hand, the dealer will be dealing cards faceup in the middle of the table, where everyone can see them. This isn't a mistake: these later cards are *community* cards, and I'll explain how they fit into the dealing and the betting in just a moment.

The Player to the Left of the Two Blinds Acts First

Now the blinds have been posted, and the dealer has dealt out each player's first two cards. Then, to begin the first round of play, the player to the left of the big blind acts first. Technically, the two blind bettors have "acted" first, by posting their bets, but because their "action" is involuntary, the player sitting to the left of the big blind is really the first player who faces a decision, and the first who will take some kind of voluntary action, as he sees fit.

Note that the blinds are posted only before the very first betting round. After that, the player closest to the button's left (the one who had posted the small blind on the first round) is the first to act, if he is still in the hand.

During the first betting round, the player to the left of the posted blinds has just three options: calling the bet (matching the big blind), raising the bet (to exactly double the big blind), or folding his hand. (All calls or raises are placed in front of the player, in the pot, so that you can keep track of who has put in what: when the betting on a round is done, then you drag it all into the pot.) Usually, players fold by gently tossing or sliding their cards into the middle of the table facedown, without comment; but a verbal declaration—saying simply, "I fold"—is also acceptable and is considered binding: you must then release your hand. Although poker involves a great deal of deception, if you state that you're taking an action, you must follow through. You can't say "I fold" and then, after hearing a sigh of relief, push chips into the pot to make a bet. Similarly, you can't say "I raise" and then toss in your cards instead.

The next player to act has the same three options as the preceding player: he may call, raise, or fold. The next player to act also has the same options—call, raise, or fold—and so on until the action in the first round of betting is complete. Once the action is completed, the first round is over. (By the way, if you follow my advice in the chapters on strategy, you will be folding frequently on the first round of betting, as Hold'em is a real game of patience.)

One More Circumstance of the First Round of Play

The only other betting rule you need to know about in the first round is that the two players in the blinds have the option of raising the bet, just as anyone else in the hand does when it is his turn to act. In an unraised pot in our hypothetical $2–$4 game, the small blind may come into play by adding $1 to complete his bet to the full $2 size, or $3 ($3 + $1 = $4) to complete one full raise, and the big blind, even though he already has his $2 in, has the option of raising the pot another $2. In fact, a pro dealer will always ask the big blind if he wishes to raise it if the big blind hasn't made a motion one way or the other. I know that this may sound complicated at first, but after you've played about four hands it will seem very simple. (My parents played in a poker tournament the day after I taught them how to play, in September 2000.) Put more simply, when it's your turn to act during a Hold'em hand, you will always have the option of betting (when no one else has bet yet), checking (when no one has bet and you don't want to bet either), calling, raising, or folding.

Second Round of Betting

After the first round of play is complete, the dealer flips three *community cards* faceup in the middle of the table. These are available for use by everyone (as we shall see), and they stay there throughout the hand. We call the three community cards (and the moment they are dealt) the *flop*. In every hand of Hold'em, the flop is a signal moment; for each player still in the hand, these three new community cards are likely to confirm his high hopes for the hand or all but shatter them, since there are just two cards still to come. Since the blinds are used only during the first round of betting, the first remaining player who is closest to the left of the button begins the action in the second round. You might suppose that this is the same player who had to post the small blind before any cards were dealt, but it's quite possible, even likely, that the small blind, the big blind, and other players have folded during the first round because the early-position players didn't like their own hands or because someone raised.

This person, the one who begins the second-round action, may now check (make no bet at all, but not fold his hand either; in effect, he is saying, "I'm not betting right now, but I retain my option to call bets or even to raise, later in the hand"), fold (you should never fold until someone has made a bet that you would otherwise have to at least call), or bet. It's possible that everyone will check, the pot remaining just as it was; in this case, too, this round of play is complete. But the appearance of the three flop cards on the table will change everyone's view of the hand.

Hold'em Flop

Third Round of Betting

After the second round of play is complete, the dealer flips up a fourth community card faceup. This card, which also stays on the table throughout the hand, is usually called either *the turn* or *fourth street*. Then the third round of betting begins. Again, the person closest to the left of the button who still has a live hand (hasn't folded) begins the betting, and, take note, *the stakes are now doubled*. (The bets are larger, but there are, in nearly all hands, fewer players—the others have folded.)

Fourth Round of Betting

After the third round of betting is complete, the dealer flips up the fifth and last community card, faceup in the middle of the

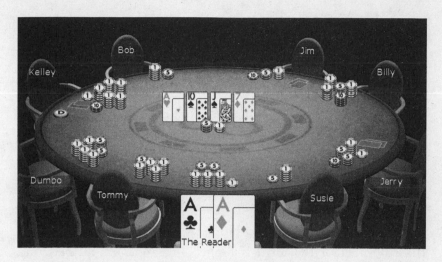

Hold'em 4th Street

table. This card is usually called either *fifth street* or *the river* (much more often). Now we have the five community cards in the middle of the table plus the two that you have in your hand: seven cards total. Each of you will settle on the best five cards out of the seven available to you (including one, two, or neither of the cards in your hand) to make your best possible poker hand. Now the fourth and final round of betting begins. After this round is completed, you will all flip up your *hole cards* to determine who has the best hand. Usually, once someone has shown a hand that no one else can beat, no one else bothers showing his hand at this point. (Sometimes a player who feels he got unlucky on the turn or the river may show a good hand that "went bad." We call this a "sympathy show.")

A Short Review of What a Hand of Limit Texas Hold'em Looks Like

There are four rounds of betting in limit Hold'em. The first round plays out before the flop (before the first three community cards are dealt, faceup), and on that first round you can bet and raise in one-unit increments. The second round occurs after the flop, and you can still bet and raise in exactly one-unit increments. The third round of betting occurs after the fourth card (fourth street or the turn) is flipped up, and now all bets and raises are made in two-unit increments. The fourth and final round of betting occurs after the fifth and final community card (the river) has been flipped up, and again you can bet and raise in two-unit increments.

Starting with the setup that I've illustrated (on page 19) in an eight-handed limit Hold'em hand, let's run through a $2–$4 sample hand. The dealer has dealt out two cards each, facedown, and the small blind of $1 and the big blind of $2 have been posted. Player one (P1) folds his hand, P2 (who holds, let's say, ace-jack, a hand that we will be referring to as A-J) raises, making it $4 to call the bet. P3, P4, and P5 all fold. P6, holding K-Q (king-queen), calls $4. The dealer and the small blind (SB) fold. The big blind (BB) calls the bet holding 9-8: because he already has $2 invested in the pot, it costs him only $2 more to see the flop. Now the dealer turns up a flop of 2-4-9.

Although P2 held the best preflop hand with his A-J, fortunes have changed on the flop. The player who sat in the BB with 9-8 is now the only player who has a pair (though he has no way to be certain of this), and suspecting that his pair might be

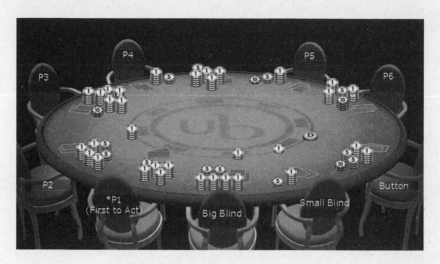

First Round of Betting—P2 Raises

the best hand, he bets $2. P2 and P6 somewhat loosely and stubbornly call the $2 bet, even though neither yet has a pair.

The turn card proves to be a 10, for a *board* of 2-4-9-10, and although the BB is a bit concerned by both this *overcard* (a board card higher than his pair) and the fact that two players called his opening bet, he decides to stay aggressive and bets $4 (recall that third-round bets are doubled). P2 folds (wisely, because there are now only six cards in the deck that can save him—three aces and three jacks), and P6 (who now needs a jack for a straight, or a Q or a K to make him a pair) calls the $4 bet. P6's call is good, because with any jack, queen, or king probably winning for him, he has 10 probable winning cards, which are usually called *outs* in poker slang.

Fate isn't always just, however, and even though the odds were against it, the river card is a Q, for a 2-4-9-10-Q board, and the BB simply checks, figuring there is a good chance that if he wasn't already beaten by a starting hand like J-J or A-10, he is now vulnerable to any hand containing a queen. Now P6 bets $4, and BB sighs and calls the $4 bet. P6 shows his Q-K, for a pair of queens, and BB shows a 9-8 for his pair of nines. The pot is awarded to P6, who, perversely enough, had the second-best hand before the flop and the worst hand on both the flop and the turn!

Two Important Aspects of Hold'em Etiquette

The game does involve some points of etiquette, and I would be remiss not to mention two issues at this point. For one, be sure you avoid "slow rolling" an opponent in a casino. When you're virtually certain you hold the winning hand (and it won't take you very long in your poker education before you know when you probably hold the winner!), and you then hesitate for a moment before you flip your hand up—clearly grandstanding and probably trying to make your opponent think he holds the winning hand—that's slow rolling.

Usually, a hesitation on the end by the bettor means that the bettor's hand is weak, and the players hate it when you then flip your strong hand up slowly. When a player perceives that he has won the pot, because you've stalled, but then, "bang," you tear his heart out and take the pot away from him, you're not making a friend; indeed, you're probably making an enemy who will have an elephant's memory and will look for revenge someday.

Another important point of etiquette is to be sure you always act in turn. Players are supposed to act one at a time, in a clockwise direction. If you look at your hand and realize you have nothing and are planning to fold, you still have a duty to the other players to sit there and look as interested or uninterested as you usually do, rather than folding out of turn. Why? I could give you many examples, but they mainly add up to this: your premature fold gives the other players information to which they aren't entitled. Your early display of weakness may encourage someone to play who might otherwise have been bluffed out by the play of an opponent.

This may seem a bit picky, but I promise you that the further you progress in your poker career, the more important you will realize this is, and the more likely it will be that at some time in your career someone will cost *you* a pot by giving away *his* weakness too soon. Suppose, for example, that you've correctly figured out that one of your opponents has nothing. You then decide to bluff at the pot with your own very weak hand in order to get rid of a third opponent whose turn to act arrives before the opponent that you think is weak can act. The man you are bluffing starts to study you and begins to fold, partly out of fear of your bet, and partly fearing that even if you're bluffing, the opponent behind him may have him beat. Now if that later opponent—the one you read as being weak—folds out of turn, and the opponent that you so skillfully bluffed at decides to call you, instead of folding, you have just lost a pot that you would have won, if only your weak opponent had played in turn!

Introducing Limit Hold'em into Your Private Game

If you've followed me to this point, you'll be able to play Hold'em in your own home game. At first it might seem hard, but after less than an hour of playing Hold'em, you'll have the basics down.

How much should you play for? In $1–$2-limit Hold'em, the big winner for the night might win $100. (Notice that this figure is 50 times the largest bet allowed in the game; expressing expectations in terms of x number of big bets per session or per hour is pretty common in poker.) But $20 to $40 wins (just 10 to 20 big bets) will be far more common. Wins equivalent to more than 50 big bets do happen, but they are very rare, and you could play a long time without seeing one and a much longer time without experiencing one yourself! If you've understood what I've been saying about predicting wins and losses in terms of number of big bets won, you can probably figure out that in a $2–$4 game you can expect the big winner to win around $200, but that more commonly you will see a lot of $40 to $80 wins and losses at this limit (again, 10 to 20 big bets).

So what limit should your poker game be? You'll have to answer this for yourself. You can play with a limit of 25 cents and 50 cents if you're a poor college student and take $5–$10 swings on average. If you're an investment banker, perhaps you would enjoy playing with a limit of $300–$600, with average swings hitting $6,000 to $12,000 and the big winner sometimes winning $60,000! If your group normally takes swings of about $20, then I would suggest that you play at that level (75 cents and $1.50) for Hold'em. Remember that the stakes can be changed very easily just by changing the size of the blinds. Note that if your group really plays Hold'em poorly, then the swings will be about twice as high. Speaking of playing Hold'em poorly brings me to the next section.

The Advantage of Position

As I've been teaching you the setup and basic play for Hold'em, I have referred to the advantage of position many times. Having position in Hold'em or being one of the last players to act in a hand is a great advantage. You can just sit back and wait for everyone else in front of you to act. If your opponent bets and you are strong, then you can raise, effectively doubling the amount of money that is put into the pot and raising other strong hands out of the pot by making it twice as expensive for them to call. If your opponent bets and you are weak, then you can fold. If your opponent checks (in this case he is showing you some weakness), now you can act on your hand accordingly. By acting last, you get a better feel for the strength of your opponents' hands. I will really get into the differences between being in or out of position in the chapters on strategy.

No-Limit Texas Hold'em Structure— The Cadillac!

No-limit Hold'em (NLH) is considered the Cadillac of poker games, because most professionals believe it involves more skill than any other modern-day poker game. The structure of

no-limit Hold'em is exactly like that of limit Hold'em, except
that when it is your turn to act you can bet any amount at any
time during the hand! In plainer language, the game is still dealt
the same way, but now you can bet any amount at any time. It's
pretty exciting to watch someone push a mountain of chips into
one pot! At the World Championships of 2001, I pushed in
almost $1 million in one hand, and lost!

After a flop of Q-9-3, I bet out $70,000 and Carlos Morten-
son raised it to $270,000 to go. I studied awhile and then
reraised all of my chips (about $1 million total) with Q-10 (top
pair), thinking that Carlos had at best Q-J, and that he couldn't
call me even if he did have Q-J. Carlos did have Q-J, but he made
an incredible call on me! No-limit Hold'em is treacherous; I had
survived for five days in the World Championships, only to get
blown out in one single spectacular hand!

Pot-Limit Hold'em

Again, the structure of pot-limit Hold'em (PLH) is the same,
except that the betting is limited to the size of the pot. So if the
blinds are $10–$20, and you want to *raise the pot* (make the
maximum raise), you can call $20 and then raise $50 more ($10
small blind + $20 big blind + your $20 call = $50), making it $70
to go. When it is your turn to act, you can always bet or raise the
size of the pot. Because it is almost always correct to bet the size
of the pot, you see a lot of big bets in pot-limit Hold'em—especially on the last round of betting when the pot is huge—just as
in no-limit Hold'em.

Because the differences between PLH and NLH aren't very significant, especially to beginning and intermediate players, I'll treat the games the same way in the chapters on strategy. However, I will point out some of the subtle differences in strategy along the way.

Chapter 3

Limit Hold'em:
Beginners' Strategy

I remember well my introduction to Texas Hold'em at the Memorial Union on the campus of the University of Wisconsin (UW). I was a poor (OK, broke!) undergraduate student at UW then, with nothing to lose (literally). Amazingly enough, the game was played right in the middle of the Student Union, infamous for its relaxed mores. For some reason, the powers that be didn't think students should be playing poker there, but because we used some old Austrian coins as chips, instead of the usual red, white, and blue plastic chips that were the standard for the time, none of the authorities seemed to notice what we were playing. The game of choice offered additional camouflage: we were playing Texas Hold'em instead of the much more easily recognized Seven-Card Stud.

I fancied myself a great poker player at the time, and when I heard about the game, I hurried down to play. Of course, I wasn't even a good player then, because I'd had very little experience. It seems that everyone overrates himself when it comes to playing poker!

The players were quite an eclectic mix: taxi drivers, students, professors, lawyers, and even a prominent psychiatrist. When I sat down and bought in for $20, I was warmly welcomed by the group, because every game needs some new blood (and fresh cash) once in a while. I quickly learned that I had a lot to learn about Texas Hold'em. I had a great time, but my $20 didn't last long, and it was all I could afford to risk. Although I didn't know much about poker yet, I at least had the good sense not to risk more than I could afford to lose, or borrow money I'd have trouble paying back.

Still, I thought I was gaining a feel for the game and its nuances, and, with so much money flying around down there, I thought I might one day begin paying my tuition with my poker profits. So I struck up an acquaintance with the best player in the game and set out to learn how to play Texas Hold'em the right way.

My new acquaintance, Tuli Haromy, ended up becoming my best friend for the next eight years. He was also the best player and banker for the game. (The banker is responsible for passing out chips, cashing checks, judging how much he can lend various players, and making sure that everyone is paid at the end of the night.) That made sense, because the best player has a vested interest in making sure the other players have access to cash to play with (and lose to him). It turned out that Tuli was originally from Las Vegas, which explains why we were playing Hold'em in Madison, Wisconsin, in the first place. Without

someone with Tuli's Las Vegas background, the chances of finding a Hold'em game in Madison in the early 1980s would have
been slim to none!

Tuli had a basic theory about Hold'em: "Tight is right."
"Tight" means that you drop out of most hands before the flop.
It was good advice. After studying the game with Tuli's tutoring
and playing with the group for about three months, I found that
I'd surpassed Tuli and become the best player in the game. After
all, I had no job and no money, which meant that I had a lot of
time on my hands and a strong motivation to learn the game.
The amount of money I was winning each week was pretty good,
too. In fact, from my modest perspective, the money was phenomenal. After about 18 months, I'd put more than $20,000 in
the bank, and I paid off all my student loans! The bigger poker
game on campus included mostly successful faculty and staff
members, doctors, and lawyers. The money, combined with the
fact that my ego felt great competing with and beating successful
PhDs, JDs, and doctors twenty years older than I was, caused me
to devote a lot more time and energy to learning Texas Hold'em.

While I was crushing the games in Madison, I began developing my own basic theory of Texas Hold'em. I had taken Tuli's
theory and moved on: supertight was better than tight. In other
words, playing even fewer hands than Tuli had suggested was the
way to go. Another skill I had developed was an ability to read
my opponents (to analyze how strong or weak their hands were,
from subtle clues of behavior). Reading players, though, is a
more advanced concept, so for now let's just take a look at my
theory: "Supertight is right."

To make "supertight" something that you can sink your
teeth into, I'll begin by identifying my top ten hands for

Hold'em—the 10 strongest Hold'em hands out there. I'll then teach you how to play those top ten hands before the flop, on the flop, on fourth street, and, finally, on the river—in other words, on all four rounds of betting. I'll teach you how to use well-timed raises on the flop to gain information that will help you judge, in the final rounds, whether or not your opponents have you beat. I'll show you how to make good use of that information when you're on fourth street. Finally, I'll show you that folding your hand on the river is usually not a good idea, because of the amount of money that's already in the pot by then.

Before we get into analyzing tactics in actual hands, I'll also introduce certain "animal types" that describe many of the people you will be playing against. Through examples, I'll show you when to raise, reraise, call, or fold your hand, depending on what types of "animals" your opponents seem to be, and thus what their tendencies are likely to be.

If you can truly absorb all the information I'll be offering in this chapter, and act on it under game conditions, you will already be capable of beating most small-limit Texas Hold'em players all over the world! I will now teach you how to play limit Texas Hold'em—a variation of Texas Hold'em in which the size of the bet in each round is preset. This is the most popular game in the world today.

Remember to read Chapter 2 before you read this chapter.

In this chapter you will learn:

▮ Preflop limit Hold'em for beginners: the top ten hands only.

▮ My "animal types": jackal, mouse, elephant, lion, and eagle.

▮ How to play the flop for beginners: the power of the raise.

▮ How to play A-K on the flop.

- How to play the top ten hands on fourth street.
- How to play the river: call because of pot odds.

Preflop Limit Hold'em: Lessons for Beginners, Top Ten Hands Only

To begin with, I recommend playing *only* the top ten hands and folding on all others. The top ten are, in order of relative promise: A-A, K-K, Q-Q, A-K, J-J, 10-10, 9-9, 8-8, A-Q, and finally 7-7. Experience has shown me that these are the strongest starting hands in limit Hold'em. This beginning "strategy for survival" is designed to keep you in the game while you learn the more subtle techniques that are necessary to beat tougher games, or to extract more money from weak games. And in *some* games using just this strategy will make you a winner. With this patient strategy alone, and really not much else in the way of poker instruction, I was able to crush the games in Madison. What happens is that when you consistently play only the top ten hands, your opponents will begin to fear your bets and raises because they'll see that you're always playing something powerful. This fear gives you some leeway to make a few different plays later on, when you've absorbed the intermediate and more advanced advice I'll be giving you later. In other words, the "top ten hands" strategy teaches the right fundamentals. You will need these fundamentals when you do add some intermediate and advanced strategy to your arsenal, because playing supertight alone just won't get the pots in these tougher games: the good hands don't come along often enough, and perhaps even more important, you risk becoming a bit too predictable.

Top 10 hands in Hold'em

When you break limit Hold'em down to its basic elements, good game theory suggests that you wait for big starting hands before you get involved in a hand, because the blinds are relatively small compared with the size of the pots, unless you're playing in a very tight game (which is rare at low stakes). It may seem a bit boring to play only these top ten hands; after all, most of you play poker just to have a good time and socialize—that is, for entertainment. Fair enough, but if you want to win the money, then you need to show some patience and entertain yourself in another way. And, anyway, how entertaining is it to play all the hands and lose most of them?

In general, I recommend playing the top ten hands regardless of your position in the betting order or the number of bets it will cost you to get involved in the hand. Always raise with these hands, no matter what it costs you to get involved. Of course, if you have a lot of evidence to suggest that your 7-7 is beaten (perhaps the tightest player in the game has just re-re-reraised the hand, making it, as we say, "four bets to go"), then you might do well to fold the hand. But in general, playing these hands aggressively is a good way to play Hold'em.

I know that you're probably thinking right now, "Is it really that easy? All I have to do is play Phil's top ten hands?" The answer is basically yes, at least as far as your *starting requirements* (your first two cards) are concerned! Yes, because it will be easy for you to play before the flop (on the first round of betting) when all you have to remember is to play only the top ten. (Playing after the flop is much more complicated, I'm afraid; but don't worry, we'll cover that as well.)

In what follows I'll be giving you a number of examples of hands that will help you understand the best courses of action for a beginning player to take. But before I give you these examples, it's time to introduce those "animals" I promised you. I cannot go much further in teaching you how to play poker without characterizing some of the personality types that you will inevitably face as you play Texas Hold'em, because no matter how much you may want to think of Hold'em as a card game played by people, in many respects it is even more valid to think of it as a game about people that happens to be played with cards. This becomes more and more true as the stakes get higher and the games get tougher.

Phil's Animal Types

Phil's "Animal Types"

These are the five animals: the *mouse, lion, jackal, elephant*, and *eagle*. I have created these animals because they seem to be the most common types out there right now.

The mouse is like your old aunt Edna, a conservative type who probably wouldn't even approve of your reading this book. The mouse—like you—plays only the top ten hands but hates to invest any money with a hand as weak as 7-7 or 8-8. The mouse hardly ever raises someone else's bet; but when he does raise, look out, because he has the goods!

The lion is a tough competitor who plays fairly tight poker but doesn't limit himself to the top ten hands. He bluffs with excellent timing and seems to know when the other players are trying to bluff him. Though he plays pretty tight, he's occasionally out on a limb with a bluff or a semibluff. You could do worse than play like the lion.

The jackal is loose and wild, and some days it seems as though he's just giving his money away. Because he's involved in so many pots and raises so often, his play can take some pretty big swings. The jackal's logic seems at odds with the logic of all the other players. He just seems crazy! (He's what many of us in poker call a megalomaniac, or sometimes just maniac.) The jackal can hurt you and himself too with his crazy play, because he puts in so many bets. But there is some method to his madness. He's good at raising the pots at the right times (his style of play gives him many occasions to think about what's going on), and when he does at last win a pot, it's generally huge! If a jackal runs hot by catching good cards for a while, you may become convinced that he's the best player in the world, but when his cards come back to earth, he can lose money as fast as he won it.

The elephant is fairly loose (which means he plays a lot of pots) and seems to be from Missouri, the "Show me" state. He's what we refer to in poker as a "calling station": he never folds when he is supposed to fold, because he doesn't ever believe that you have the goods. Because he's impossible to bluff, no one with much experience ever tries to bluff him—with one exception: can you guess who that is? The elephant keeps feeding the other players his chips, slowly but surely. The elephant isn't very sharp and isn't a very dangerous opponent for most players, but he seems to do well against the jackal, because the jackal keeps on trying to bluff the elephant.

Finally, we have the eagle. The eagle is a rare bird, and you might not ever play with him, because he's one of the top 100 poker players in the world. You'll find the eagle wherever high-stakes poker is played. He flies around high in the sky and swoops down to eat other animals' chips when he's hungry! You'll find the eagles competing every year at the World Series of Poker (WSOP), trying to win world championships and the money and prestige that come with winning them—if not in the tour-naments, then perhaps in the big-money side games the WSOP always generates. Learning how to play like an eagle is a lofty and worthwhile goal, but it is beyond the scope of this book. (In fact, if you're able to absorb everything in this book, then per-haps I'll see you sitting across the table from me soon.)

Now that we've pondered the personalities of most of the animals (players) that you'll be playing against, it's time to move forward with some examples of how to play the top ten hands to perfection. (As we proceed, you'll see the value of recognizing these personality types.) Again, the basic premise in playing the top ten hands is this: always raise or reraise with these hands before the flop, no matter what the action has been before it's your turn to act. (While I lay out these examples, I'll begin to weave into the equations some ways to play the hands somewhat differently, depending on which animals you're playing against.)

Raising with a Top Ten Hand in Late Position

The game is $2–$4 at your local bar. You hold J-J on the button. The player in the first position (see the illustration) has raised, making it two bets, or $4, to go, and the jackal, in the second position, has reraised (The jackal reraised! What a surprise!),

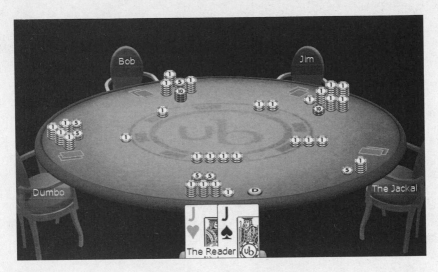

Re-Raise—"Four Bets"

making it three bets, or $6, to go. You then raise it again to make it four bets, or $8, to go. This hand is easy enough to play because you have one of those top ten hands and also have the advantage of late position.

Beware of the Mouse

The game is $5–$10 at the local businessmen's club. You have 9-9 in the small blind, and the jackal, in the third position, has raised it to two bets, or $10, to go. Then the lion, in the fourth position, makes it three bets, or $15, to go. Now, the mouse on the button makes it four bets to go! Yikes, what to do? You know that the lion probably has a strong hand, but the mouse making it four bets, even over the top of the lion? That is big trouble!

You decide that the mouse probably has A-A or K-K, and you throw your hand away right then and there, because you figure that you're a 4½-to-1 underdog (a small pair is roughly a 4½-to-1 underdog against a big pair). I know that I've said you should always play these hands, but sometimes a little discretion is the better part of valor. If no animal personalities had entered the picture, you could play this hand—but poker is about people as well as game theory. Deciding to call the four bets in this case wouldn't actually be foolhardy—but it would be a pretty weak play, one that would lose money over the long run. Many players who consider themselves experts would call this a terrible play, but they're forgetting to consider the very large pots you're likely to win in such cases if you do happen to "flop a set" (three of a kind, in this case three nines).

Reraising the Jackal with a Top Ten Hand in Cyberspace

The game is $10-$20 limit (which means you could win or lose $1,000 on any given night) at UltimateBet.com, an online poker site. You have A-K in the second position and with your raise you make it $20 to go. The elephant, in the fourth position, calls the $20 (that's what elephants do, after all), and then the jackal makes it $30 to go from the small blind. What should you do? You make it $40 to go, figuring that you have both the jackal and the elephant beat. The elephant has probably called with a hand too weak to call with, and the jackal has probably raised with a hand too weak to raise with.

If either of them has a pair, then you will need to make a

hand, but this is still a good time to play aggressively. Making it four bets here is an especially good play because the jackal could have anything. And putting in those extra bets now will make the pot so large that you'll probably be forced to play the hand farther than you might want to, making it easier to call the jackal down with ace high. This is good, because no one will be able to bluff you off your A-K if you miss the flop. The pot will be large enough to make it right to call even if you miss the flop.

A Top Ten Hand against a Mouse

The game is $15–$30 limit at the Mirage poker room in Las Vegas. The jackal in seat one raises the bet, making it $30 to go. The mouse on the button makes it three bets, or $45 to go. You have K-K in the big blind, so you make it $60 to go. Yes, the mouse's raise is ominous, but you have K-K, the second-best-possible hand, and you need to raise with it no matter what the hand looks like otherwise.

Pocket Aces

You have A-A in any position before the flop. Put in as many bets as you can before the flop, regardless of what your opponents do! This is the best possible hand in Hold'em!

Kings, Queens, and A-K

You have K K, Q Q, or A-K in any position before the flop.
Again, put as many bets out there as you can before the flop! With
any of these you have one of the four best hands in Hold'em!

Pocket Jacks

You have J-J before the flop, in any position. OK, you have the
fifth best hand in Hold'em, and in general I would say never fold
this hand before the flop in limit Hold'em. But there may come a
time or two, as you become a lion, when you choose to fold this
hand before the flop. Maybe, for example, the tightest mouse on
the planet has made it four bets to go, and you just have a strong
feeling that you're beat. After all, what hand would encourage
the tightest player in the world to make it four bets to go? Probably A-A or K-K. But because this is the beginners' section, I'd
advise you to put in your four bets anyway; when you are a lion
you will know when the time is right to fold this hand.

Before the flop, then, successful play in Hold'em is pretty darn
easy using the top-ten-hands strategy. In general, you raise or
reraise every time you have a top ten hand, and you fold the rest
of your hands. The exceptions are: when a mouse makes a raise
or reraise (two bets or three bets), a lion makes it three bets (a
reraise), or an elephant makes it three bets (since it is out of the
ordinary for the elephant ever to bet his own hand). In these

cases, you might want to back off if your top ten hand is 9-9, 8-8, 7-7, or A-Q.

Notice that I'm not diagramming the way you should play every hand. There are just too many variables for me to attempt that. The fact is that the play of some of these hands depends on the opponents involved. But I've given you a few things to think about, and you will develop many more things to think about as you gain more experience and a greater feel for the game. It's time now to move on toward the next step in playing a limit Texas Hold'em hand: how a beginner should play limit Hold'em on the flop.

Playing the Flop for Hold'em Beginners: The Power of the Raise

The principle that I am going to teach you in this section is how to use a raise on the flop to find out "where you are at" in a hand. I'll show you how to use the raise or reraise on the flop to gain information, so as to learn, perhaps, whether you have the best hand or not. Learning that is crucial to your decision-making process for the rest of the hand, and sometimes you have to pay heavily for the information! Another great thing about using a raise or reraise on the flop is that even though your purpose in betting was to find out if you had the best hand, your aggressive betting often causes a better hand to fold. Aggressive play in Hold'em is often rewarded in ways you weren't anticipating at the time; this is one of the reasons why jackals have developed their particular playing style, and why they seem to win more often than they should.

After all, most of the time the flop that you are hoping for in Hold'em just isn't there. When I make it three bets to go in a Hold'em hand with K-K, I'm hoping that no ace will hit the flop! And yet an ace does fall on the flop roughly 30 percent of the time. When I have Q-Q in a big multiway pot (with two or more opponents), then I'm hoping for neither an ace nor a king on the flop, because an ace or a king on the flop is the most likely way for me to lose the pot (to someone holding A-K or something similar). Yet often the ace or the king does come on the flop. But when you have Q-Q, and three small cards beneath the queen come on the flop, the hand is easy to play on the flop: just jam (raise and reraise) the pot!

I've been telling you to "ram and jam" (raise and reraise) with my top ten hands before the flop, but what happens when you've made it four bets to go with 10-10 and the flop comes 2-Q-K? This situation is a good bit trickier than one where you make it four bets to go with 10-10 and the flop comes down 10-7-2 (you have flopped the best possible hand in this case): there, you just jam it.

You'll be able to handle the dream flops, or even the really terrible flops, but what do you do when you're heavily involved in a hand before the flop but then have what for you is a marginal flop? What you do is raise your opponents as if you have hit the flop perfectly, and then watch to see how they react to your raises. If you get the strong impression that you're beaten, on the basis of your opponents' reactions to your raises, then fold. But if you're pretty sure you still have the best hand, then keep on betting or calling.

Notice here that woven into the principle of using raises on the flop to gain information about hands is the idea of using the occasion to read your opponents. I don't want to be teaching you just plain old boring game theory without also showing you how to take into account your opponents' moves, tendencies, and expressions. Poker is a lot more about reading your opponents than it is about how to play pocket eights against four opponents! If you do learn how to read someone, then everything will fall into place as you read this book. But if you don't know how to read someone (or think you don't), don't despair: reading people is also a skill that can be learned.

Now that I've shown you some of the power of the raise on the flop, I'm going to walk you through some examples that will help you learn how to play hands *after* the flop. But before I introduce these examples, I think it will be useful to tell a little story about a hand that I played at Foxwoods Casino (in Connecticut) in late 2001 during a $2,500-buy-in "World Poker Finals" Hold'em event. We were playing $300–$600 limit Hold'em when the following hand came up. I sat in the big blind, and three people called the $300 bet before the flop. Because I held 8-8, I raised, making it two bets, or $600, to go. My three opponents all called my raise, and the flop then came down A-9-5. I bet out $300, and everyone folded! This was terrific news for me, since most of the time in a big-buy-in poker event someone would have an ace in this situation. Four people times $600 each equals $2,400. I won $2,400 because I'd made the right bet on the flop and the right raise before the flop! If I hadn't bet on the flop, but had just checked, I probably would have lost this pot.

A lot of world-class players wouldn't have raised before the flop on this hand, and therefore would have missed out on the extra $900 that I got the others to put into this pot before the flop. Some other strong players wouldn't have bet on the flop either, figuring that someone had to have an ace! I assumed or gambled (hoped) that my opponents had cards like K-10, Q-J, or 🔟♣-9♣, and for a $300 bet on the flop I earned $2,400.

If I had simply checked on the flop, rather than betting, then someone else might have tried to bluff, and I would have had a tough call, since I couldn't beat a pair of nines or aces. If I had checked and everyone had checked behind me, and then a king, queen, jack, or ten had come off on the turn, then I would probably have been beaten and would not have wanted to call a bet! Through playing this hand properly and making the bet on the flop, I won a pot that many players would not have won. Andy Glazer says this is a "Smith Barney pot," in the sense that I got my money the old-fashioned way: I earrrnnned it!

This is the principle I'm trying to illustrate, the principle of betting or raising on the flop, when you have a top ten hand, to find out if yours is the best hand. In this case I was representing an ace with my bet, and fortunately no one had an ace or a nine. If someone had raised me on this hand after I'd bet my 8-8 on the flop, then I most likely would have had to fold my hand, but the $300 bet was going to give me some valuable information, or a better chance of winning the pot (if it drove out someone who held something like K-Q and who might have caught that king or queen on the turn or the river), or, as wound up happening here, the whole pot.

Although I won the battle in this hand, I ended up losing the war in this particular tournament, going on to finish in twentieth place in a field of 100. Unfortunately for me on this day, poker tournaments usually conclude by paying only one table per hundred players, and here it was only the final table of nine players who "cashed."

Examples

Now let's take a look at the examples I've promised, situations that will teach you how to play your top ten hands after the flop. Seven assumptions will apply to the four examples that follow:

1. You're playing a $5–$10 online game at UltimateBet.com.
2. You have J-J, also known as pocket jacks.
3. Jim (a jackal) raises before the flop in the first position (the first player to act after the blinds, usually referred to as "under the gun").
4. You reraise, making it three bets ($15) with your J-J in the third position.
5. Dumbo (an elephant) calls on the button.
6. Jerry (unclear profile) calls in the big blind.
7. Jim (the jackal) calls your raise.

The Flop Comes Down 10♦-7♦-4♠

Jerry checks and Jim bets out $5. This is a very good flop for you, because there are no "overcards" (Q-K-A) to your pair of jacks (an overcard creates a reasonable possibility of a pair for someone who entered the pot with two big cards in his hand), and therefore there is an excellent chance that you still have the best hand.

Clearly a raise is in order here. You raise because you probably have the best hand at this point, but your hand is vulnerable to overcards, and you want to try to drive out (force the player to fold) a hand like Q-K that can hit a queen or a king on either of the next two cards, and thus beat you. Your raise may also drive out someone with 5-5, who would otherwise call for the relatively cheap $5 and perhaps end up beating you because he hit a five on the next card or caught a six and then a three to make a straight. In other words, right now your raise is all about "protecting" your hand from losing by driving out opponents who, though trailing at the moment, have reasonable chances to beat you on the turn or river, if you let them stay in the hand. Your raise makes it too expensive for players facing weak draws to stay in the hand.

The Flop Has Come Down A♦-10♠-4♦

Jerry bets out and Jim calls. Now what do you do? A raise at this point is a great idea. Clearly, you cannot fold right here, because the pot is fairly large and you may still have the best hand. As long as you're going to play, you might as well raise it and find out if you have the best hand. You already know that you probably have Jim beat, because he's a jackal who always raises when he has any kind of hand and he didn't raise Jerry's $5 bet.

Assuming that you do raise, if Jerry reraises you here, he probably has you beat, but it's not a certainty: he could have a hand like a pair-and-a-flush draw, such as 10♦-Q♦, or a straight-and-a-flush draw with a hand like Q♦-K♦. You should call his reraise on the flop, since it is only $5 more to you, and you want to see what he does after the next card is turned. If Jerry then bets out after the next card, where the limits are now doubled (he can bet $10 now and on the last round of betting), then it is time for a decision. You have to analyze what kind of hand Jerry is likely to have.

Does he have a drawing hand that you can beat or a hand like A-Q (a pair of aces; remember the flop is A-10-4) that beats you? Did the flush card or a king or queen hit the board on the turn? (Note, by the way, that even though a jack on the turn would appear to be a great card for you, because it would give you three jacks, it could also present some danger, if it is the jack of diamonds, or if someone had K-Q and has now made his straight.) If so, then can you beat anything anymore? Perhaps a "blank" card (a harmless card that helps neither a straight draw nor a flush draw) like the 6♣ comes off and Jerry checks his drawing hand to you. Why has he checked? Because your raise on the flop scared him off from betting the 6♣. (If so, then your raise on the flop has accomplished its mission!) If he does bet here after a "blank," then you must watch the way he makes the bet (look for body language that might show confidence or fear) and make your best decision.

On fourth street (after the fourth up card is dealt), if something in your head (intuition or instinct) tells you that Jerry is bluffing, then call. If you feel that he has a real hand, then fold. Trust your instincts and you will find that they keep improving as you continue to play Hold'em.

You will also find that your ability to read others will get better as you gain experience, especially if you work specifically on watching how people bet their hands. One of the best times to do this is when you have folded your own hand and so no longer have to concentrate on your own tactical considerations: you can focus entirely on studying your opponents (and the outcome!) for information that will come in handy later.

The Flop Is A♣-K♦-4♣

Jerry bets out $5, and Jim raises it to $10 to go. In this case there is no flush draw, and it's hard to imagine that both of your opponents have a straight draw with a hand like Q-J, Q-10, or J-10. Although one of your opponents might have a hand like that, what does the other one have? Almost certainly the other opponent has a pair of kings or a pair of aces, because people holding high-rank cards like that tend to stay in hands. In this case, the two overcards on the flop make folding your hand an easy choice. This is one of the worst possible flops for a pair of jacks, especially in a three-bet pot where your opponents probably hold A-something or K-Q, K-J, or K-10.

"But wait a minute," you might ask; "if my opponent can get lucky by hitting the ace he was drawing to on the flop, why can't I get lucky and hit a jack on the turn or the river?" If one of your opponents does have a pair of aces or kings, then you can win only by hitting a jack (don't even factor in the extremely unlikely chance of hitting two perfect cards in a row to make a straight); and because there are only two jacks left in the deck, the odds against that happening are about 22 to 1 on the next card. Just say to yourself, "OK, I've played this hand perfectly so far, so even though I've waited a long time for a pair of jacks, it's time to fold them. Next time I have a big hand, I hope I have a better flop to it." Then simply fold your hand and forget about the outcome of that one. (But again, see what the outcome tells you about Jerry or Jim.)

Of course, the jack sometimes hits right away, and sometimes you would have won the pot because your opponents have Q-10 and ♦4-♦Q. (Obviously the jackal has this hand!) But regardless of the outcome, you made the right move by folding. Sometimes people drive themselves crazy by second-guessing their plays. The next thing you know they're staying in pots trying to hit the shots that are 22 to 1 against them, and virtually giving their money away! Sometimes poker will drive you batty or, in poker terms, put you on "tilt."

If you can keep your emotions in check when bad luck smacks you hard—if you can avoid letting a bad break in one hand affect the way you play your next hand—you will have an excellent chance to become a winning poker player. But if you find that you can't get the last hand out of your mind, and you're vulnerable to tilt, you will probably find it impossible to win over the long haul. In the long run, I'd rather invest my money in a "good" player who never goes on tilt than in a "very good" player who is vulnerable to going on tilt.

The Flop Is ♦K-♦Q-♠7

Jerry checks, and Jim bets out $5. A lot of us would be tempted to think, "OK, I'm probably beaten in this hand because I cannot beat someone who has a K or a Q in his hand and I'm facing three opponents in this pot. But I'm not convinced yet that I'm beat, so I'll just call the $5." In fact, a "mouse" might even fold his hand at this point! But this is the wrong way to look at it. Yes, you probably are beaten, but for an extra $5 (raising instead of calling) you can gain a lot of information, and because of your raise you might even win this pot. Assuming that you do make the correct raise, making it $10 to go, you might:

1. Have Jim the jackal beaten and force Dumbo to fold his Q-J (even though it has you beat with a pair of queens, Dumbo will be afraid you have a king in your hand). This is an example of winning a pot through aggressive play. The beautiful thing about this scenario is that you were really just making a raise to gain information about the strength of your hand, but as a by-product you forced the best hand to fold!

2. Have Jim the jackal beaten and force Dumbo to fold his A-10, a hand he might have played for $5 trying to hit an inside straight, and lo and behold, the play saves you a fortune when your third jack comes off on the next card, because it would have given Dumbo an ace-high straight (10-J-Q-K-A)!

3. Find out that Dumbo has you beaten when he reraises the pot behind you, making it $15 to go. Now you can call $5 more on the outside chance that a jack will hit the board or that Dumbo is sitting on a big draw like A♦-J♦ and will check it on the next two streets if he misses his hand. But if he bets again or if Jim calls the $15 total on the flop, you will have to fold. At least you will know that you are beaten at this point in the hand, and you can avoid calling the next two $10 bets.

4. Find out that you are beaten because all three of your opponents called your $10 bet on the flop, and it's just too unreasonable to think that your pair of jacks is the

best hand after they all call a bet and a raise. (All three
would have to be on either a smaller pair than jacks, or
a straight draw, or the flush draw, and this is pretty
unlikely.)

5. Eliminate all the other opponents in the hand, but find
    that Jim does have you beat. In this case, you will prob-
    ably wind up losing some extra bets to Jim because he's
    a jackal! This is an example of what I mentioned ear-
    lier—of how jackals don't lose as much as their wild
    play would seem to indicate, because they get paid off
    big-time when they actually do make a strong hand.
    But you will have ample opportunity to get those bets
    back from Jim later on, in another hand!

You can now see why raising Jim's bet here on the flop may
win the pot for you, or at least give you the additional information that says your hand is beaten. Of your three options, raising
is best, folding is second best, and calling is the worst! Your raise
on the flop will set up the way you play your hand on the next
two rounds of betting, and it may bluff out a better hand.

Playing the Flop, for Limit Hold'em Beginners: The Special Case of A-K

It's time now to tackle an old problem in the Texas Hold'em
game: how to play A-K after a bad flop. Since you will be putting
in a lot of bets before the flop with A-K, you can usually play this
hand pretty aggressively after the flop as well (because you've
already built a pretty good-size pot, one worth going after).

Even though we are only in the beginners' section for limit Hold'em, I want to talk briefly here about the historical significance of A-K in no-limit Hold'em tournaments. The classic hand to come up between two players in big no-limit Hold'em tournaments is A-K versus Q-Q. Many times one of these tournaments is decided because a great player has hit or missed his A-K versus Q-Q for a mountain of chips! At the 2001 World Series of Poker, which is the poker world's world championships, I had Q-Q early in one event and was "all-in" (all my remaining chips were in the pot) against my opponent's A-K. I put my last $2,000 in before the flop with my Q-Q, and my opponent called me with A-K. If I had lost this "coin flip" (actually, Q-Q is about a 13 to 10 favorite), then I would have been eliminated and would not have gone on to win the event and $305,000 for first place. This is a fairly common occurrence late in these events. It makes sense, considering that the hands J-J, Q-Q, K-K, A-A, and A-K are the top five hands in Hold'em. The trick is to "finish the job" and go on to win the event if you are lucky enough to win a big coin-flip pot.

Examples

Now that I've shown you the key role that A-K often plays in no-limit Hold'em events, it's time to set up the next five examples. Here are your six assumptions:

1. You have A-K in the small blind in a $2–$4 game at your house (someone may win or lose up to $200, but usually $50–$100 wins and losses are to be expected at this limit).

2. A jackal named Joe makes it $4 to go in the third position.

3. An elephant named Earl calls the $4 on the button.

4. You reraise, making it $6 to go from the small blind.

5. The big-blind lion named Leo calls the $6 bet.

6. Joe the jackal and Earl the elephant also call the $6 bet.

The Flop Includes an A or a K (For Example, A-9-4, K-10-7, A-2-3, or K-Q-J)

You bet, raise, and reraise quite a bit because you have hit "top pair" with "top kicker." In every case where an A or a K hits the flop you will have top pair with top kicker (A-A-K or A-K-K), and this is a very strong hand in Hold'em! For example, if the flop is A-9-4, then you have a pair of aces with a king kicker. This hand will beat all other pairs of aces like A-Q, A-J, A-10, A-8, etc.

But let's suppose now that the flop is A-9-4 and someone is holding A-9. Your A-K would be losing on this flop, because A-9 now makes two pair, aces and nines. Still, for every time someone who plays a weak A-9 against your powerful A-K and beats you, you'll beat him more than two other times (that is, the A-K is slightly more than a 2.5 to 1 favorite heads-up against A-9). The point I'm trying to make is that A-K becomes very powerful when you catch an A or a K on the flop, and you should put in a lot of betting and raising on the flop when this is the case. Fortunes have been won and lost with A-K!

Now let's move on to a few examples of how to play the A-K when you miss the flop.

The Flop Is J-5-2

You bet out $2. The lion, Leo, raises, making it $4 to go; and the elephant, Earl, calls the bet. In this case you figure that one of your opponents has you beat, but you call $2 anyway, on the chance that an A, K, Q, or 10 will hit the board on fourth street. If an A or K hits, then you should bet out $4 on fourth street. But if a Q or 10 hits, then you will want to call a $4 bet (check and then call $4 if your opponents bet) because you have picked up a straight draw. Since you know you will call $4 when a Q or a 10 hits, you may choose to bet out $4, attempting to win the pot right there (but right now we are talking about play on the flop). So the play on the flop here is fairly simple: you bet out $2 and call the raise of $2.

The Flop Is 7♦-8♦-9♦ and You Have A♠-K♣

You bet out $2, and the lion raises it to $4 to go. The jackal calls $4. Now what do you do? Folding here isn't a bad option, because two of the cards that under other conditions you would like to see on the turn or river, A♦ or K♦, would make four diamonds on the board, so they're very likely good cards for someone else, bad cards for you. Still, it costs you only $2 to see if you can hit your hand. I would probably just fold for $2, but an expert could call the $2 bet, because he feels that he reads his opponents well enough to avoid getting too involved later on in the hand. The point I'm trying to make is this: sometimes, even though you have A-K, you have to fold your hand on the flop when the others raise you. You're not folding often, mind you, but situations where you face three suited connected cards like

7♦-8♦-9♦ or 8♥-9♥-10♥ on the board, and you have none of the suited cards in your hand (like with A♠-K♠), are just too likely to have helped someone else in the hand. Those two examples are the worst possible flops for your A♠-K♣, and it's probably right to just fold your hand on the spot.

The Flop Is Q-10-2

You bet out $2, the lion raises it to $4, and then the elephant reraises it to $6 to go. In this case, you need a J for a straight or an A or a K for a pair. You have to call the $6. You have to figure that at least one of your opponents has you beaten, even though one of them may have a hand like K-J, an open-ended straight draw. (You may even consider raising it again to make it $8 to go! Whoops, never mind, that's a play for the advanced discussion, still to come.) The point of this example is that if what turns up on the flop gives you a straight draw, then you need to play your A-K. Three available aces, three available kings, and four of whatever card completes your straight draw (in this case four jacks) give you too many winning possibilities (pros call this having 10 "outs") to fold right away.

The Flop Is 6-5-2

You bet out $2, and the lion calls. Then the jackal makes it $4 to go, and the elephant folds. What do you do now? You probably have the lion beaten, since he only called the $2 on the flop, and lions usually don't merely call when they're pretty sure they have the best of it. The jackal could easily have you beaten with a pair of deuces, fives, or sixes, and jackals play a lot of strange hands. But he *is* the jackal and he could just as easily have 7-8, A-4, A-3, 7-9, or 8-9, all of which give him a straight draw of one sort or another. If this is the case, then you are a favorite over his hand. (He has to hit something with only two cards to go, while you're already winning and don't need to improve to beat him.) You're going to call the $2 raise anyway, so why not reraise, making it $6 to go?

The reraise will probably cause the lion to fold his hand, isolating you (getting it down to just the two of you) against the jackal. If you don't reraise, and the jackal does have 8-9, and the lion does have $\boxed{Q_\blacklozenge}$–$\boxed{J_\blacklozenge}$, you might end up losing the hand to the lion because you let him in cheap! This is the advantage of being the jackal; his erratic play sometimes causes you to put in extra bets against him. But aggressive play against the jackal is a good thing! Since he will play his drawing hands "fast" (raising and reraising), you will have a chance to win some big pots when he misses his hand. What I'm really trying to say is this: play your "A-K high" (the best nonpair hand) aggressively on the flop against the jackal when you think there is a decent chance he's drawing. You can always fold your hand on fourth street or the river if you think the jackal has you beat.

We'll talk more about how to play A-K on the flop in the intermediate discussion of limit Hold'em, to come.

How to Play the Top Ten Hands on Fourth Street

One great benefit of the style that I'm teaching you to use in Texas Hold'em is that fourth street and the river are now easier to play, because you will have done some good work on the flop (raising) to find out whether or not you have the best hand. Fourth street is the time for you to use the information you've learned on the flop. Because the bets are now doubled on this round of betting, a well-timed fold will save you at least two big bets, perhaps more. On the other hand, a well-timed raise may win the whole pot for you! If you believe you have the best hand after the fourth card is turned up, then you need to make a bet or a raise. If you've learned that you are beaten, now is the time to fold your hand.

First, let's take a look at some obvious plays (obvious to an expert, at least) and how they may affect the outcome of a hand.

Protecting Your Hand

You have K-K. A jackal raises before the flop, you then make it three bets (reraise), and an elephant behind you calls the three bets "cold" (without having any money already invested in the pot). The jackal then calls the one additional bet.

The flop comes 10-9-2 and the jackal bets, you raise, and the elephant calls the two bets. The jackal also calls two bets. The turn card comes up a 2, for 10-9-2-2, and now the jackal bets out into you. At this point you should be thinking, "Raise it!" But you're distracted by the conversation going on across the table, and you just call the bet. Now, the elephant calls the bet as well.

This is a most costly mistake, since you've now let the elephant call only one bet with his A-9, and the last card off is an A, for 10-9-2-2-A. Now the jackal checks and you decide to check as well, because you fear the A may have hit the elephant. Then the elephant bets and the jackal calls, and you call as well. The elephant then says, "I have two pair, aces up." You think, "Man, am I unlucky, I cannot believe that he hit an ace on me here!" Wrong! You misplayed this hand! All you had to do was raise after the two came up on fourth street, and the elephant would have been forced to throw his hand away! Your call on the end might also fall into the mistake category (even though I've said you should generally not be folding on the end), because the one card you had legitimate reason to fear, the ace, hit the board, and a bet *and* a call were already in front of you.

Let's rewrite the script, then, so you're making the obvious raise on fourth street. A deuce comes off the deck for 10-9-2-2, and the jackal bets out into you. You don't really think the jackal has a deuce, so you raise and the elephant reluctantly folds his hand. The jackal calls your raise. The river card is an ace, for 10-9-2-2-A, and the jackal checks. You conclude that the jackal has a pair of tens, so you bet out, and then the jackal calls you. You say, "Pocket kings for me" and the jackal says, "Nice hand." You then pile all the chips onto your stack as the elephant loudly complains, "Darn it, I would have made aces and nines if I'd stayed in, but I couldn't call, because your raise on fourth street told me you had me beaten!" You just smile and finish stacking the chips, thinking, "Looks as though I played that hand perfectly!"

This first example is about "protecting your hand" with a raise on fourth street. If you fail to do that, you give your opponents a chance to outdraw you for just one bet. The next example is another fairly obvious play, but in the other direction—folding!

Knowing When to Fold 'Em

Two opponents have called the bet before the flop, and now you make it two bets to go with [J♠]-[J♠] on the button. The big blind and both other opponents call the raise, and the flop comes [2♦]-[3♦]-[Q♠]. The big blind checks, the first "limper" (caller) bets out, and the second limper folds. You then raise to find out "where you're at" (great strategy!) and the big blind calls. The remaining limper, whose play falls somewhere between that of a lion and that of a jackal (he's a fairly strong player who's sometimes unpredictable), now reraises, making it three bets to go. You call, and now the big blind calls as well.

Fourth street brings [4♦], for [2♦]-[3♦]-[Q♠]-[4♦], and the big blind checks and the limper bets out. You fold because you can't beat a pair of queens or a flush (the flush draw hit!) and you're afraid of both the limper and the big blind. What hand could the limper make it three bets with on the flop, and nonetheless be a hand you can now beat?

If he has a flush draw, then he hits his flush. If he has a pair of queens, then you're already beat. If he has a "set" (trips made with a pocket pair like 2-2 and a 2 on the board, then you're also beat). Of course it's possible that the limper is overplaying a pair of threes, like A-3 (with 2-3-Q on board) or something similar, but it's very unlikely that he would reraise on the flop with that hand. About the only realistic hope for you is that the limper three-bet with A-K, a hand your jacks still beat. That's certainly not an impossible holding, but are you willing to pay off big bets on both the turn and the river to find out if you're right? If the limper is willing to push A-K on the turn, there's a very realistic possibility that he will push one more time with it on the river. I won't carry the script of this hand further, but suffice to say that you made the right play, because there is almost no hand that you can beat at this point in the hand. Chasing (calling) on the strength of the slight hope that the limper is playing like a maniac and pushing his A-K will gouge big chunks out of your bankroll over the long run.

Folding Down Your Hand

With a hand of 10-10 you've made it three bets to go over the top of a lion before the flop, and two other opponents have called. This means you have four players putting in three bets each. The flop comes up A♣-4♦-5♣, the lion bets, and you raise him, but this time he reraises you (assume that everyone else folds on the flop).

Fourth street is the time to fold this hand. The lion can't be drawing here, because there is no draw, and you can assume the lion isn't playing 6-7! The jackal might have 6-7, but the lion wouldn't. So when the lion bets out again, into you, after the 9♦ comes up, for A♣-4♦-5♣-9♦, it's time to fold your hand. The lion's response to your raise on the flop lets you know that he has you beaten! Now act on the information you've paid for, and fold your hand. You may even want to show the lion your hand and say, "OK, you win because I fold." Although you are giving away free information when you show your hand in this spot, sometimes this sort of ad hoc play encourages your opponent to show you his hand for free (now or in some later hand), and you may wind up collecting a lot more free information than you've given away.

Examples

Let's now revisit an example we looked at earlier and consider a
few different possibilities.

Assumptions for the following five examples:

1. The game is $5–$10 at UltimateBet.com.
2. You have J♣-J♠ (pocket jacks).
3. Jim (a jackal) raises before the flop in the first position.
4. You make it three bets ($15) with J-J in the third position.
5. Dumbo (an elephant) calls on the button.
6. Jerry (unclear profile) calls in the big blind.
7. Jim calls your raise.
8. The flop comes down A♦-10♠-4♦.
9. Jerry bets out and Jim calls the bet.
10. You raise with your J♣-J♠, making it two bets to go.

Folding Your Hand Because a Bad Card Came on
Fourth Street

Jerry makes it three bets, and Jim calls three bets. Now you
call three bets, but you now believe that Jerry has some kind of a
strong hand. You aren't sure if Jerry has an ace, or a flush draw
and a straight draw (like K♦-Q♦, K♦-J♦, or Q♦-J♦), or a flush
draw and a pair like 10♦-Q♦, 10♦-K♦, or 10♦-xd (x is a random card).
The next card is the 6♦, for A♦-10♠-4♦-6♦, and Jerry bets out into
you and Jim folds. OK, the flush draw has hit, so you fold your
hand, because you figure that Jerry has either an ace or a flush.

Protect Your Hand

Jerry and Jim both call your raise, and the next card off the deck is the 8♣, for A♦-10♣-4♦-8♣. Jerry and Jim now check to you. They probably aren't checking an ace (a pair of aces) to you, and you don't want to give them a free draw at their flush, or at an overcard hand like K-Q. So you bet to protect your hand.

The Elephant Scares You Off

Dumbo makes it three bets to go, and he isn't the type to raise it unless he has a big hand. Dumbo makes a lot of calls but doesn't raise too often. Jerry now folds, and Jim calls the $15 bet. It is only $5 more to you to call, so I would call, but I'd be ready to fold my hand on fourth street for one bet from Dumbo. I would be thinking that Dumbo has at least a pair of aces with a high kicker, and probably two pair, aces up with A-10 or A-6.

Raising the Jackal on Fourth Street When a Good Card Hits

Jerry and Jim both call your raise on the flop, and now the A♠ comes off the deck for A♦-10♣-4♦-A♠. (This is a good card for you: first, because now there are only two aces left and the chances that one of your two opponents has it are decreased; second, because this isn't a straight or a flush card.) Jerry checks and now Jim bets out into you. You decide that you have Jim beat and you raise to protect your hand, because there is a chance that your raise here will cause Jerry to fold his flush draw. If Jerry does have an ace, you will know when he raises it to $30 to go, and now you can fold your hand. Either way, you're pretty sure you have Jim beaten here, because he's a jackal who hasn't made a bet or raise until now! Don't be afraid to raise Jim on fourth street if you think you have him beat.

A Tough Situation

Jerry reraises you on the flop, making it three bets, and Jim calls the three bets. You also call the three bets. Now 6♠ comes off the deck, for A♦-10♠-4♦-6♠, Jerry bets out into you, and Jim calls the bet. Now you have a tough situation to deal with! You really aren't worried that Jim might have you beaten. The question is, does Jerry have you beat (as he would with an A or three fours) or is he holding a big draw like 10♦-Q♦, 10♦-9♦, J♦-Q♦, Q♦-K♦, or something similar? I would lean toward folding my hand here, but everything would depend on my read of the player. Is Jerry the type to try to bluff me here? When I look straight at him, what do I sense he is pondering? Does he want me to call or to fold right now? Just make your best guess and go with it! You will find that the more often you're put in this situation, the better you become at reading your opponents.

Playing the River with the Top Ten Hands: Call for the Pot Odds!

In general, if you've made it all the way to the river with your top ten hand, then it's probably correct to call one bet on the river. The concept of "pot odds" will help me explain to you why I like to make a lot of calls on the river in Hold'em. In poker slang, I'm a "calling station" on the river in limit Hold'em; I'm from Missouri, the "Show me" state!

If the game is $5–$10, and I've played my top ten hand aggressively throughout the pot, then the amount of money already in the pot might be $140. For example, I make it $15 to go with three opponents ($60) before the flop, and now I raise on the flop and two opponents call my raise ($30). Then I bet out and two opponents call my bet on fourth street ($30), and finally one opponent bets out into me and my other opponent calls ($20). So the pot holds $60 + $30 + $30 + $20 = $140. Now, my $10 call gives me a chance to win $140!

If you do decide to fold here, then you must be at least 93 percent sure that you are beat (10/140 = 0.0714, and 1–.0714 = 92.86). That's why I don't lay down too many hands on the river! Of course, when the worst possible card for my hand hits on the river and a mouse bets into me, then I'm 98 percent sure that I'm beaten! So the $140 *pot* is laying me 14 to 1 *odds* on my call. $140 to $10 is pretty strong pot odds! This is why I encourage being a calling station like me in limit Hold'em!

Examples

Having said all that, I'll start with two examples of where I would fold a hand, even on the river.

Folding on the River

Let's assume that you have Q-Q in a four-way-action pot with a board of 5♦-10♦-J♠-7♠, and that there has been a lot of betting and raising on the flop during this hand. Say now that A♦ comes off the deck and a mouse bets into you. You'll want to fold your hand without further thought. The A♦ makes a flush, a straight, and a pair of aces all possible. That combined with the specter of a mouse betting into you is a scary scenario! You'd probably have to fold even if a jackal bet into you, especially if there are other opponents in the hand behind you yet to act. It is also a bad sign for you that there was so much betting and raising on the flop; this suggests that there are straight and flush draws out there. Some cards are just so bad that you have to fold.

The Board Is So Bad I Surrender!

Suppose you have A♠-A♦, the flop comes 8♥-9♥-10♥ (this is one of the worst possible flops for your hand), and two opponents are really "jamming it" with you on the flop. Say 2♠ hits on the turn, they both check, you bet, and they both call you. Now you know that you probably have the best hand at this point, since no one has raised you, but you're also sure that your opponents have big draws. (What else could they have been jamming it with on the flop?) So when J♥ pops up on the river, for 8♥-9♥-10♥-2♠-J♥, what can you beat? Any heart makes a flush and any seven or queen makes a straight. How can you call even one bet on the end, especially given the way the others have played the hand? You can't even beat an opponent who holds 10♠-J♠ (that hand makes two pairs). Even though you waited hours for your

A-A, and even though the pot odds are pretty good, sometimes you just have to surrender!

Now let's take a look at some situations where, most of the time, you just have to call on the river because of the pot odds.

The Following Hand Has Three Different Endings

Here's a familiar situation, involving Jim (the jackal) and Jerry (unknown profile). You have J-J and you've made it three bets over the top of Jim's two bets (reraised) before the flop. Jerry calls you from the big blind, and the flop is [A♦]-[10♠]-[4♦]. Jerry bets out on the flop, Jim calls the bet, and you raise it, to find out what they really have. Both players call your raise, and then [6♠] comes off on the turn and they both check to you. You bet out, thinking your J-J is still the best hand, and they both call again.

The last card is [K♦], for a final board of [A♦]-[10♠]-[4♦]-[6♠]-[K♦]. Jerry bets out and Jim calls. The [K♦] was probably the worst possible card for your hand, other than [10♦], because now you can't beat a flush, a straight, or a pair of kings. Jerry probably has you beaten, but how about Jim? It looks to me as if Jim has you beaten here as well.

Here, I'd put Jim on K-Q, which makes a pair of kings for him on the end. Think about it. If Jim has a flush, then he would have raised on the end. If Jim has kings and tens (another possibility, given the way the hand unfolded), then he would probably have raised on the flop himself, with his pair of tens. Whatever the case may be, it looks as if Jim has you beaten. It's true that there is already $125 ($45 + $30 + $30 + $20) in the pot, so you need to be over 92 percent sure that you're beaten before you decide to fold. But given this situation, I would have to fold, because I'd be convinced that both players have me beaten. Both players expect you to call on the end, and the chances that both of them are trying to bluff you therefore seem very remote to me.

Let's suppose now that the last card is [6♣], for [A♦]-[10♠]-[4♦]-[6♠]-[6♣], and now Jerry bets out into you and Jim folds. This bet would seem very suspicious to me, and I would call it very quickly. I would be thinking, "Why did Jerry decide to bet right here and now? I don't think that the six helped him, so he's either bluffing or holding an ace." If I'm facing an either-or situation and getting this kind of pot odds, I'm going to call without hesitation.

Let's suppose again that the last card is [6♣], for [A♦]-[10♠]-[4♦]-[6♠]-[6♣], and now both opponents check to you. Do you bet here or check? If you bet here, you have to be hoping that either Jerry or Jim will call you with a pair of tens or worse. I wouldn't be worried about Jim in this case, but Jerry would concern me a little bit. (Could Jerry have an ace with no kicker, like A-2, A-3, or A-5, which would explain why he just called on the flop? Did he fear an ace with a kicker on the flop?) This "value bet" that you're considering making (a bet you make believing that it will earn slightly more than it will lose, over the long run) is one that needs a little bit of reading ability as well (a little finesse). If you decide to bet, then that's fine; if you decide to check, that's fine too. I would bet it myself unless I felt strongly that Jerry had me beaten. We'll talk more about value betting in the intermediate and advanced sections.

Pot Odds Say, "Close Your Eyes and Call"

You're holding K-K, and you three-bet an elephant before the flop. The flop then comes down [5♦]-[6♣]-[7♥], and now you make it four bets (a raising war on the flop). The next card off is

[10♠] and he checks and then calls your bet. Now [8♠] comes off on the river, for [5♦]-[6♠]-[7♥]-[10♠]-[8♠], and the elephant bets out into you. In this case, any four or nine makes a straight, but you call the bet quickly because you can still beat a lot of hands. The pot odds are heavily in your favor for a call here—there is already $7 from the blinds that folded, $30 from before the flop, $40 on the flop, $20 from fourth street, and $10 from the elephant's bet on the end. One $10 call to win $107! I'd call quickly as well.

Suppose it's [A♠] that comes off on the river, for [5♦]-[6♠]-[7♥]-[10♠]-[A♠], and the elephant bets out into you. I'd call quickly here as well, because of the pot odds (there is a lot of money in this pot).

Calling Two Bets on the River

The question here is whether or not you should call on the river when calling costs you two big bets. In general, when you have to call two bets (someone bets and then someone else raises) on the river in a Hold'em pot, it's a good idea to fold. Usually, the only hands that you can beat on the end, when it costs you two bets just to call, are bluffs. You will rarely see an experienced player bluff raise on the river in low-limit Hold'em! It's just not a very profitable play. To return to a familiar example: let's assume that the hand has been played out among Jim, Jerry, and you, as detailed above. When Jerry bets out into [A♦]-[10♠]-[4♦]-[6♠]-[K♦] and Jim raises, it's a good idea to exit stage left with your modest little J-J.

If the last card is [6♣], leaving [A♦]-[10♠]-[4♦]-[6♠]-[6♣], and, as before, Jerry bets out and Jim raises, then get out of that one too. Even though [6♣] seems a harmless card, all you can really beat here is a bluff by both players. Is it really possible that both Jerry and Jim are bluffing? I don't think so! (If you want another reason to fold this hand, suppose now that you call, and Jerry really has the goods, something like A-6, and reraises! Now what are you going to do?

Folding A-A for Two Bets on the End

When John bets out into [5♦]-[6♦]-[8♣]-[10♠]-[4♦] on the end and Frank raises to two bets, then it's a good time to dump your A-A even though the pot is huge! When they bet and raise at this point in the hand, what can you beat? It seems likely that one of your opponents has made a flush or a straight (he needs to have only a seven in his hand for a straight) or at least two pair. I'm assuming in this example that you played your A-A very aggressively and put in a lot of bets, which would have discouraged them from thinking that they could bluff you on the river.

When the Last Card Is Bad for Your Hand

Let's assume that you have put in a lot of bets with your Q-Q (pocket queens), that two opponents have called, and that the board has developed [4♣]-[5♣]-[9♥]-[J♠] on the turn. Let's consider two scenarios.

In the first scenario, both opponents have just called you on fourth street and now the last card is [9♣], for a final board of [4♣]-[5♣]-[9♥]-[J♠]-[9♣]. Your first opponent then bets out into you, and now it's your turn to act, with your other opponent waiting behind you. Wow, what an awful card [9♣] was for your hand! You can't beat anyone who is holding either a nine (he now has *trips*, or three of a kind) or two clubs (he now has a flush), and either of those is a hand pretty likely to have withstood your heavy raising on the flop. A nine would have given him top pair on the flop, and the flop presented a flush draw.

I might lean toward folding here for the first bet (I would fold to a mouse, but not to a jackal), but let's assume that you call and now the opponent behind you raises and the other opponent calls. In this situation you can be almost certain you are beat. Judging from the fact that they have bet into you, raised you, and then called the raise, you can suppose they pretty much know your hand! (By the way, my guess here is that they both have your Q-Q beat.) Yikes, you had better fold, even though the pot odds are huge. The point is that you need to be very concerned when someone raises on the river! Ironically, the great size of the pot (which so powerfully entices you to call) demonstrates that they almost certainly have you beat, because they will have assumed you would call them with such a large pot staring you in the face. In very-high-stakes games, this isn't always going to be true, but when you're starting out, you aren't going to be seeing very many bluff raises on the river.

Let's assume now that 6♣ comes off on the river, for a final board of 4♣–5♣–9♥–9♠–6♣, and that the first opponent bets out into you. The second opponent is sitting behind you, waiting for you to act. This card is bad for you, because it completes the flush draws, but not nearly as bad as the 9♣ we looked at in the preceding example, because it doesn't give trips to those folks who may have started with top pair. Here, you have to call your first opponent. But if the second opponent raises, then you have to fold, regardless of whether the first opponent called the second opponent's raise or not. It's just too hard for the second opponent to bluff here. What's he going to do, raise hoping that both of you will fold?

In general, when you aren't sure whether or not to call one bet on the river, then call. The pot odds support a whole lot of calling on the river, because in the long run you don't often have to be too successful in picking off a bluff for this call to prove profitable! Generally, though, I would fold my hand on the river for two bets, since rarely do you see someone making it two bets to go on the river on a bluff. Of course, if your instincts say fold, or call, or raise on the river, and you've begun to trust your instincts, then follow them!

So, before the flop in limit Hold'em, play only the top ten hands, and make sure that you play them very aggressively. On the flop, remember to raise to find out "where you're at" so that you can make the right moves later on in the hand or possibly win a pot through your aggressive play that others wouldn't have won. On fourth street make sure that you protect your hand, or fold it, depending on what you learned on the flop, what card came off, and the way the betting came down. On the river, look to call down your opponents because of the pot-odds principle, but be leery of calling two bets on the river.

You've now learned enough to win money playing poker in most small-stakes games. Remember, though, that it may take a long time to digest all the information I've given you so far. Before you rush on out and play, keep in mind that you need to learn to walk before you can fly. You're not ready to play with Junior's graduation money just yet.

Chapter 4

Limit Hold'em:
Intermediate Strategy

If you have a really steep learning curve, and the ability to read players well, then you may be able to move up rather quickly from the beginners' level to the next, intermediate level of limit Hold'em. But usually, in order to reach the intermediate level, you will need to play for at least a few months and absorb the nuances of limit Hold'em.

The intermediate-level limit Hold'em player does extremely well in low-limit games. In fact, he does so well that he wants to test himself at the next level up. For example, if you begin to beat your $2–$4 home poker game consistently, then it is time for you to try a higher-stakes home poker game (or casino game)—perhaps $4–$8 or $5–$10. If you're only breaking even or losing at this higher level, then you need to drop back down and continue to win at the lower levels for a while before you test your game again. But if you're a good intermediate-level player and you do well in the $4–$8 games, then you will want to try playing $8–$16 or $10–$20 limit.

Every great player that I know of has moved up through the limits in this way, with some drop-offs along the way. You start out playing $1–$2 limit Hold'em with your friends, and the next thing you know, you're playing $400–$800 limit at the Bellagio with Phil Hellmuth, Johnny Chan, and Doyle Brunson! I personally won about $20,000 in home games in 1986, but when I stepped up to Las Vegas casino play, I slowly lost the whole $20,000 and went broke for the first and (so far!) last time. A bumpy road on the way up is to be expected—no one climbs Mount Everest with ease!

Extending Your Play beyond the Top Ten Hands

It's time to add a few more hands to the mix. I call the new group of hands the "majority play hands" because you can play all of them in the majority of the Hold'em games you find yourself in. Recall that the top ten hands in Chapter 3 were A-A, K-K, Q-Q, A-K, J-J, 10-10, 9-9, 8-8, A-Q, and 7-7. The majority play hands are 6-6, 5-5, 4-4, 3-3, 2-2, A-x suited, and K-Q. "A-x suited" simply means an ace and any other card of the same suit, like 🂡-🂤, 🂡-🂥, 🂡-🂢, 🂱-🂳, etc.

In this chapter you will learn:

▌ How to "steal the blinds"
▌ Phil's "majority play" hands
▌ The "calling" theory on how to play small pairs
▌ The "reraising" theory on how to play small pairs

- How to play K-Q
- How to "trap" players ("slow playing" and "smooth calling")

The intermediate-level majority-play-hands strategy will be more "swingy" than the top-ten-hands strategy. By swingy, I mean that you'll find that your chip stack goes up and down both more frequently and for higher amounts when you use this intermediate-play strategy along with the top-ten-hands strategy. For example, you may now lose a small pot or win a big pot when you play A♣-3♣ against your opponent's A-Q (most of the time you'll lose). Using just the top-ten-hands strategy, you would never have gotten involved in this hand, so your chip stack wouldn't have had to endure the swings up or down that this confrontation can create.

Similarly, you will lose many small pots when you play hands like 2-2 or 3-3, but you will also win some really big ones when you *flop a set*, the poker slang term for three of a kind. Of course, you're not guaranteed to win when you flop a set, but I like your chances! The problem is that you will flop a set only one time out of every 7½ attempts. That's why playing this hand will cause you to lose a lot of small pots: most of the time you'll miss the flop, but you'll be smart enough to fold when you do, and when you do hit the flop, you'll probably score well.

Stealing the Blinds

We'll get into the play of these majority play hands soon, but first I need to introduce a strategy called "stealing the blinds," one that can yield a few chips in certain circumstances, even with a worthless hand, and at minimal risk. In most tough games, you'll see a lot of folding before the flop. When everyone folds up to the player on the button, then that player will usually raise in the hope that the small blind and big blind will fold their hands too. If they do, then the button player gets to keep the blind money. Even if the player on the button has something like 5-8, he will often raise in this situation in order to try to steal the blinds. Experienced opponents will know that the button player who raises at this point might be attempting to steal, but if their hands are just as bad, they'll fold rather than get involved with a bad hand in bad position. You can see how the term "stealing" would have arisen when players put in a raise with a hand this weak!

The power of the blind steal is related to the fact that the button player has the best position. Being on the button gives a player the advantage of position, in that he will act last during the whole hand. In Hold'em acting last (having position) is a huge edge. If you're powerful, weak, or somewhere in between, you can sit back and wait for all the other players to reveal their strength or weakness before you act on your hand. Two good reasons for you to fold a marginal hand in the blinds when the button raises are that you're in bad position and that the button may actually have a real hand instead of a weak hand.

Weird Things Can Happen When You're Stealing the Blinds

I still remember a hand that came up with 11 players left (five at one table and six at my table) in a limit Hold'em event at Caesar's Palace in 1991. With the limits at $1,000–$2,000 I decided to raise in late position with [Q♦]-[7♠]. The poker legend Hans "Tuna" Lund (twice a final-table finisher at the World Series of Poker!) decided to call me with 10-J in the big blind, because he thought that I was just trying to steal his blind.

The flop came up Q-10-7, which gave me a very powerful two pair, and Tuna checked and then called my $1,000 bet. When a jack came off on fourth street, giving him two pair (tens and jacks), he bet out $2,000 and I raised him to $4,000. He then reraised me, and I just called his three bets ($6,000), thinking that he probably had me beat. Tuna then bet out $2,000 on the end, and I called. He then stated, "Two pair, jacks up," and I responded, "No good, I have queens up." Tuna replied, "You lucky puppy, I knew you were just trying to steal the blinds!"

It was indeed a very lucky hand to have come up with, when 11 players were left in the tournament and the limits were as high as they were. I won a $22,500 pot all because I was trying to steal the blinds! Of course, although an attempt to steal may lead to either a successful steal with nothing or a big win like the one I got against Tuna, you can also end up losing a big pot if you flop something good in that endeavor and it loses to something better.

In another tournament, this one at the U.S. Poker Open at the Taj Mahal in Atlantic City in 1997, I kept trying to steal the blinds, and I kept getting crushed! I would steal from a position one off the button (you will observe that a steal attempt looks less like a steal attempt the farther you are from the button) with 9-10, and I'd get called with K-10. Then the old 10-4-2 flop would hit and I would lose the maximum. Or I would raise with 8♦-9♦ stealing on the button and be called with Q-J. With a flop of J-10-2, I then had to play my open-ended straight draw all the way. And boom—an eight would come up on the last card and I would call that bet too! After repeatedly getting crushed stealing the blinds that day, I decided to be more careful in the future, both in using that play and in how aggressively I would continue on after I got called, and so should you. So again, blind-stealing can cut both ways. (It will crop up in various examples in this chapter, and you should already understand the strategy when it does.)

Playing the Majority Play Hands before the Flop

Now it's time to examine the play of the majority play hands of 6-6, 5-5, 4-4, 3-3, 2-2, A-x suited, and K-Q before the flop, all of them weaker than the "top ten" hands in Chapter 3. Common sense and deception are two important concepts in the play of these hands. I view the pairs 2-2 through 6-6 as basically being of the same value before the flop in limit Hold'em. A-x suited is slightly below the value that I assign these pairs, and K-Q is the weakest.

Calling with Small Pairs

Most theories agree that you should be the first raiser with a pair before the flop, that is, that with your small pair you should usually make it two bets to go. But when it is already two bets to you, a popular theory says you can either call the two bets or fold. Some top pros want you to call two bets with these pairs in order to lure other players into calling and therefore "build the pot" before the flop in the hope that you'll flop a set. So they'll have you passively call someone else's raise before the flop, leaving you hoping that others will call two bets before the flop as well.

Although this sounds good on paper, keep in mind that you'll flop a set roughly once in every eight tries. Now what do you do with your 3-3 when the flop comes down J-10-2? You're forced to fold, because you've let other people into the pot, some of whom probably have you beaten at this point. (If you'd reraised, they would probably have folded.) One advantage "calling to build a pot" does have going for it is that if you miss the flop, you can generally just fold your hand and be done with it. In other words, no thinking is required. If you flop your set, then you jam it, but if you have a bad flop, then you just fold your hand right away. Generally, this is a relatively easy way, and not a bad way, to play limit Hold'em.

Reraising with Small Pairs, before the Flop

I have a different preference. I like to reraise with a small pair before the flop and then "represent" whatever hits the flop (to your opponents, you *seem* to have started with something before the flop, and to have hit it on the flop). This is a more deceptive approach, allowing a chance to win every pot you play. Imagine having made it three bets with 4-4 over the top of your opponent, and now the flop comes down A-8-2. Your opponent checks to you, and then you bet out with your 4-4, just as if you have A-K. Your opponent now folds his K-Q, and you have won this pot fairly easily.

But let's suppose you play this hand according to the mainstream "calling" theory. You call the two bets with 4-4, and one other player and the big blind also call. The flop comes down A-8-2, and now the big blind checks. Now the original raiser bets out with his K-Q, hoping that no one calls him. By just calling the preflop raise, you've given the K-Q the chance to use deception. The K-Q is now representing an ace! You have to fold your hand right here. You can't call the first bet, because you have to fear that someone has an ace, or maybe the big blind has an eight. You have gone from a position of power to a position of weakness simply by not reraising before the flop—quite a difference.

By reraising, you'll win more pots, but you'll also get yourself into trouble more often. Consider the following scenario. You have three bets in with 4-4, but the original raiser has K-K. He decides just to call your raise and then play his hand hard on the flop if an ace doesn't come. This is a common strategy for people who hold aces or kings. The flop comes down 7♦-8♦-2♣. This appears to be a good flop for you. After all, it's unlikely that the original raiser has a seven or an eight in his hand, so unless you're up against a big pair instead of the more likely two big cards, you're winning at this point. The K-K bets out and you raise him, and now he reraises (three-bets) you.

You have a fair amount of money already invested in this pot. If you had known your opponent had kings, you would have thrown your hand away, but it's also possible that he could have been playing a big flush draw this way. You end up calling him all the way down, only to have him show you K-K. You have just lost a fortune using my reraising approach! Every approach offers its own risks and its own possibilities.

Now let's look at the play of the hand using the mainstream calling approach. You just call two bets with 4-4 before the flop, and now both blinds call. The flop is $7\diamondsuit$-$8\diamondsuit$-$2\clubsuit$, and the big blind (who wouldn't have been in the hand using my approach, because the reraise would have pushed him out) bets out, and now the K-K raises to protect what he correctly feels is currently the best hand. You now fold, having lost only three small bets. Clearly the mainstream approach has done well in this situation.

But if the original raiser had A-K rather than K-K, then my reraising approach would yield better results here. I like my approach because it is mathematically more likely that the first raiser has two big cards than that he has a big pair. But remember, my aggressive approach does lead to more fluctuation in the size of your stack across time, and if you don't have much of a bankroll, pursuing it may put you in an awkward spot.

Now let's look at a few other examples that compare the two approaches to playing small pairs, using my "three bet" theory with the mainstream theory of calling to build a pot.

Examples

Make It Two Bets with No Callers

You have 4-4 and the two people have folded in front of you. According to both theories you make it two bets to go, so that you have a chance to win the blinds before the flop. No need, then, to discuss this case further.

Making It Two Bets with Callers

You have 2-2, and two people have "limped in" (simply called the bet before the flop). My theory says you should raise here. The mainstream theory—"call to build a pot"—can go either way here, but it leans more toward just calling, since two other players have already called ahead of you. The "call" theory is thinking: let's get by for one bet before the flop; then we can fold if we don't flop a set. Not bad thinking, but why not put in one raise and represent something strong with a bet after the flop? For one more bet before the flop and one more after the flop, you may win the whole pot on the flop. And raising does accord nicely with the "building a pot" part of the "calling" theory.

Small Pairs When the Mouse Has Come in Raising

You have 3-3 in late position, and a mouse has raised in front of you (types of players are discussed in Chapter 3, page 33). A mouse raising, as you will recall, is a scary thought indeed! Both theories are now in agreement: the mouse probably has your 3-3 beat with a higher pair. So what to do? My reraising approach doesn't advocate reraising when you're almost certain that you're beat. Folding your hand at this point is clearly the best idea. Why put in your money as a 4½-to-1 underdog to the mouse's higher pair, which he probably has? You can throw away a lot of "majority play hands" and some "top ten hands" when the mouse comes in raising!

But if you feel that others will call the mouse's raise behind you (something possible to probable in a low-stakes game where the other players haven't even noticed that the mouse is someone who doesn't raise very often), then calling is OK. If you do flop a set, then you'll probably win a big pot. Frankly, I would probably call the mouse's raise, thinking that the most I could lose would be two small bets, but the most I could win would be a lot of bets. In this calling scenario, I'm looking to collect from the other players more than from the mouse. In other words, I would be thinking that if I flop a three, I win big; but if I don't, then I'll just fold my hand, having lost little.

Raise and "Isolate" the Jackal

You have 3-3 in the fourth position and a jackal (see page 33) has raised in the second position. My theory says reraise (three-bet) and "isolate" the jackal (play the crazy player one on one) with your 3-3. The "call to build a pot" theory says just call the bet. But even if you subscribe to it, that theory and the notion of isolating the jackal aren't mutually exclusive. Nonetheless, people who like to call and build large pots tend not to use the more aggressive isolation play.

Small Pairs—Don't Call Three Bets!

You have 5-5, and it has been two bet and then three bet in front of you. For the "majority play hands," as opposed to the "top ten hands," calling three bets is a bad idea. Just fold your 5-5 and live to fight another day. Still, if nearly every hand in your game is being three-bet, then by all means call the three bets! (In a crazy game like that—which by the way, I love to play in—sets tend to play well and win huge pots.) Even at low stakes it is unusual to play in a game where every pot is three-bet, so folding small pairs for three bets is the norm. In general, then, fold all small pairs for three bets unless you know three things: that more or less every hand in your game gets three-bet or four-bet; that your bankroll can handle the wild swings this is almost certainly going to create; and that your emotions can handle things like flopping sets and losing to people who make straights with hands like 2-3 off-suit (this can be tough to swallow!).

How to Play A-x Suited before the Flop

Once you add A-x suited to the arsenal of hands you play, you need to pursue this hand within certain constraints:

1. A-x suited is not a hand you would ever want to call three bets with before the flop. Perhaps if your hand is A-10 or A-J suited, and you're in the big blind, then it's OK (recall that we covered A-Q and A-K in Chapter 3). But with only a very few exceptions, you don't ever want to call three bets with A-x suited.
2. When no one else has entered the pot in front of you, you should usually make it two bets with this hand. This way your raise seems to be representing a strong hand, and you may just end up winning the blinds if no one calls your raise. With these types of weak hands, picking up the blinds is a good result.
3. When anyone else has already limped into the pot in front of you (just called one bet), you should call that one bet. For the intermediate-level player, this play is

slightly better than making it two bets. If you then hit the flop, you can play your hand hard, but if you miss the flop, you can fold your hand, having lost only one bet.

4. If someone raises in front of you, then just call the two bets. The one exception is that you could three-bet a jackal with A-10 or A-J suited.

I don't think giving you any more examples of what to do before the flop with A-x suited would help very much at this point. You now have the basic principles. (I hope, by the way, that I'm not driving you crazy with all these rules followed so closely by all these exceptions! That's just the way poker is. Personality and relative hand strength are always factors.)

Playing K-Q before the Flop

I think we can safely move on now to the play of K-Q before the flop. When you're considering calling a raise with K-Q, pause and consider some more, because most of the time your hand is beaten! In fact, if a mouse were to raise, I would just throw this hand away before the flop. A certain small percentage of the time, the first raiser will have A-K or A-Q, in which case you're in particularly bad shape! Let's look at a quick list of rules for K-Q:

1. Never call three bets with K-Q. You just don't want to get yourself in too deep with this hand before the flop. If it's three bets to you to go, then you can be almost certain that your hand is beaten, and probably in bad shape.

2. Always raise it to two bets with K-Q before the flop. Whether someone else has limped in front of you or not, make it two bets to go. Representing hands in Hold'em is a strong way to play poker.

3. If it's two bets to go to you, then use your best judgment regarding whether you should call the two bets, raise it to three bets, or fold. If a mouse made it two bets, then fold your hand; if anyone else made it two bets, then call; if a jackal made it two bets, then sometimes you might make it three bets to go (this is more of an advanced play). But what if an elephant made it two bets to go and then a mouse called the two bets? Here, too, use your best judgment. Calling and folding are both OK, but when you're on the fence, don't forget to take position into account (it's a much easier call on or near the button).

The play of K-Q before the flop is thus relatively simple. Notice that it is almost exactly like playing A-x suited before the flop. The only difference is that with A-x suited you should call just one bet when there are limpers before the flop, whereas with K-Q you should make it two bets with other limpers. (When you have A-x suited you're hoping for more opponents.)

Playing before the flop is the easiest part of the "majority play hands" approach. Now it's time to move on to the most difficult part of playing these hands: how to play on the flop.

Playing the Majority Play Hands on the Flop

Although you can still use "raise to find out where you are" as a strategy with "majority play" hands, it's not as powerful a move as it was in playing the top ten hands. Now that we're playing the majority play hands as well, two things will change dramatically. The first is your table image; the second is the power of the hands you're playing.

Your *table image* is the way the other players in the game are likely to be viewing you. When you're playing the top ten hands only, people will fear your hands when you raise the pots, because you're playing only very powerful hands—if they've been paying attention (but remember, some people won't pay attention, no matter how consistently you play). Now that you're playing some weaker hands too, your opponents will fear your raises less and therefore call (or raise) you more.

When you add the "majority play hands" to your acceptable starting-hand list, you'll find yourself playing well over twice as many hands as before. Therefore the power of the average hand that you're playing will go way down, and in time your more astute opponents will begin to perceive that as well (your table image is now altered). Both of these changes will have a direct impact on the way you should play your hands on the flop. You should continue to raise to find out where you are in some hands, but now discretion and deception become very important.

Shakespeare, as we know, wrote that discretion is the better part of valor. In poker, valor (courage) and aggressiveness are winning traits. You will win many more pots by playing your hands aggressively, but it takes a lot of valor to raise someone on a flop of Q-J-2 when you're holding pocket tens! Shakespeare never played poker, but in Hold'em there are indeed times when discretion is the better part of valor. There is a time to throw your hand away after the flop, rather than putting up a fight. Sometimes, "saving bets" is the name of the game in Hold'em; and the only way you can save them is by folding your hand in a timely manner.

For example, if you three-bet with 4-4 and three opponents take a flop, and then the flop comes down Q-9-2, you're better off not calling any bets or making any raises. Folding is a pretty good choice at this point. Even if somehow your 4-4 was the best hand preflop, when you're facing three opponents who have hung in to play for three bets, and you see two high cards on the flop, there's a pretty good chance that your little pair is now losing. Yes, you could be up against A-K, 7-6 suited, and J-10 suited, which would technically mean you're still winning. Notice, though, that even if that rather unlikely "best-case scenario" was in fact what you had wandered into, you will lose if any A, K, J, 10, 8, or 6 hits on the turn or the river. Save your valor for another hand.

Examples

To give you a greater sense of what you need to do on the flop while playing the "majority play hands," I'll lead you through several examples.

Playing Small Pairs (2-2 through 6-6) on the Flop: Pump It or Dump It

In general, if there are four people in the pot when the flop comes down and you have a small pair, you need to flop a set in order to continue playing your hand. Of course, if you have 6-6, and the flop comes down 3-4-5, this too is a good flop, although certainly not as strong as flopping the set. When you have this kind of flop, you want to raise to protect your hand, because although there's a reasonable chance that you have the best hand at the moment, all you have at this point is a pair of sixes, a hand clearly vulnerable to overcards that could give someone else a higher pair. Of course, if you get callers and then make your straight (preferably with the deuce, because then you'll get a lot of action from anyone holding an ace), you'll want to continue raising—for the same reason you want to raise when you flop a set: you have the best hand and want to "pump it."

When the flop comes down J-Q-2 to your 6-6 with four players in the pot, then use some discretion and (in most cases) fold your hand: "dump it." The "pump it" tactic is used either to protect your hand, by raising to eliminate your opponents on the flop, or to get more money into the pot when you have a strong flop. "Dump it" is used to save bets, by using your best discretion to fold your hand on the flop, thus losing no more bets.

Playing Small Pairs on the Flop

You have 4-4 in the fourth position, and the player in the second position (two seats to the left of the big blind) makes it two bets to go. You're playing my theory—"three-bet with small pairs"—before the flop, so you make it three bets. No one else calls, and the flop is Q-10-3. The player in the second position then bets out into you and you raise him, thus "representing" a queen (or perhaps K-K or A-A) but also gaining information. If your opponent reraises you, then either you're already beaten (this is more likely) or your opponent has a straight draw, and it's time for a decision. If you feel you have him beat at this point, then you may want to reraise him. Or you might decide that your opponent has you beaten and fold your hand on the flop. You might decide simply to call his reraise on the flop and defer a decision to call or fold when you see what drops on fourth street. I would call one more bet and make a decision on fourth street heavily weighted toward folding, but trust your instincts here.

If your opponent just calls your raise, then he may still have you beaten, with something like A-10 or Q-J. But if he doesn't have you beaten, then he most likely has some sort of straight draw like K-J, A-J, or A-K. Therefore, any 9, J, K, or A would be a terrible card for you on fourth street.

Let's look at the way this hand would be played on the flop if you had just called the two bets with your 4-4 before the flop. In this case, it's likely that at least one other player will have called the two bets before the flop. Suppose one of them was the big blind, since it costs him only one more bet. Now the big blind checks after the Q-10-3 flop, and the preflop raiser bets out. You have to use a bit more discretion here because you also have to worry about the big blind behind you. I would probably just call the bet in this case and see what the big blind does. If the big blind were to fold, then I would make a decision about this hand later, on fourth street. (In this case, it's all about how you read your opponent on fourth street.) But if the big blind were to raise the bet on the flop, then I would just fold my hand right there. And if the big blind were to call the bet, then I would assume that he has some sort of straight draw, or maybe a mediocre piece of the flop with something like 10-8 or 3-A.

Suppose now that the button player and the big blind both call the two bets before the flop. So we have the second position making it two bets, you calling the two bets with 4-4 in the fourth position, and now the button and the big blind calling the two bets as well. The flop comes down Q-10-3. Now the big blind checks and the original raiser bets out on the flop. What do you do? With three other opponents still in this hand and two over-cards on the board (Q-10), folding is the proper play. Moreover, the fact that the second-position original raiser has bet out into you, and there are two other people behind you yet to act, is a little bit scary in this scenario. You just have to give up and fold.

Playing Small Pairs: Flopping a Set

You have 2-2 on the button, the second position raises, and then the fourth position calls the two bets. You play in my style and make it three bets to go, everyone calls, and the flop comes down 2-4-J. You have flopped a set! You should put in as many raises as you can, both to build the pot and to protect your hand.

If you've used the other approach and just called before the flop with your 2-2, and then get your 2-4-J flop, nothing changes in your postflop approach. You still put in as many bets and raises as you can in order to build a pot and protect your hand. No matter how you play your small pair before the flop, when you hit a set it's time to "ram and jam" (raise and reraise). Sets usually win or lose (a majority of the time sets win) pretty good-size pots.

Playing Small Pairs: Good Flops, Protecting Your Hand

Assume that you have 6-6 in the small blind, the third position has raised before the flop, the fifth position has called the raise, and now the flop comes down 2-4-5.

Now it's your turn to act. You bet out, and the third position calls the bet. Now the fifth position makes it two bets, so you reraise (making it three bets) in order to protect your hand. This is a great flop for your hand, and you need to reraise in order to get rid of the original raiser. At this point, the only hands that can beat you are overpairs, and in any case, you have a straight draw to go with your hand. Maybe the original raiser has K-Q and your reraise forces him to fold his hand. If you don't drive him out, you may lose the pot to him by allowing him to call just one more bet in the hope of catching a king or a queen.

Suppose you're taking the approach where you just call the two bets before the flop, and the big blind calls. Now it's your turn to act. Because you haven't shown too much strength before the flop, you might want to try checking with your now powerful hand, and then raising when someone else bets out into you. Sometimes the "check-raise" plays can help you eliminate your opponents and therefore help you protect your hand. But betting out into the flop works well also. In either case, you want to "ram and jam" (raise and reraise) your hand with this flop in order to protect it.

Playing Small Pairs: Terrible Flops

Some flops are so bad for small pairs that you should just run for cover, no matter whether you've just called two bets before the flop or made it three bets. If the flop comes down Q-K-A, it's time to fold as soon as possible! Of course, if I had been using my three-bet approach I would bet on the flop when it was my turn, on the off chance that all my opponents might fold their hands, giving me the pot right there. It could also happen that I get called on the flop and then hit my set card on either fourth street or the river. Such things are possible. But I would not call a bet on this flop; I would not call a bet on the turn; I would not call a bet on the river; I would not bet on either fourth street or the river. All I would do in this case is make that one bet on the flop when it's my turn to bet.

Playing Small Pairs: Good Flops

When you have 4-4 in a pot, flops like J-J-3 or 10-10-2 or 9-9-3 are good for your hand; there is in fact an excellent chance that your two pair are the best hand at the table at this point. So put in some bets and raises, for two reasons: first, to find out if you do have the best hand; second, to protect your hand. When you face mixed overcards like J-10-3, you're in trouble, but when a big pair lands on the flop, it's much less likely that someone already holds the key card. For example, in the J-J-3 flop, there are only two jacks left in the deck; had the flop come J-10-3, there are six cards—three jacks and three tens—in the deck that would beat you. So with the J-J-3 flop, your pocket fours are the best hand unless someone has a higher pair or one of the two remaining jacks (both are unlikely).

Reraising before the Flop Leads to Betting on the Flop

When you're playing the small pairs the way I suggest (reraising with them before the flop), a lot of times you'll end up playing three-bet pots against only one or two opponents. When this happens, be sure you bet the flop aggressively, so as to gain information about what your opponents may have. Suppose for example that you've made it three bets before the flop with 3-3, and then the flop comes down A-K-9. If your lone remaining opponent checks, then go ahead and bet once. You never know—he may just fold for the one bet. Perhaps he too has a small pair, or he holds 10-8 suited or something of that sort.

Playing A-x Suited on the Flop: Hit It or Fold It

In the discussion of preflop situations, I said that if no one else has raised the pot before the flop, and you have A-x suited, then you should make it two bets to go. In general, if you've done that but missed the flop, you should bet out once anyway, thus representing that you've hit it. If an opponent calls your bet on the flop when you've missed the flop, prepare to fold your hand soon. There is no need to get too involved with A-x suited if you miss the flop, and no warrant for bluffing off too much money with this hand. If you're the raiser before the flop, then take one "shot" (bluff) at the pot and give up if you get called.

Where someone else *has* raised the pot before the flop, I've been recommending that you just call his two bets. In general, if you've done that but then missed the flop, then you should fold your hand. Again, there's no need for you to get involved in such a pot by calling or raising. Just throw your hand away, save some chips, and forget about it.

With A-x suited you'll see a lot of different flops that hit part or all of your hand. You may have $A\spadesuit$-$7\spadesuit$ when the flop comes down J-10-7; this one is trouble for you (because you hit just enough of the flop that you may decide to play on until the end and lose a bunch of chips). You may have $A\spadesuit$-$7\spadesuit$ when the flop comes down A-7-4, a terrific flop for you. You may have $A\spadesuit$-$7\spadesuit$ when the flop comes down 8-7-2, a reasonably good flop for you. You may have $A\spadesuit$-$7\spadesuit$ when the flop comes down 7-5-2, a strong flop for you (top pair with top kicker). Finally, there are dream flops for $A\spadesuit$-$7\spadesuit$ like $K\spadesuit$-$J\spadesuit$-$2\spadesuit$ (ace-high-flush) and A-A-7 (top full house).

So there are a lot of ways to hit A-x suited, some of them good and others bad. The interesting thing is that you may win your biggest pot with the 7-5-2 flop! Why? On those two "dream flops" I just mentioned, how much action can you expect to get from other players? You already have most of the cards that would get someone interested in playing. But on the 7-5-2 flop, people may sense a bluff and try what they think is a *resteal* (they raise on a bluff because they believe you're trying to steal the pot). In poker, you never know which hands or flops will win you the biggest pot of the night. Just be prepared to play your hand as well as you can.

I'll never forget a pot I once played holding A-7 at the World Series of Poker. The year was 1994, and we were down to about 40 players left in a no-limit Hold'em event. First place was $220,000, and as with any WSOP event, both money and history were at stake.

Two players to my right was a jackal from Europe who was reraising everyone while holding any kind of hand. He was a real nuisance to me, because he kept reraising me and stealing all the pots that he and I were going after. In fact, he was reraising everyone at the table and outplaying us all after the flop with his big bluffs. He had played this very dangerous style to near perfection, parlaying his chips to over $65,000. I also had about $65,000 in front of me, which is a ton of chips. This jackal and I were the chip leaders at a time when the average chip stack in the tournament was less than $15,000. Conventional wisdom at this point would suggest that neither one of us should play a big pot against the other. Why risk a boatload of chips in a single hand, when we could both just coast in to the final table with our huge stacks of chips? A cardinal sin at this point would be to get involved in a big pot with each of us holding really weak hands.

So much for conventional wisdom and cardinal sins! I soon found myself raising it to $2,000 to go before the flop with my A-7. The jackal was sitting in the big blind this hand, and he decided to reraise me by making it $8,000 to go. Perhaps he smelled my weakness and was just trying to force me out of the pot with his weak hand. He was right—I was weak—but he didn't count on the fact that I had smelled the weakness in his reraise. So I reraised it again to $20,000 to go before the flop. Again, I think the jackal smelled some weakness in me, and in any case he decided to call my $20,000 bet. Now the flop came down 7♣-5♦-4♦, and he bet out $15,000. I decided that top pair was enough to allow me to move all-in against him because I thought

I had the best hand. Frankly, I wasn't hoping for a call. So I moved all-in for $45,000. (I raised him $30,000!)

The jackal then called me quickly, and the next two cards to hit the board were the two worst cards I could think of! First the 6♣ came off the deck and then the Q♦ (7♣-5♦-4♦-6♣-Q♦), so that the flush draw and a straight draw had both hit the board! I stared in disbelief at the board. What had I done? I had just put in $65,000 with an incredibly weak hand! I could have waited patiently for some strong hands and made the final table fairly easily. I couldn't beat anything anymore. The flush draw beat me, some straight draws beat me, a set beat me, and an overpair beat me! But he was the first guy to flip his hand faceup, and he was taking a long time to do it.

I was thinking, "Just show me your hand, and I'll leave this tournament feeling sick about my awful play." With $130,000 in the pot in a tournament where no one else had even $30,000, the winner of this one pot would have an excellent chance of winning the tournament. Finally, he flipped up his hand and said, "One pair." I stared in amazement at his hand: 7-9 off suit, which gave him a pair of sevens with a nine kicker! I had a pair of sevens with an ace kicker, and the pot was mine! My good read of this jackal paid off, and from there I cruised easily down to the final three players. My attitude quickly changed from, "Phil, you idiot, how did you let yourself get $65,000 into this pot with this hand?" to, "Phil, baby, great play, great read, well done!" Eventually, I finished in second place and collected $110,000. Here was a story illustrating how an A-7 can pay off big when you merely hit a good flop with it. But please don't try this at home.

Examples

Now it's time to move on and give you some examples of how you should play A-x suited on the flop. In general, with A-x suited, we "hit it or fold it."

Playing A-x Suited on the Flop: Flush Draw

Suppose that an elephant has made it two bets in the second position before the flop and then a jackal in the fourth position has called the two bets. Now you call on the button with A♥-3♥, and the big blind calls as well. The flop is 9♥-Q♥-2♠, and the big blind checks. The elephant bets and the jackal raises. What do you do? You have flopped the "nut" (best) flush draw. If another heart comes off the deck, then you have made an ace-high flush.

This is a reasonably strong flop for your hand. With this strong draw, you'll make the flush about one-third of the time, and occasionally you may win simply by hitting your ace, so you must either call the two bets or raise it to three bets to go. My instinct in this case would be to raise. Who knows what the jackal has in this hand? He may have a flush draw or a straight draw, in which case you have him beat with your ace high at this point. Your raise may eliminate the elephant (who may have the best hand!) and get you one on one with the jackal, whom you may have beaten. The worst-case scenario for you, if you make it three bets to go, is that the elephant makes it four bets to go and you end up having to call one more bet.

In general, I recommend playing a nut-flush draw very aggressively on the flop, especially when you have position, as you do in this example. This hand all but requires that you call a bet with it on fourth street, and if it were mine I would want to put in a lot of bets on the flop and then bluff at the pot on fourth street even if a bad card comes off. Alternatively, I'd put in a lot of bets on the flop and call down one opponent on the end with my measly ace high if there's any chance that this opponent was drawing to something as well. Sometimes the size of the pot that you create by playing the nut-flush draw aggressively will necessitate your calling on the river with merely ace high, because the size of the pot may tempt other players who are on inferior draws to make desperation bluffs at you. You win these often enough, with your ace-high river call, to justify this play.

Playing A-x Suited: Bad Flop

Suppose that a jackal has raised before the flop, and you have called his raise with [A♦]-[5♦], and then the big blind calls as well. If the flop comes down [J♠]-[Q♥]-[3♦] and the big blind checks and the jackal bets, fold your hand. You have missed the flop (you don't have either a pair, a straight draw, or a flush draw); you have only two bets in the pot at this point; and you were the caller before the flop, not the raiser. There is no warrant for getting further involved in this hand.

Suppose now that a jackal has called one bet before the flop, and you've raised it with your [A♦]-[5♦]. Then the big blind and the jackal both call and the flop comes down [J♠]-[Q♥]-[3♦]. If they both check to you on the flop, then go ahead and bet once on the flop. They may both fold at this point. If one of them does bet into you, just fold your hand. Other than taking one shot at the pot on the flop when you were the preflop raiser with A-x suited, what you really want to do when you miss the flop is fold your hand.

Playing A-x Suited: Hitting Second Board Pair

A jackal in the second position raises before the flop, and you call with [A♠]-[9♠] in fifth position. The button and the big blind call as well. The flop is [10♥]-[9♥]-[2♠], and the jackal bets out into you. This situation seems to be a good time for a raise. To have you beaten right now, someone has to have a ten in his hand or an overpair (a set or two pair are also possible). You also know that the jackal could have anything at this point in the hand.

Let's try the same situation, but let's say that the big blind bets out this time and then the jackal raises on the flop. What do you do? It's time to use that newly developed reading power you've been working on. There are two possibilities here: you have the best hand or not. With this flop ([10♥]-[9♥]-[2♠]), it's possible that you still have the best hand with your [A♠]-[9♠]. Perhaps one of your opponents has J-9, and the other has the J-Q for an open-ended straight draw. Maybe one of your opponents has a straight draw and the other has a flush draw. But you may also be in a lot of trouble with the way that the action came down on this flop. Perhaps one of your opponents has a ten (for a pair of tens) and the other has a flush draw. If this is the case, then you need to hit one of two aces left in the deck (the [A♥] makes a flush), one of two nines left, or consecutive spades (called "runner-runner," not something you want to depend on!) for a backdoor flush. So if one of your opponents has you beaten, then you're really an underdog to win this pot. Whether you call two bets or fold in this case depends on how you read your opponents.

Playing A-x Suited: OK Flop

Suppose you've called an elephant's early position raise with A♣-6♣ on the button. The big blind calls the raise as well, and the flop comes down J♥-J♦-6♥. Now the big blind bets out and the jackal raises. What do you do? Read, read, and read your opponents. If it were my hand and if I didn't have a read on my opponents, I would reraise (make it three bets) to find out where I am, especially given that the raiser was a jackal. Your opponents need to have an overpair or three jacks to have your two pair beaten at this point in the hand. They may have the three jacks, or they may have 6-7 or K-6 or a smaller pair or a flush draw. Raise it in this spot, unless you have a strong feeling that you're beaten, in which case fold.

Playing A-x Suited: Marginal Flop

Suppose you've called an elephant's early-position raise with A♠-10♠ and then three other players call, including the big blind. The flop comes down J♦-10♥-8♣, and the big blind bets out and the elephant calls. What do you think, and what do you do? I wouldn't raise, because I figure that there is an excellent chance that the big blind has me beaten, and with five players in the pot, what are the chances that I have the best hand? But calling and folding are reasonable options. I would lean toward calling, but with two other people behind you and the big blind leading out, I could also make a pretty reasonable case for folding your hand right there. What did the elephant, the original raiser, call the one bet with on this flop? It seems pretty likely that he has A-Q, A-K, or K-Q, all of which would give him a straight draw. The reasons why I lean toward calling a bet on the flop in this situation are these:

1. You may have the best hand.

2. There are already six big bets in this pot.

3. Calling will cost only one more small bet, and perhaps both opponents behind you will fold their hands.

4. You may hit an ace or a ten on fourth street and wind up winning this pot because you called that one bet on the flop.

5. It's possible that everyone will check the rest of the way (no one will bet on fourth street or the river) and that you win the pot because you called one small bet on the flop. (Don't hold your breath hoping for this to happen!)

Playing A-x Suited: Flopping a Draw

Suppose that a mouse in second position has raised it up before the flop and the jackal on the button has called. You then called as well in the big blind with [A♦]-[8♦], and the flop is [5♦]-[6♣]-[7♠]. Generally, when you flop an open-ended straight draw (you need a four or a nine to make your hand) in Hold'em, especially when you're drawing to the big side (in this case a nine-high straight as opposed to having A-4 and drawing to the small side or eight-high straight), you're well advised to play this hand all the way to try and hit it. What do you do now?

You know that you are going to have to call on the flop, and on the turn as well, if you miss making the hand on fourth street. You also know that the mouse has a strong hand and that the jackal could have anything. I would be thinking, "I hope the mouse has A-K so that I can bluff him out of this pot." (We all know how tightly the mouse plays!) I would also be hoping that the jackal has a hand that I can beat, but that he can bet with, for example A-4 or K-8 or J-8 or some other straight draw. Perhaps I would check with my hand, hoping that the mouse checks and the jackal bets. Then I could check-raise, making it two bets to the mouse and therefore forcing him to fold his A-K or A-Q. Of course, what I really want to do is complete my straight on the turn or the river.

You could also decide to bet right out into the mouse on the flop, to see what he does. The mouse would either call you or raise you; it's hard to imagine him folding this flop, just because he's a mouse, which means he had a pretty strong hand before the flop. If he were to call me, I would try to bluff him out on the next two rounds of betting, thinking he couldn't call me down with A-K—because he's a mouse! If he were to raise me on the flop, then I would call him and check to him on the next two rounds of betting (unless I were to make my straight). I'm assuming that the mouse would just call on the flop with A-K and raise me with any overpair.

Playing A-x Suited: Second Pair with Mouse

Suppose that a mouse has raised in the third position and an elephant has called on the button, before the flop. You call with A♠-8♠ in the big blind because it's only one more bet to you in the big blind. Normally you wouldn't call the mouse's raise with this hand, but you're getting a discount! The flop comes down 9-8-3. What do you do here? I'd want to bet out here to see what the mouse does. If the mouse were to raise me, then I'd probably call the bet, but I'd fold my hand if the mouse bet on fourth street (unless I'd caught an A or an 8). If the mouse just called me on the flop, then I'd figure that I have him beat (I'd put the mouse on A-K or A-Q) and I'd continue to bet with my hand all the way.

If the elephant were to put in a raise on the flop, then you'd have to read him the best that you could. You'd want to call his raise on the flop and see what card comes up on fourth street and whether the elephant bets on fourth street or not.

Playing A-x Suited: Strong Flops, Slow Play

When you hit a really strong flop for your A-x suited hand, you have to decide how to collect the maximum number of bets. Usually, you can win the maximum by jamming the pot (putting in as many bets and raises as you can) after the flop. But sometimes, in order to give the impression that you're weak, you need to *slow-play* your hand—put no bets or raises in on the flop. If you've just flopped a "monster" (a huge hand) and someone bets out into you on the flop, you might want to just call one bet in order to draw your other opponents into the pot. Why raise everyone out of the pot when you flop a big hand? If your table image is weak or wild, you can raise on the flop because no one thinks you have anything anyway. If your table image is strong or tight, you're better off letting someone else bet your hand for you, even at the cost of missing some bets on the flop, in order to increase the chance that you can collect lots of bets on the last two rounds, when the limits are doubled. Let's look at some more examples.

Playing A-x Suited: Strong Flop, Slow Play or Not

Suppose that a jackal in the first position raises and you call with A♣ 4♣ in the third position (even in this early position, this is a pretty easy call against a jackal). Now the fifth position and both blinds call the raise as well. The flop comes down 10♣-9♣-6♣, and now the big blind bets out and the jackal raises. What do you do now? You have flopped the nut flush! The others can't beat you unless they flopped a set and the board gives them a pair, or unless they catch perfectly on both of the next two streets (you can't live in fear of runner-runner).

If you reraise and make it three bets to go on the flop, you might drive out the fifth-position player and both blinds, and that's not what you want. You're not going to drive out anyone who flopped a set (that is, anyone who has a reasonable chance to beat you); you're going to drive out only people who need a miracle to beat you. This is the time when you should just call the two bets and hope that everyone else calls as well. Or better yet, just call, hoping that everyone else calls, and hope that the big blind reraises it. This is a time to keep as many players in the pot as you can on the flop, because in the next two rounds of betting the limits are doubled.

If everyone checks to you on the flop, then you should bet out one bet rather than checking. After all, you have to give the other players a chance to check-raise you on the flop! You have to start building a pot sometime, and the flop is the place to make sure that you get at least one bet in the pot. Making the pot larger now may encourage people whose hands are still trailing badly to call for the size of the pot later (they may call bets later because they want to try to win the big pot out there), when they (although they won't know it) have little or no chance to win.

Trying to lure in the maximum number of bets in a hand is a nice problem to have, but doing it well every time can be tricky. Most of the time, in most pots, no one gets the maximum anyway when playing with a monster hand. After all, we can't see everyone else's hole cards. So just strive to get as close to the maximum as you can.

Playing A-x Suited: Strong Flops, Slow Play?

When you have A♦-7♦, and the flop is A♥-7♥-3♠, you want opponents in the pot, but you want to make sure that you protect your hand as well. In other circles, this would be known as wanting to eat your cake and have it too. Suppose that four people are in the pot, and the player in front of you bets out. What do you do? You could just call and let people in for one bet, but you might then let 8♠-8♥ in the pot for one bet and then lose the pot to the 8♠-8♥ when an eight comes off (in this case you'd lose a lot of chips as well!) or lose it to a heart-heart finish. I would raise on the flop to protect my hand and build that big pot right there and then. Maybe your surviving opponent has A♠-K♠, and maybe he'll reraise you on the flop.

When you flop the nut flush or a full house with your A-x suited, it's time to try to extract from your opponents all the bets you can. This may well include slow-playing your hand on the flop. When you flop two pair with your A-x suited, then it's time to protect your hand by jamming the flop as much as possible. You've flopped a strong hand, but it's still much too vulnerable for slow-playing. If you flop trips (three of a kind) when it comes 7-7-J and you have A-7, then it's time to examine the situation more closely. Should you slow-play or not? How many opponents are there in the hand? Are there two to a suit on the board on the flop? Generally, I will jam it with my trips in order to protect my hand. Most people slow-play too much, and they risk letting opponents back into positions where they can beat the slow player. Not only is this a big financial setback; it's the kind of defeat that can put a player on tilt. (You will hear the word "tilt" every time you play poker in a casino. It is a very common poker word that means being too troubled to play your usual game.)

We could talk all day about how to play your A-x suited after a marginal flop. What it really comes down to, though, is this: when you have a marginal flop with A-x suited, try to read your opponents to decide what to do with your hand. If you feel that they are weak, raise. If you feel that they are strong, fold. Don't forget to raise to find out where you are at if you aren't quite sure. This play is a great way to sort things out in your mind.

Playing K-Q on the Flop: Hit It or Fold It

I consider K-Q the weakest of my "majority play hands." Some pros may consider A-6 suited the weakest, because one might make a straight with A-2 suited. Others may consider 2-2 the weakest. A good argument can be made for any of these hands being the weakest of the majority play hands. Be that as it may, K-Q gets my vote for the weakest hand of the lot. This is a hand you need to hit on the flop if you are going to continue playing it.

Of course, when the flop is 4-10-J, and you hold K-Q, then

you have an open-ended straight draw. In this case, you need to play the hand all the way to the end, in the hope of hitting your straight. The trouble flops for K-Q are something like A-Q-2 or A-K-5. You have flopped second pair (the kings or queens) with top kicker, and this hand is just strong enough to get you into trouble. You can't beat any ace, but you can beat almost every other hand. Of course, it's always nice to see K-Q-4 (top two pair) or 10-J-A (nut straight) when you have K-Q! (Andy Glazer just elbowed me in the side and told me that the first time he ever played no-limit in a live game, he had K-Q and the flop came K-Q-4. His opponent had been holding pocket fours, and you can probably envision the ensuing carnage. Notwithstanding Andy's traumatic introduction to no-limit, if you flop top two pair in limit poker, you should push pretty hard.)

When you do hit K-Q, it is important to protect your hand by jamming the flop. K-9-2 and K-J-4 are pretty strong flops when you have K-Q. Without going into any further examples, suffice to say that K-Q is the kind of hand that you fold if you miss the flop, but jam with if you hit the flop, period.

How to Play the Majority Play Hands on Fourth Street

If you have made it to fourth street with any of these hands, then presumably you've hit something on the flop. Fourth street is the time to dump those hands that you decided were no good on the flop, now that the bets have doubled in size. This discussion will be rather short, since judgment is now the key to whether or not you continue to bet, call, or raise with your hand. Obviously, if you've hit a strong hand or a good drawing hand on the flop, then you'll continue to play the hand in some manner. If you flopped a set, two pair, a straight, or a flush, then you'll be doing a lot of betting and raising (jamming the pot) on fourth street. If you have flopped a strong draw, then you'll either be in the lead in the betting or just calling other people's bets at this point in the hand, depending on how you played your draw on the flop.

Fourth street is also the time to evaluate whether or not your opponent has hit his draw. Sometimes it's obvious that he's hit his hand; he'll reveal that by being easy to read. Perhaps he'll all but jump out of his seat when the card comes off the deck! At other times, the card that comes off the deck is the one you knew would be the worst possible card for you, and now you're almost certain you're beaten.

Sometimes, of course, you're the one who hits the draw on fourth street, and now you have to decide how to win the most from your hand, from here on out. Of course, this is a nice problem to have! Maybe you need to jam the pot, or perhaps you need to "smooth-call" someone else's bet—merely call when you have a raising hand—in order to lure other players into the pot at this point.

Examples

The following are examples of smooth-calling, jamming the pot, raising to protect your hand, and folding.

Smooth-Calling

When you have A-x suited and you hit your nut flush draw on fourth street, you may want to smooth-call someone else's bet in order to win the maximum with your hand. Let's say there are four opponents in the hand against you. The first opponent bets out into you, and you decide to raise him in order to build the pot. Now the next two opponents fold, and the original bettor looks you in the eye and says, "I know you wouldn't raise me here unless you had a flush, so I fold." How much money have you made after hitting your nut flush? One big bet! Why did you raise out the two opponents behind you?

If you were the last person to act and someone bet out into you, then I can understand the raise, because you would already have several people in for one bet, and people who have called one bet rarely drop out for one more. Now suppose that instead of raising, you smooth-call your opponents' bets. Now one of the two other opponents behind you calls the bet as well. On the end, the first opponent bets into you again, but this time you raise (smooth-calling the river bet is rarely if ever a good move), and you get called by both of your remaining two opponents. How many bets have you won this time? Six big bets! All because you smooth-called the bet on fourth street, and, presumably, allowed your opponents to hit good cards for their hands on the last card. (Of course, it's actually a bad card for them, because it didn't improve them enough to win, only enough to lose more money!)

In 2001, in the $7,500 buy-in no-limit Hold'em championship event at the U.S. Poker Championships at the Taj Mahal in Atlantic City, a smooth call worked for me to perfection. I called a $200 bet with A-A in the first position before the flop. Now Men "The Master" Nguyen, in the small blind, called with 5-6 off suit, and the big blind checked. The flop was A-7-3, and we all checked again; this was the second time this hand that I checked with the best possible hand in order to "trap" my opponents. The next card was a 7 for A-7-3-7, and I had made top full house (aces full of sevens).

My opponents both checked to me again, and now I bet out $200 into the $600 pot. Men called the $200, trying to hit a four for a straight, which would have cost him thousands of dollars more if he had hit it, since I already had a full house. The big blind now raised me $500 (this hand was developing beautifully for me). I decided that I needed to reraise right here in order to give the big blind the chance to give me all his chips (in case he had a seven in his hand), but I didn't want to reraise too much and lose him either. So I reraised $1,000 more, Men folded, and the big blind called me.

On the end, a harmless card came off the deck and my remaining opponent checked to me. I went ahead and bet $2,000, hoping for a call, and my opponent called me very quickly. So I won the hand, and it's very unlikely that I could have extracted another $3,000 from this opponent if I had bet aggressively from the beginning. In fact, if I had raised before the flop in this hand, all my opponents would have folded their hands then and there.

Tricky plays like smooth-calling and slow-playing generally offer bigger payoffs in pot-limit or no-limit than they do in limit, where you can't grab one giant bet from someone on the end; but even in limit these plays are an important part of the good player's arsenal.

Jamming the Pot

This is the counterpart of the example of slow-playing given above. Sometimes, when you hold the nut hand, you just need to jam the pot on fourth street, in order to make the pot as big as it possibly can be. But it's hard to know the right time to jam the pot, rather than smooth-calling someone else's bet. Generally, it depends on whether someone has bet right in front of you or not. If someone has, then you usually want to smooth-call the bet. But if someone has bet and several others have already called that bet, then it's time to go ahead and raise it up.

Protecting Your Hand with a Raise

The principle of protecting your hand by way of a raise is also very important in Hold'em. ("Protecting your hand" is all about making raises when you have a strong hand, so that you can eliminate players, thus giving yourself a better chance to win that hand.) It can mean the difference between winning and losing a pot. Suppose that you have A♣–3♣ (A-x suited), and garner two pair with A♦–10♦–3♠ on the flop. Now on fourth street 9♣ comes off the deck for A♦–10♦–3♠–9♣. Someone now bets into you, and you just call the bet. But because you just called the bet, you let a jackal in with K-Q, and he hit a J on the end to make a straight. Clearly, even the jackal would have folded his "belly buster" (inside-straight draw) for *two* big bets; but for just one, he was able to dream about a jack and convince himself that hitting a king or queen might win also. Because you didn't protect your hand here by raising, you wound up paying the ultimate price in poker; you lost a pot that you should have won.

Folding Your Hand

When you're involved in a big multiway pot and there's been a lot of raising on the flop, watch out for indications that the drawing hands have hit on fourth street. Suppose you have 6-6 and the flop came down 2♦-3♠-4♦. On the flop you have three opponents all putting in some bets. Still, you're pretty sure that your hand is the best hand on the flop. But what if the worst possible card for you comes off on fourth street? Then what do you do? To me the worst possible card here is A♦. If A♦ comes off the deck, then the straight draw (any five in your opponent's hand), the flush draw (two diamonds in an opponent's hand), and any ace (like A-K or A-4) all get there and beat you. If this card comes off of the deck, then you'd better look to exit stage left immediately.

When you face a situation like this, ask yourself, "What are they holding that's driving them to put all this money into the pot on the flop?" Probably straight draws, flush draws, pairs, and ace high. Folding your hand on fourth street wisely when the draws appear to have been hit is considered an art form.

Playing the Marginal Play Hands on the River

In the discussion of beginners' strategy for the top ten hands on the river (Chapter 3), I advocated making a lot of calls on the river, because of the large size of the pots with the top ten hands. In other words, the "pot odds" are there for you to call on the end with a top ten hand. This thinking is still somewhat applicable here, but now we're dealing with some weaker hands. Often, in my advice to beginners, my examples would have you in the lead with a strong hand (you're the bettor), and it would be your opponents who were calling *you* down. Now, with the weaker marginal-play hands, you will often be calling your opponents' bets.

Sometimes, situations will come up where you're calling someone down with your A-3 (calling all the way to the end) and a board of A♠-K♠-4♥-7♣, and then the last card is J♠ and someone else bets into you as well. In this case you were calling just one opponent, whose hand probably had your pair of aces with a weak kicker beaten. Now, when a third party bets out into both of you when the flush card hits, folding your hand would seem to be the wise move.

But you may also end up with A-10 and a board of 10♠-J♠-4♠-5♥, and then see the river produce Q♥. Now what do you do? If there had been a lot of action on the flop here, then you were probably playing against either a spade flush draw, a straight draw, a pair of jacks, or an overpair. With Q♥ on the river, you can now beat only the flush draw, assuming that the flush draw didn't have a Q with it. The point is that you may have already been in trouble with the A-10, but with this last card and two other opponents still in the action, you shouldn't even think about calling on the river. Again, playing the marginal play hands, as opposed to the top ten hands, may put you into some bad situations when it's time to ponder calling on the river.

You're still getting pot odds to call someone on the river—the payoff could be huge—but if you can make four or five prudent and well-timed folds a night, that will add up to some serious money by the end of the year! Learning when to call with your marginal-play hands on the river, or fold them, will become clearer as you gain experience.

Whether or not you make a call on the river depends entirely on how you read the situation. Reads, reads, reads, and a little "pot odds" math should be your guide. (I showed you how to calculate the pot odds earlier, on pages 62–63.) Only through practice will you be able to make good decisions on the end. Pay attention to how often you're right and how often you're wrong with your calls on the river. Was there a good reason that you called? Did you read your opponents well? Keep in mind that the idea is to constantly improve your reading skills along the way.

Chapter 5

Limit Hold'em:
Advanced Strategy

Take note: because the concepts presented in this chapter are both subtle and complex, the beginning or intermediate player really shouldn't race right out to try them in serious games. Successful application of these concepts involves not merely knowing and understanding them but possessing the judgment to know how and when to apply them.

Your typical megalomaniac player (a jackal type) may well appreciate advanced limit Hold'em theory more than most of the rest of us. Which is to say, when using advanced limit Hold'em theory, you can often find yourself skating on very thin ice. Pursuing play in this fashion is often thrilling and dangerous, both to the user's opponents and to the user himself!

In this chapter I'll show you how to reraise opponents who are stealing blinds. Essentially, I'll teach you to steal from the stealers! You won't quite be Robin Hood, because while you'll be stealing from the rich, you won't be giving the plunder to the poor: you'll be adding it to your own stack.

We will also talk about adding "suited connectors" like 8♦-9♦, 4♠-5♠, and 6♣-7♣ to the mix of hands that you can play before the flop. We'll talk about reraising people with nothing, in order to bluff them out. We'll talk about trapping and check-raising opponents, and more.

In this chapter you will learn:

- How to play suited connectors.
- How to use suited connectors to "advertise."
- The "fire up the table" strategy applied by Spencer Ouren.
- How to steal from the blind stealers.
- How to trap with big hands: the John Bonetti story.
- How to play advanced Hold'em on the flop: anything goes!
- Having position is always good.

All these advanced concepts should be used with great caution. Most of them shouldn't be used by anyone other than the top pros, because most of them are highly "read-dependent." In other words, when you've advanced to the stage of your poker career when you're able to read your opponents well, then your chances of using these concepts successfully will be greater.

Playing Suited Connectors

Now that we're contemplating advanced play, we'll add suited connectors to the mix of hands that you'll sometimes play before the flop. Notice that I said "sometimes." There is very little advice in the way of "always" or "never" when one reaches the advanced strategy concepts in Hold'em.

Generally, in order to play suited connectors, you need to have multiway action (at least three players in the pot). Generally, you don't want to call three bets with these types of hands. Nor do you want to play these kinds of hands too often. The best time to consider playing suited connectors is when you decide to reraise (three-bet) someone you feel is weak, before the flop, in the hope that you'll be taking the pot away from this player later in the hand. Stealing the pot with these suited connectors is quite similar to the concept of stealing from the blind stealers.

The problem with playing suited connectors is that they don't win the pot very often. You might, for example, play 7♦-8♦ or 9♠-10♠ and hit a hand that will just get you into a lot of trouble. You might make top pair or second pair or even a flush and still lose a big pot. So the best way to play these kinds of hands is very carefully! If you're an advanced player, you understand that it's very difficult to fold the 7♦-8♦ when the flop comes down 2-6-7. If you're trying to play suited connectors, you have to learn how to fold them at the right time. This takes finesse, skill, and, above all, reading ability.

Three Limit Hold'em Situations Appropriate for Playing Suited Connectors

Situation 1: One situation conducive to playing these hands is when someone has raised and two or three players have already called in front of me. Here I'm investing two bets with at least three other opponents. In this situation, I like to have at least 5-6 suited or higher. I don't see much value in 2-3, 3-4, or 4-5 suited: the pairs, straights, and flushes these hands might make are all too low. To show you what I mean, if I'm playing a hand like 3-4 suited, I'm hoping to make a straight. It's not that I object to making a flush, but mine would be the worst possible flush, and I could easily lose to a higher flush. So I'd rather make a straight, but unless I hit the hand absolutely perfectly with A-2-5, my straight is probably going to be on the low side of what's available.

For example, if the flop comes 5-6-7, I have indeed made my straight, but I'm vulnerable to people who are playing higher suited connectors: 8-9 just buries me, 7-8 gives my opponent top pair with an open-ended straight draw that can easily beat me, and both 5-6 and 6-7 leave me vulnerable to losing to a full house. Someone with pocket eights will be trouble, too. But if my suited connectors are a little higher, I'm not quite as vulnerable to losing a big pot. I'm not going to hit a suited connector hand too often anyway, and when I do hit it, I want to be reasonably sure I'm going to win with it.

Playing suited connectors, I'm hoping to hit the flop pretty solidly; if I don't, I just surrender my two previous bets on the flop and fold the hand. I'm also prepared to jam the flop if I think I've flopped the best hand, in order to protect it.

Situation 2: The second favorable situation arises when I have suited connectors in the blinds, because I get in for a discount. In other words, calling two bets in the big blind amounts to calling just one bet, since it was I who posted the first bet in the blind.

Situation 3: The third situation involves messing with other players' heads and making myself more unpredictable in other players' eyes. In this situation, I'll make it three bets over the top of someone who I think is raising the pot with a weak hand in front of me. I may three-bet (reraise) a jackal when I'm on the button with 5♦-6♦ in order to try to steal the pot from him.

If I *am* able to take the pot away, by forcing everyone to fold, then I'll just place my winning hand facedown. But if I get caught bluffing, then I'm more than happy to show the whole table my hand and say, "Six high." When the other players realize that I reraised with 5♦-6♦ before the flop, then I can expect to receive a lot of extra action for a while! After I've shown down six high once or twice, then it's time to play the top ten hands only, for a while, and wait for the players to give me their chips. They'll still be thinking that I have nothing (six high!), but I'll be showing them some real hands for a while. This pattern tends to keep many players off balance, and eventually they may decide they don't want to mess with me.

Calling with Suited Connectors

The idea behind calling two bets with suited connectors is to try to win a big pot. So I'm looking for a lot of opponents when I consider calling two bets with this hand. It doesn't make sense to me to call two bets with 8♥-9♥ when no one else has called before the flop. In other words, I'm looking for good pot odds for this type of drawing hand. An occasional big pot pays for a lot of failed attempts.

Suppose that someone raises before the flop in early position and now two other people call the raise in front of me. I'm on the button with 4♦-5♦. I simply fold this hand, because 4-5 is below the suited connector line that I like to maintain. In this same situation, if I have 7-8 suited, then I'll go ahead and call the raise, trying to get lucky on the flop or later.

Suppose that a mouse in early position makes it two bets to go and now two other players call the two bets in front of me. I'm on the button with 9♣-10♣. In this case, although two other players have already called the raise, I'll probably fold my hand because the original raiser is a mouse. (When a mouse raises in early position, I'm always looking for an excuse to fold as soon as possible!) Of course, if the original raiser isn't a mouse, I would call with my 9♣-10♣. My rule for playing suited connectors is this: if two other people have called two bets (a raise), then I'll call with my hand (assuming that it's above the 4-5 line).

Calling with Suited Connectors in the Blinds

Usually, I will call two bets in the big blind with any suited connectors, even the weak ones like 2-3. After all, in the big blind it will cost me only one more bet to call, since I have posted one bet already. In the small blind, too, I will defend with most suited connectors, but I'll usually draw the line at 4-5 suited because it will probably cost me 1½ bets more to call the two bets in the small blind. With 10-J or J-Q suited, I'm usually willing to call three bets in the blinds.

If I have 6-7 suited in the big blind and a mouse has made it two bets to go, then I will call if at least one other opponent calls, and I may call if I'm the only one left in the pot. Although I don't like to mess with a mouse's raise, the 6-7 suited in the big blind may bring a big reward for me if I hit the flop, and of course it will cost me only one more bet to see if I hit it. Moreover, a mouse is generally easy to read: he probably has a big pair or A-K high when he raises before the flop.

By risking one more bet to call before the flop, I may win a lot of bets from the mouse. And if I run into a troublesome flop like 10-6-4, then I can usually figure out fairly easily whether the mouse has me beaten or not. Again, in general I don't like to mess with a mouse's preflop raise, but being in the big blind (a discount) with suited connected cards is the time and place to do it.

If I have *any* suited connected hand in the big blind before the flop, then I'll call someone's raise (two-bet), period.

If I have J-Q or 10-J suited (they're both worth about the same before the flop) in the blinds, then I will in general call three bets (a reraise) before the flop. Of course there are exceptions: a mouse's three bets will force me to lay down my hand for sure! I have learned that it's very hard to beat Q-Q, K-K, A-A, or A-K with Q-J or 10-J suited! Use your own discretion when you're deciding to call three bets with J-Q or 10-J suited in the small blind. If you have a bad feeling that the three-bettor has a big pair, then just throw your hand away before the flop. Remember, you're getting only a half-bet discount, not much compared with the 2½ bets you would need to add, and you'll be playing the hand out of position for every betting round. The same thing applies to Q-J or 10-J suited in the big blind, although calling isn't ever a terrible play unless it's against someone who is a consistent mouse.

Three-Betting with Suited Connectors: Messing with the Other Players' Heads

It's time now to talk about advertising   a way of messing with players' heads in order to confuse them and induce action later on: three-betting someone with a suited connected hand like 6-7 suited. Why suited connectors? A suited connector is the kind of hand that you might hit easily when you're out there making a play. It's said that timing is everything in life, so how do you time this crazy move?

Before I go any further, I want to stress that it is a play you shouldn't use too often, and, further, that it's important to use this play against the right people. I would never use it on a mouse, for two reasons. First, the mouse is set in his ways and won't give you any extra action no matter what you do. Second, why take 6-7 suited against a big pair (which is probably what he has), when it's so hard to win that pot? Early in the evening is the perfect time and situation to use this play, because then you may get extra action all night long! Why use it when only a few more hands are to be played, when you won't gain the benefit of extra action?

In general, three-betting an opponent with suited connectors is a losing play for that one hand, but you make the play occasionally anyway because it will bring you extra action for another hour or two. This extra action will ultimately bring you more money, but it may also cause you to lose some pots that you ordinarily would have won when someone who now thinks you might be in there with any piece of junk runs you down with a really weak hand. Still, reraising with this type of hand will mess up the other players' attempts to read you. In the future when you three-bet preflop, they will begin to wonder whether you have 6-7 suited.

If you win one of these pots without having to show down your hand, then I recommend folding your hand facedown and trying the same play again soon. As long as the play keeps working and you don't have to show your hand, continue to use it. But when you've been caught bluffing with one of these hands on the end, then flip it faceup and say, "I have nothing." Even better is when you do hit your hand and flip it up at the end of the hand and say, "I have a straight!" It's pretty funny to watch the players at the table study your hand and realize that you three-bet before the flop with your 8-9 suited! When you show down weak suited connectors that you three-bet with preflop, make sure that you're ready to play really tight for a while, since you will get extra action for a time afterward. Just make sure that you have a strong hand when they do call you down later.

Suppose that you're about one hour into a poker game that figures to last six hours or so. You have 8♦-9♦ in late position and a jackal has just made it two bets in front of you. You now decide to make it three bets, and everyone folds except the jackal. The flop comes down A♥-K♠-4♦, and the jackal bets out into you. Of course, you now go ahead and raise the jackal on the flop, attempting to take the pot away from him right then and there. If the jackal folds, just throw your hand away facedown. But if he calls, make sure that you try to bluff him on fourth street and the river. If he calls you down, then say, "Nine high" and flip your hand faceup. Just the look of the other players at the table will be worth the money that you lost on this hand! Well, maybe not just the look, but the look combined with the advertising is welcome!

If the jackal folds his hand at some point, then fold your own hand facedown and try the same play again soon.

Suppose that the jackal calls preflop and the flop is $6\heartsuit$-$7\heartsuit$-$2\spadesuit$ (assume that you've three-bet him preflop with $8\diamondsuit$-$9\diamondsuit$). This is a great flop for you because if you hit a five or a ten you make a straight, and if you hit an eight or a nine you've made a pair of eights or nines, which would be top pair on the board. Of course you need to play this hand aggressively (ram and jam), and whether you hit the winning hand or miss your hand, just flip it faceup on the end when the jackal calls you down. Obviously, it works out pretty well for you when you do win the pot while making your "suited-connectors three-bet advertising play." Just remember that advertising is usually pretty expensive, so make sure to look for ways to make it pay big dividends. And don't advertise too often.

Spencer's Approach: "Fire Up the Game"

Some years ago at the Bicycle Club Casino in Los Angeles, there was a regular named Spencer Ouren (he was very well liked). Spencer was about my age and was on his way to becoming a poker legend before his untimely death in 1992. Spencer would sit down at the $80–$160-limit Hold'em table and raise every hand *in the dark* to the maximum before the flop (he wouldn't even look at his hole cards!) for one round. He did this every single time he sat down in a high-limit game.

Players began to expect this seemingly suicidal move, and some of them would decide to reraise Spencer with a weaker hand than they would usually play. Others, realizing what was happening, would then call three bets with weaker hands than *they* would normally play. Before long, all those in the game were caught up in playing hands that they didn't normally play. Spencer would thereby open up the game every time he sat down to play in it! Imagine what would happen. Often, the game might not have even been worth playing in before Spencer sat down, because everyone was playing tight (like a mouse). Then out of nowhere, Spencer sits down and all this craziness begins!

The players at the table would be playing hands that they didn't normally play for large amounts of money preflop. Invariably, some players would lose big pots with big pocket pairs like Q-Q, K-K, or A-A. Some of these players would then "go on tilt" and begin to play outside their normal, more successful style of play. Spencer was very good at shaking up a game by giving everyone a lot of action in the first round of play.

Usually, playing this way is a losing proposition, but because everyone knew what was coming (and then began to play out of character), if Spencer could win just one pot, he stood a good chance of losing only a little bit for the whole round. After all, these were pretty huge pots for the first round of deals he sat in! If he won just two pots, then he'd win (or break even) for the round. In any case, Spencer would then settle down after his "cap it in the dark" round and play supertight for a couple of hours afterward.

Invariably, the other players would continue to give Spencer too much action, and he was very successful because of this. His unique brand of firing up the table—thus messing with the other players' heads—by giving them a ton of action for one round is something worth looking into for even the greatest players in the world today. Sometimes, it would be a pretty expensive round for Spencer, but he would calmly sit back and take his $3,500 "start-up cost" loss, knowing that everyone was now perfectly set up to be crushed for a couple of hours.

Spencer was thus a real master at "advertising" that he played weak hands. Usually, advertising costs money, but every marketing department in the world will tell you that well-placed advertising eventually pays big dividends!

Stealing from the Blind Stealers

Stealing from the blind stealers is a very advanced Hold'em play. I'm not sure that it's a winning play, but it definitely falls into the realm of advanced Hold'em play. Personally, I like reraising players whom I suspect of stealing the blinds with a hand like any two cards ten and above (called "20" in honor of its value in blackjack), such as 10-K or 10-Q. I also like reraising with any ace. This play is a lot more effective if you reraise in a better position than the original raiser. (If the raiser is two or three off the button, then being on the button—and acting behind the raiser—gives you an edge, because you act last.)

Reraising with 20 is a lot more solid than just reraising with 5-7 off suit, because you have a playable hand when you get called (and everyone will call one more bet when he's already made it two bets). Nonetheless, it is important to talk about stealing from the blind stealers with a really weak hand. I know of a couple of world-class limit Hold'em players who absolutely love to reraise the "live" (weak) player in the game with nothing at all in their hand, in order to steal the pot from him or outplay him later on in the hand. This reraise of the live player in the game also causes them to isolate themselves against the live player because the reraise usually drives the other players out of the pot. So the reraise (three bet) of the live player isolates that player and gives the better player a chance to outplay him later on in the hand. And when you give this kind of extra action to the live player, he also gives you extra action, and believe me, he's the fellow you want extra action from!

A lot of good things can happen when you reraise the blind stealers preflop. If the blind stealer misses his hand (and remember, it's hard to hit a hand in Hold'em—you miss many more flops than you hit), then he'll often have to surrender his hand on the flop. You can also get lucky and win a big pot when you hit your own hand restealing.

On the other side of the ledger, you can get yourself in a heap of trouble making a three-bet resteal with a weak hand. If the alleged thief has your hand beat, you've already put in three bets to little purpose when you were losing, and he still has both position (when you reraise out of the blinds) and has just as good a chance as you do to hit something on the flop. It just seems counterintuitive that you should be putting in three bets with 5-7 just because you suspect that someone is making a blind steal. Why not wait for a decent hand, one that is probably the best hand at the table preflop, before you three-bet it? This play may work best of all late in a Hold'em tournament when your opponent is more likely to throw his hand away on the flop, rather than risk going broke with a weak hand on the flop. (If I seem to be sending mixed signals, that's just poker; some advice is reliable, some is a crapshoot.)

Trapping with Big Hands before the Flop

We have already talked about trapping players on the flop. I've seen my good friend John Bonetti, a world-class poker player at the age of 73, trap players *before* the flop beautifully! In 1996, in one memorable hand in the World Series of Poker championship event, John decided to try to trap the defending world champion, Dan Harrington, when there were still about 25 players left.

Dan opened the pot for $6,000 with K♠-10♠, and John smooth-called the $6,000 bet with A-A. The flop was 6-9-10, and Dan bet out $25,000 into John. John again just smooth-called the $25,000 bet. I've got to tell you, I would have had to raise Dan's last $100,000 right there. I mean, I understand the smooth call before the flop, though I rarely do that myself, but no way would I have just called the $25,000 bet on the flop! I would have been too scared that Dan had a pocket pair and would hit it for a set, just because I smooth-called his $25,000 bet instead of moving him all-in right there and then. The next card was an A, for 6-9-10-A, and now Dan moved all-in for his last $100,000. John called Dan's $100,000 bet so quickly it gave me chills!

Then John looked up at me and winked. I was watching the action from about 20 feet away from the table and I had 50 percent of John that year (I had purchased 50 percent of his action). Having a piece of a player (sharing his wins and his losses) is often more brutal than being there at the table yourself, because you have no control over what's happening. Worse, first place was $1 million, which means I could have won $500,000 for my half! But I knew it was OK when John looked up and winked at me, and I wandered over to the table to see the upturned hands. Three aces for John and one pair of tens for Dan. John had had him drawing dead! No matter what the last card was, John would win the pot!

In this case, John had trapped Dan at just the right time. Sometimes traps trap the user, of course, but this one worked out perfectly. By the way, John went on to finish third that year, when the young and talented Huck Seed took first place. Having my two best friends at the time finish first and third was awfully cool. With John's second-place finish in the second to last event (for $140,000) and his third-place take in the main event ($680,000), we walked away with over $400,000 each! I always tell my poker friends when they visit my house, "This is the house that Bonetti bought!"

A good time to trap is when you are sitting in late position with A-A or K-K and you suspect that both blinds will fold if you make it two bets to go. By just calling the one bet, you allow the players behind you to call before the flop. By slow-playing with A-A or K-K and looking for action, you'll often get it. Sometimes, you need to be careful what you ask for! You may let the big blind play his 2-6 off-suit hand free by not raising before the flop, and then the flop may come 2-2-J and you are stuck in there losing a lot of bets because you trapped yourself. Still, sometimes I like to trap in this situation, and it usually works out pretty well for me (it's pretty tough to beat pocket aces or kings).

Advanced Hold'em on the Flop

Advanced Hold'em on the flop is really all about reading other players. If you read your opponent as weak and think you might be able to take the pot away from him, then do it! If you have flopped a big hand and you feel that betting will drive out your opponent when what you want to do is keep him in the pot, then go ahead and trap your opponent by checking on the flop. Use your reading ability on the flop to determine what you can and cannot do. You may have flopped top pair, but if you read that your opponent has you beat, just fold your hand, having lost the minimum number of bets. If you read your opponent as being weak before the flop and you are making a steal on him, then make sure that you follow through on your steal attempt, unless you then have a strong read that he has hit the flop well. Again, advanced Hold'em on the flop is all about reading your opponents.

I know I keep mentioning reading the opposition, and I can't teach you how to be intuitive. I can, however, tell you that a lot of the information going into my reads comes from working hard at studying my opponents, both when I'm in a hand with them and when I'm out. Intuition springs from a combination of matters that you can understand and explain, and others that you can't. In the discussion of no-limit and pot-limit Hold'em (Chapter 6) I talk about a game I play while I'm at the poker table. The object is to try to determine someone's exact two hole cards in a hand. Through practicing guessing at what my opponent's cards are, even when I'm out of a hand, I increase my own reading abilities. (Flip on over to the material on no-limit for more details.)

Suppose that you have K-K before the flop and two opponents are also in the pot. If the flop comes down A-7-2, the advanced player makes his money by knowing what to do, on the strength of his read of his opponents. Does either of your opponents, or do both of them, hold an ace, a set of sevens, or a set of twos? How does the betting on the flop come down? Are your opponents capable of raising on the flop with just a pair of sevens or worse? If it does come bet and raised to you in this spot, will you three-bet it or fold? Odds are that you probably have to fold in this case, but what does intuition tell you to do?

I have played with advanced players who have bet out 8-8 on the end with a board of A-Q-7-5-3, simply because they thought they had the best hand, and they proved to be right! In fact, their bet was called on the end by someone who couldn't beat the 8-8! How did they know that the 8-8 was the best hand? How could they possibly have value-bet their hand in this case? Perhaps they knew that their opponent would never check a Q or an A to them. In advanced Hold'em play on the flop, anything goes! As you try different things, you will find that the basic top ten strategy is a pretty good way to play Hold'em, with a twist—some well-timed intermediate and advanced moves along the way. The jackal lives in the advanced, wild, dangerous realm all the time, and it's very difficult to win when you play this way time in and time out.

Dangers of Resteals and Suited Connectors

I'm not going to spend any more time in the realm of restealing and suited connectors in Hold'em, because it really is for expert players only, and it isn't to be dabbled in lightly! I would recommend that all beginners stay away from this advanced strategy, since they will find it very hazardous to their bank balances, with one exception: the suited-connector reraise (advertising) before the flop once or twice a night. I think this play is good for a beginner, because it makes him more difficult for the rest of the table to read.

The real problem with advanced play—for all of us, whether

we are world-class or beginners—is that it causes us to play too many hands. When we begin to win pots with 7♦-8♦ (or see other players win with this hand), then we start to play 7-8 suited far too often before the flop. Pretty soon, 6-8 suited looks good as well. Playing suited connectors is like eating potato chips: once you eat one chip, you can't help eating many more! Once you start to win with suited connectors, you begin to play them all the time. I've seen people think this way many times in the past, "Three bets to me when I have 9♦-10♦; sure I'll call. Why not, when I've been winning with these types of hands all night?" Beware of overplaying suited connectors. If you're not careful, before long you'll tell someone, "Man, was I unlucky with 6♠-7♠ today. I called three bets and the flop was 8-9-10, and then . . ." Buddy, if you called three bets with 6♠-7♠, then you got what you deserved!

Position in Advanced Play

Note that most of the plays I have talked about involve having the advantage of position. Being able to act last is a huge advantage in all forms of Hold'em. Imagine, you can just sit back and wait for all your opponents to act in front of you. "Just sit back and all will be revealed to you" isn't exactly the case, but it is nice to know where the other players stand. If the others check, then they're generally weak. If you have a powerful hand, then you can raise it when they bet. If you have a weak hand, then you can check behind them when they check. Having position in Hold'em is always good.

Chapter 6

No-Limit and Pot-Limit
Hold'em Strategy

It's time now to talk about the Cadillac of all poker games, no-limit Hold'em (NLH), and its brother, pot-limit Hold'em (PLH). In NLH you can bet any amount of the money in front of you on the table at any time! Imagine this concept: any amount at any time. If you sense weakness in your opponent, then go ahead and bet $100,000 on a pure bluff. Of course, if you bluff $100,000 at someone who has only $50,000 left in front of him on the table, then he is allowed to call for his $50,000, making your bet effectively $50,000. If we didn't have that protection in place, whereby you can only bet as much as your opponents have in front of them (called "table stakes"), then Bill Gates would win every pot! Bluffing is a much bigger part of NLH and PLH than it is in limit Hold'em. The great bluffs, the great "reads," and the massive amount of strategy involved in NLH make it the most interesting and most strategic game that we have in poker.

PLH is similar to NLH after the flop play, because by that

point the pot in a PLH game has usually grown large enough to make huge bets possible. Before the flop, there are a fair number of strategic differences between the two games, because big bets aren't possible immediately in PLH. But in most respects PLH and NLH are roughly the same game.

In this chapter you will learn:

I The difference between no-limit Hold'em (NLH) and pot-limit Hold'em (PLH).

I How to introduce NLH into your game—"cash downs."

I Phil's "NLH fifteen."

I How to trap with A-A and K-K.

I Three theories on how to play pocket 2-2 to 8-8, and A-Q.

I Phil's game—"Guess your opponent's exact two hole cards."

I Phil's NLH theory.

I The "bet it all" NLH strategy—yuck!

I The "suited connector" NLH theory that Huck Seed uses.

I The superadvanced "Calling with nothing" NLH theory.

I Dave "Devilfish" Ulliott's NLH theory.

Pot-Limit Hold'em (PLH)

In PLH you'll often be able to look at a flop, because the preflop raises are limited to the size of the pot. In fact, all bets are limited to the size of the pot. So, if the blinds are \$1–\$2, then the first raiser can only make it \$7 to go: \$1SB + \$2BB + \$2 call = \$5 raise, so \$2 call + \$5 raise = \$7 to go. (SB is small blind; BB is big blind.) If you've got \$200 in front of you, wouldn't you like to take a $7 flop with a pocket pair? If you hit a set, then you may get the other $193 into the pot when you're a huge favorite. Let's take this example further and suppose that someone did open for $7 and two players called the $7, one of them the big blind. How much can then be bet on the flop? Well, $7 from the raiser + $7 caller + $1SB + $7BB (caller) = $22. Suppose that the big blind bets out the maximum $22. How much can the original raiser make it? Well, $22 in the pot + $22BB pot-size bet + $22 pot-size call from the raiser (he has to count his own $22 call before he makes a raise) = $66. So the original raiser can call $22 and raise $66, making it a total of $88 to go. The betting can escalate quickly in PLH.

Some world-class players believe that there is more skill in PLH than in NLH because there is more play on the flop in PLH. I believe that it is very close, but I will say that playing flops takes a ton of skill. The way some players play NLH today, folding or betting it all before the flop—without ever taking a flop—does take some edge away from the more skilled Hold'em players.

The Biggest and Most Prestigious Poker Game: No-Limit Hold'em (NLH)

Of the 10 most prestigious poker tournaments today, six are NLH. There is a list of the 50 most prestigious events in poker in Appendix 3. The biggest two—the World Series of Poker (WSOP) and the Poker Million—each pay roughly $1.5 million for first place!

Imagine the scene in 2001 at the World Series of Poker

when we were down to six players left in the tournament. I was still playing. The Travel Channel had a battery of cameras covering the table and the surrounding standing-room-only crowd. (Most of the crowd had to watch the action on television monitors set up throughout the room.) Two live Internet broadcasts were going on, one at my site (philhellmuth.com) and one at Mark and Tina Napolitano's site (PokerPages.com). With a first-place prize of $1.5 million and $6,130,000 in tournament chips lying on the table, we engaged in some pretty spectacular clashes that day.

In one hand, I opened the pot for $90,000 on the button with 9♣-9♠ (exactly the same two cards that I won the WSOP with in 1989!) and Phil Gordon moved all-in in the big blind for about $550,000 total. I called his $450,000 raise so quickly that I freaked out everyone at the table! I just knew that he was going to move all-in with a weak hand, and I was ready for him. It turned out that he had 6-6, which made me a 4½-to-1 favorite to win the $1.1 million pot and bust him (I still had $500,000 in chips left if he won).

Unfortunately for me, the flop was 6-8-K, and his three sixes wound up winning the pot. If I had won this pot, then I would have had at least $1.6 million in chips and perhaps would have won my second "big one." My friend Andy, reading this book in draft, remarked that there's very little "perhaps" to it, although he was extraordinarily impressed with Dewey Tomko's play at the final table (Tomko finished second). Oh, well, either way, it was an exciting hand to be a part of! The two black nines lost the $1.1 million pot, but in 1989 they had held up for a $1.2 million pot and given me the WSOP title. So, 9♣-9♠ is still my favorite hand, and I'd had a really good chance to immortalize it that day. Winning the most prestigious NLH event in the world is the best way to achieve poker immortality!

Introducing No-Limit Hold'em to Your Home Game

Now is the time to tell you that if you introduce NLH to your own home poker game, watch out! The money won and lost can escalate pretty quickly. Before long, the size of the pots will be more than you bargained for. As a brake against this tendency I recommend that you introduce NLH in a "cash-down" format, which allows people to take a portion of their chips off the table at a certain predetermined chip total.

For example, you could require everyone to keep at least $50 in chips in play (making that the maximum they could lose in one pot), but allow them to take off the money above that amount. If someone wins a $110 pot, he can remove $60 in chips and put it in his pocket while keeping $50 in play in front of himself. In this way, the stakes won't go up and up and up after a few hours of NLH play, as they usually do.

This system also allows the players to play an amount they feel comfortable with. You might have two business owners keeping $2,000 apiece in front of themselves, and a couple of other players with only $70 each in front of themselves. It's also possible that one player has a mere $17 left, because he started with $50 but lost down to this point. How does the pot work if the two $2,000 players move all-in along with the $17 player on the same hand? The player with $17 is entitled to $17 each from the big stacks if he wins the pot. His money is matched by both opponents. In fact, the $17 player may well make a straight flush and lament the fact that he won only a $51 pot! Meanwhile, the nearly $4,000 side pot may be won by a player holding merely top pair! Ironically, the straight flush wins $51, but one pair wins a $3,949 side pot on the same hand.

If someone starts with $50, and loses $20 in one hand, then he can play the $30 until he goes broke. Again, the cash-down format also allows some of your richer friends ("big dogs") to leave a lot more money in front of them. So two of the big dogs could play as big a pot as they want to between themselves, while the little dogs have all-in protection for their money. *All-in protection* simply means that if you have $38 in front of you, then you can win all the money in front of each opponent up to $38 each (each opponent matches your $38). No matter what you saw in the entertaining but extremely inaccurate movie *Big Hand for the Little Lady*, in any poker game you can't be forced out of a pot because someone else has more money on the table than you do.

I believe that if you introduce NLH to your home game, the other players will love it, especially with the cash-down feature that keeps it under control. NLH is *the game* in the poker world right now. One reason is that it opens up poker and offers the possibility of making more challenging "moves." You can now make bluffs that have teeth. If you smell weakness in someone, you can raise him right out of the pot even if you're weak. You can now bet so much money on your drawing hand that you will force your opponent to fold! NLH is poker at its best, because you don't necessarily have to hold or make a lot of good hands to come out a winner. You can win pots with your reads and understanding of your opponents. It's a bit like playing chess with a sledgehammer!

The first thing that I'm going to give you in what follows is a base of hands that you can use when you play NLH. This starting base will include the top ten hands and the other pairs. Then I will expand this base somewhat to include A-x suited hands. Along the way I will talk about how some other top pros play these kind of hands before the flop.

Beginners' Strategy for NLH and PLH

Even though there are some differences, I'm going to treat NLH and PLH as if they were the same game, for the duration of this discussion. As is always the case in Hold'em, supertight is right for beginning players while they learn to get their feet wet! Therefore I recommend that you restrict yourself to the "top ten hands" and pairs only while you learn the game. In other words, play only the 13 pairs (aces down through deuces), plus A-K and A-Q before the flop in NLH. Although my top ten hands for limit Hold'em do not include the small pairs (2-2, 3-3, 4-4, 5-5, or 6-6), these pairs can win you far, far greater pots in NLH when you "flop a set" (hit three of a kind with them on the flop)—much more than you can win in limit poker. So my "NLH fifteen" are all the pairs, plus A-K and A-Q.

The idea behind playing only the NLH fifteen hands is that you will be playing hands that will win you big pots. These are the hands that you'll most often *double up* with: put your $210 into the pot and win a pot of $420+). The NLH fifteen strategy is very conservative but very effective against other beginners. To win NLH tournaments or larger NLH side games, you would need to play more types of hands, but here I'm addressing beginners' play.

The "NLH fifteen" strategy is simple. With these hands, you'll put yourself in some very good situations. You can "double up" when you flop a set. You can double up by getting your money into the pot with A-A, K-K, Q-Q, or A-K before the flop. You can even double up with 9-9, 10-10, or J-J, after the right kind of flop. The best thing about sticking to this strategy, at least in the near term, is that the game becomes easier when you play poker this tight.

Beginners: If You Hold A-A, K-K, Q-Q, or A-K before the Flop, Bet It All

When you have one of these top four hands in NLH, you can almost always justify shoving all your chips out there before the flop. There are very few exceptions to this advice, and virtually no exceptions for the beginning NLH player. For the more sophisticated player, you will, once in a blue moon, be wise to fold Q-Q or A-K before the flop. If you're to do this, however, you should have some very strong evidence that your opponent holds K-K or A-A. The evidence might be that someone has made a big raise and then a mouse has moved all-in for a mountain of chips (for characterizations of my animal types—the mouse, elephant, lion, jackal, and eagle—see page 33 in Chapter 3). A mouse reraising someone with all his chips should set off an alarm or two in your head!

Beginners: Trapping with the Top Four Hands

The trapping theory for NLH applies mostly when you have A-A or K-K. Some players like to just call someone else's raise or reraise before the flop when holding A-A or K-K, in the hope that the move will trap someone into giving them all his chips after the flop. This is a dangerous theory with a risk-reward hazard that any expert in game theory would love to look at! Most of the time you should just go ahead and reraise with A-A or K-K and hope that your opponent either moves all-in right there with a hand like J-J or Q-Q (which makes you a 4½-to-1 favorite) or folds his hand. Reraising is the safe way to play A-A and K-K; it prevents you from losing all your chips in some situations. You'll lose them all less often when you reraise with A-A or K-K, but you'll also usually get less action on these hands. When trapping works out, you look brilliant; but when you bust yourself trapping someone, you look like an idiot!

The trap works like a charm when you have A-A or K-K and your opponent has a hand like A-J, and the flop is A♠-2♥-J♥. You may force your opponent with A-J into losing all his chips in this scenario because he may think you have K-J or a flush draw.

Trapping with aces can go badly for you, however, when your opponent hits his flop really well, as when he raises with Q♦-K♦ and you just call and the flop is K-Q-4: now you can kiss your chips good-bye. (However, think of the chips you'll win trapping with K-K on that same flop.)

Your trap could get uglier still if the raiser has 8♣-9♣, and now the flop is 5-6-7! In both these scenarios of trap gone bad, you would have won the pot had you reraised before the flop, but instead of winning the pot before the flop you have trapped yourself into losing all your chips! I rarely trap with any big hand, but some circumstances encourage me to try it. Trapping with aces is obviously safer than trapping with kings.

Beginners: Reraising J-J, 10-10, or 9-9 before the Flop

J-J, 10-10, and 9-9 are strong NLH hands, and you should reraise with them when someone raises before the flop. With these three hands you really want to use the reraise to win the pot before the flop, because you're probably winning at that point and because these hands are very vulnerable to overcards on the flop. Sometimes, when you smell weakness in your opponents, you can make a stand with one of these three hands and put in all your chips. In general, though, you want to reraise someone else before the flop, and if he or someone else puts in another raise (a third raise) over the top of you, you should just throw your hand away. These three hands are usually in a lot of trouble when an opponent puts in the dreaded third raise! You're roughly a 4½-to-1 underdog with an underpair against an overpair in Hold'em. (The exact odds depend on which two pairs you're comparing, but 4½ to 1 is close enough for most table estimations.)

Beginners: Pairs 8-8 and under and A-Q—Three Different Theories

Let's examine three ways these eight hands (8-8, 7-7, 6-6, 5-5, 4-4, 3-3, 2-2, and A-Q) might be played in NLH. In my view, these small pairs and A-Q are the kinds of hands that you want to take a flop with; thus they are hands worth one raise before the flop, or even worth making the first raise yourself. If you're raising with one of these hands, then raise about the size of the pot (this is discussed above in PLH). So you can just make the first raise with one of these hands and, hopefully, win the pot when everyone folds before the flop. But you don't want to put in very much money with these kinds of hands before the flop. Ideally, you want to call a small raise (or the initial blind bet) or make a pot-size raise yourself before the flop, and then hit your hand on the flop (a set is a great hand) and win a huge pot! Again, my theory is that you want to call a small raise before the flop or make a pot-size raise before the flop to try to win the pot before the flop.

Frank Henderson's theory about this type of hand (Henderson is a noted player on the poker circuit) is to call one raise before the flop (on this much we agree). But Frank doesn't like to try to win the pot before the flop with these kinds of hands by raising the pot before the flop. Rather, he likes to just call before the flop and hope to win a big pot when he flops his set. So Frank wants to try to lose small with these hands when he misses them and win big if he hits them, by keeping other players in the pot before the flop. Actually, this theory sounds pretty good to me! The only downside is that he doesn't win as many pots before the flop. Maybe this is OK, because the pots you win with a raise before the flop tend to be pretty small anyway.

The megalomaniac theory of playing these types of hands is always to raise or reraise before the flop. Don't discount this "megalo" theory out of hand, because it works very well for a lot of players. These megalo players are superaggressive and will try to win every pot they play before the flop. If a megalo gets hold of some chips, he can make the other players at his table miserable with his constant raising and reraising. I would rather back a megalo player than a supertight player any day in an NLH tournament. The megalos tend to do well in NLH tournaments because they're always picking up chips; but in the side games they tend to get crushed, as the more patient pros sit back and wait for the megalos to overplay their hands against them. The reason why megalos do better in NLH tournaments than in the side games is that they steal a ton of antes in NLH tourneys.

So we have three different NLH theories as far as playing small pairs and A-Q are concerned. I rarely play the megalo theory, because my opponents expect me to play that way (sometimes you need to play that way if you are at a table full of mice). Rather, I play the theory I've laid out above, and I sometimes use Frank Henderson's theory as well. In other words, most of the time I will put in the first raise with these types of hands, but sometimes I'll just call with them before the flop.

Intermediate NLH theory: Adding A-x Suited

Now we'll simply add A-x suited to the mix of hands that you play. The ramifications of adding these hands are two: you can get yourself into trouble when you hit an ace or the x with an A-x suited hand, and you will occasionally make an ace-high flush.

Try not to lose too much money when you hit an ace with your A-x suited hand. In NLH most of the value of A-x suited comes when you hit the hand hard, as when you make a flush, two pair, or trips (when you make trips with the x card, it's hard for anyone to notice). When you hit the ace only, as with A♣-3♣ and a flop of A-K-2, then watch out! Don't get overinvolved in this situation, because anyone putting in big bets against you will almost certainly have you beat, unless he's bluffing. In limit Hold'em you can just call someone down in a situation like this, without doing too much damage to your chips, but in no-limit doing that could cost you a big chunk of your chips.

When you do hit your hand hard, then you need to figure out how to win the maximum number of chips with it. You should also be thinking about protecting your hand, especially when you draw a flop of 8♣-8♥-9♣ and you have A♠-8♣. In this case, your opponents could be drawing to a straight or a flush. Keep this in mind when you think about betting a small amount to lure your opponents into the pot. The funny thing is that you want action with this hand and this flop, but you can't just let someone beat you for free. If you knew that your opponents didn't have a straight or a flush draw, then you could check on the flop, hoping for a lot of action on the next two rounds of betting. Betting out with a hand like this may cause someone with a drawing hand to raise you, and now you can reraise and win the pot right then and there.

Guessing an Opponent's Exact Two Hole Cards

Ever since I started playing NLH I have incorporated a little game in which I try to guess exactly what two cards my opponent has in the hole. I can usually narrow it down to a very few possibilities, and on occasion I have ventured a guess out loud when I feel confident about it. Boy, did I freak the other players out when I would guess my main opponent's Q-Q and he would then flip his Q-Q faceup and say, "How in the world does he do that?"

How in the world *do* I do it? I'm able to do it because I practice observation, logic, and deductive reasoning while I play in the game. By the time someone has acted on his hand three or four times, a lot of information has been made available. How did he bet it before the flop? How much did he bet, and what did he seem to want his opponent to do in this hand? Did he look weak or strong? Exactly how weak or strong did he appear? What did he have the last time he acted this way? How did the flop alter his demeanor? Was he doing any acting that I could see right through? And of course the cards on the board figure heavily in my assessments.

Usually, all the information I gather in this way helps me form a mental picture of my opponent's hand. I'm blessed with an excellent poker memory as well (I still remember hands that I played 17 years ago, and all the details—not just hands of today or yesterday), and all that helps the process too. So I could narrow it down to, say, a pair of tens, jacks, or queens. Then I would think for another few seconds and refine my guess on the basis of the way my opponent had acted in the past during a hand that I witnessed. Finally, I would throw out my guess, "You have pocket queens in the hole, don't you?" I became so good at this little trick that for a long time the other players stopped trying to bluff me. (This was awfully nice for me, but on the other hand I wasn't picking off anyone else's bluffs either!)

Trying to determine the cards your opponent holds is a great game when you play poker, and it will help your reading skills immeasurably. If you're bad at it at first, don't worry—

your reads will get better and better. Practice makes perfect! Daniel Goleman claims in his book *EQ: Emotional Intelligence* that "certain 'star qualities' are learnable." (Goleman believes that many of the characteristics that have made some people very successful can be studied and learned.) I believe that reading people is a learnable "star quality" (characteristic), although I concede that some people can take it further than others. In any case, you'll improve your reading skills a lot with practice. And when you're way off on a guess, you'll begin to see why. ("Oh yeah, I forgot that he reraised before the flop with that hand.")

Judgment is Everything in NLH

In NLH all manner of plays are possible. You can fold K-K before the flop or move all-in with 2-7 off suit, bluffing before the flop, if your judgment is good enough. By the way, I've folded K-K before the flop only a few times in my life, and every time I did, I was right, because my opponent did indeed have A-A! One thing you'll learn as you play more poker is that when someone has the best possible hand, he is often easily readable.

Quiz show hosts like to say, when the pauses are too protracted, "Go with your first gut instinct. That first instinct is always right." You'll find yourself in a lot of interesting situations in NLH where your judgment and your guts will be severely tested. Whether or not you make the right decisions will go far toward determining whether or not you'll win for the day (it helps to have good cards too). You think that you're under pressure at work? I've seen players who have all their money in the world on the table call other players' bluffs for all *their* money. In other words, if they're wrong, then they're busted!

One excellent rule for NLH is this: if you can't allow yourself to fold the best hand, then you can't win. In many of the tournaments that I've won I've had occasion to fold the winning hand. In the World Championships in 1989, when just four players were left, I folded pocket tens before the flop against Johnny Chan's pocket nines in a big pot, but I still went on to win the tournament! It's not who wins the battle; it's who wins the war. Don't be afraid to fold your hand in NLH if you think that it's beaten. If it was the winner, so what? You made your decision, and you're still at the table with chips. Stay focused on winning, not on looking back at your untimely fold.

Phil's NLH Strategy

I like to take pieces of every different strategy I'll be laying out below and keep them in my arsenal for eventual use. I like to stick to a very tight beginner-type overall strategy, one involving playing very few hands for the most part. In this way, there isn't too much pressure on me to make tough decisions all the time. So most of the time in NLH I like to play only the "NLH fifteen" hands.

When someone behind me is playing too tightly, in NLH, I like to raise the pot to try to steal the blinds from him, whenever it's his big blind.

I trust my instincts when I'm deciding whether or not a player is bluffing. My poker instincts have been very, very good to me. I hone these instincts by practicing reading my opponents when I'm out of the hand being played, to try to get a better read on them for when I need it later. (In mentioning my own play I'm trying only to show you what's possible if you practice and develop your instincts.)

If someone has raised in front of me and I feel that he is weak, I usually fold anyway. But at the end of the hand I'll watch to see if he exposes his hole cards, so that I can confirm that he was weak or see that I was wrong. If I have confirmation that I was right, then I wait for him to do it again. Anyone who makes one weak raise can be expected to make more than one. When that player makes another raise and I feel it is weak, I go ahead and reraise him, to force him to fold his weak hand. This reraise wins many more chips than a mere blind steal would win, but you're also risking a lot more chips to win the pot when you reraise on a bluff.

Phil's Strategy: Reraise with Nothing

When I teach NLH theory in seminars, I like to use an example from the World Series of Poker (WSOP) in 2001. I had been watching Daniel Negreanu very closely during the championship event on day three. In this particular hand Daniel opened the pot for $10,000. I knew he had nothing, and when it was my turn to act I made it $30,000 to go with 10♦-2♦ (bluffing). Now John "World" Hennigan decided to move all-in for $30,100, and Daniel quickly folded his hand. I called the $100 more, but I would have called another $10,000 because of the size of the pot (I had about $210,000 in front of me at the time). After all, I already had $30,000 in the pot plus John's $30,100 and Daniel's

$10,000. Much to my embarrassment, the tournament director required us to flip our cards faceup before the flop. He wasn't picking on us; that's the rule at WSOP when one player is all-in. This is a new, controversial industrywide rule in poker in 2002, and the reason that it exists is to prevent collusion. Many of the top players hate this rule because it forces them to show their hands and therefore exposes their style of play. Now players get to see, free, what the great players are doing. ("He bet all his chips with that hand?")

When the hands were announced, a lot of snickering was heard from the crowd (how did Phil get $30,000 in before the flop with 10-2?), and most of the players left in the tournament came over to watch this pot. John had 9-9 and I had 10-2! Basically, I needed a 10 to win. Anyway, the flop and the turn came 7-8-3-K, and then a 10 hit on the last card! What a lucky card for me! I don't know what John was doing putting his last $30,000 into a pot when it was raised and reraised in front of him before the flop, and I didn't like his play at all. I hadn't been making any plays that day, and even if he suspected that I was making a play, pocket nines isn't a very good hand to make a stand with, especially given that he couldn't even raise me out of the pot. Also, John had to worry that Daniel would get involved in this pot, although Daniel was probably going to throw his hand away, facing both my raise and John's call. Still, there was some chance he was going to be facing two opponents, which meant that his 9-9 was just too vulnerable. More to the point, though, John had to figure he was going to be heads-up with me, and my reraise against Daniel should have meant strength to him.

Be that as it may, John's instinct was right, so I have to give him credit for his call, and perhaps for figuring out that Daniel and I were both bluffing! Anyway, here is an example of a pot that was won while someone was making a move. Daniel later admitted having six high in this hand (he folded his hand face-down because he didn't call the $30,100 bet).

If someone raises a very small amount before the flop (less than 5 percent of my chips), I will often call with suited connectors and take the flop. When I do this, I'm putting a lot of pressure on myself to read my opponents well. Sometimes it works out beautifully and I have a huge flop and win a big pot. Sometimes I have to scramble and make a great fold in order to save chips. Sometimes I bust myself because I can't get away from (can't fold) my hand after the flop.

I'm capable of trapping with big hands like a pair of tens, jacks, queens, kings, or aces, but I'm very careful that I don't trap myself with these hands! I rarely use this play, because it can be very dangerous in NLH.

I absolutely hate getting all my chips in with *any* hand. When you are all-in you can go broke! Of course, if I have the best possible hand on the last round of betting, then I love to get all my chips in. I try to avoid getting all-in in NLH unless it can't be helped.

More often than I probably should, I will throw away the best hand when I play NLH. I will throw away very strong hands if I believe that they're beaten, no matter how much money is already in the pot. When you can do this, you can escape losing situations and even consider that you've gained an emotional win. I folded pocket kings before the flop at the World Championships in 2001 when my opponent opened for $1,200, I reraised him to $3,800, and he then moved my last $12,000 all-in. I thought he had pocket aces, so I folded my hand, rather than risk my last $12,000. As he was throwing away his hand facedown, I said, "Show me pocket aces!" Amazingly, he did show them.

The next day I folded my A-6 hand after a lot of money went in before the flop and the flop came down A♠-10♦-6♦. My opponent could have had A♦-Q♦ or A♦-K♦, which would have given him a flush draw and top pair, but that would have made me and my two pair the winner. He told me later that he had A♠-10♠, for two better pair than mine! Two days later I had more than $1 million in chips in front of me, and yet I would have been broke if I hadn't thrown away both those strong hands! The ability to throw away strong hands is a mark of an NLH champion.

I often protect my hands with huge bets and raises. At the preliminary NLH event at the WSOP that I won in 2001, I moved all-in with A-A after I was check-raised on a flop of A♦-6♥-7♠. Even though I had the best possible hand and had good reason to suspect that the opponent who had check-raised me on the flop was drawing dead (had no wins!), I decided that I didn't want to take a chance that my opponent might catch two perfect cards. This was the classic slow-play situation because we were the two chip leaders at the time. Instead of smooth-calling my opponent's $15,000 check-raise on the flop (as 98 percent of the pros in the world would do), I went ahead and raised him his last $50,000, and he threw his hand away. (Did I mention that I went on to win the tournament?) Perhaps if I had slow-played my hand, my opponent would have caught an eight and a nine to make a ten-high straight with his A-10 and a board of A-6-7-8-9.

In the World Championship event in 2001, faced with an $18,000 opening bet and a $70,000 raise to go, I moved all-in for more than $550,000 with my A-A, to send a message that I had A-A! A lot of players would have raised less, to lure their opponent in before the flop. By the way, I later did what's called *rabbit hunting*—looking at the deck after the hand is over, to see what would have happened had additional cards been dealt out—and discovered that the flop would have been K-2-3 had my opponent not folded his pocket K-K hand! I would have had one more *bad beat* (bad-luck) story to tell if I had only reraised a little bit or smooth-called his $70,000 bet. Of course, my opponent kept rabbit hunting, and he claims an ace was coming on the last card. (I didn't look beyond the flop!)

I will call someone on the end with ace high or worse if I think I have the best hand. I recently called a $30,000 bet from Carlos Mortensen (the WSOP champion in 2001) with K-Q high, and he had me beaten with a small pair.

I like to play conservatively and hang around in an NLH game or tournament until I smell blood or have a good situation come up for me. I wait for the chips to come to me. Eventually, my opponents start to make mistakes that I can take advantage of. When I feel the time is right, I will make some moves. I might call someone with a weak hand when he's bluffing, or I might bluff someone when I smell weakness. I may even try to trap someone if I make the nuts, but generally I bet the nuts to give someone a chance to break himself against me in a pot. In the hand I mentioned above, where I flopped a set of aces, I actually bet big on the flop before I was check-raised! Most players wouldn't dream of betting when they're heads up with a set of aces but no draw is on the board. If my opponents are playing too tightly, I'll start to raise every pot to steal some chips, especially when there are antes to steal as well as blinds. (Antes aren't usually used in Hold'em, but they are added to Hold'em tournaments in later rounds and sometimes to high-limit side games.)

I play NLH by feel, with some discipline, to make sure I stay around for a while. And I trust my reading powers implicitly. If they punch, then I counterpunch. If they lower their guard, then I strike. I sit back and watch what others are doing, and then I make adjustments to my play. Sometimes I play my style, and other times I play a style based entirely on my opponents' styles.

The "Bet It All" Strategy for NLH—Yuck!

In the "bet it all" strategy you raise all your chips to open a pot or to reraise in a pot. So if the blinds are $10–$20 and it's your turn to act from late position in a hand, then you just go ahead and open for the whole $1,000 you have in front of you. You will win that $30 in blinds quite often when you bet $1,000, but you're risking $1,000 in order to win $30! You do the math! Actually, a lot of poker players use this crazy strategy these days. The downside is that you're risking all your chips, and if your opponent picks up a strong hand you'll lose the whole $1,000; and for what: $30 in blinds? If someone else opens a pot for $60, and the *slider* (he likes to slide all his chips in!) decides to play his hand, then he just bets it all. ("Your $60 and $940 more.") I think the main reason these players do this is that they're afraid to play their hands *after* the flop, although some of them just fail to understand the long-term implications of betting a lot in order to win a little.

The good side of betting it all is that it prevents someone with a marginal hand from raising or reraising you before the flop. Suppose that I have A-J on the button and now you raise it to $60 to go in late position. I may reraise you, thinking that you're weak because you raised the pot in late position ("He's just stealing the antes"), and therefore I think you're just trying to steal the blinds. If you have 10-10 and decide to reraise me as well, I may have to call you if I don't have a lot of chips left. Now we're going to play an even-money pot (actually, not quite even money, because the 10-10 is about a 13-to-10 favorite over the A-J), which the champion players like to avoid. It's difficult to win consistently when you play a lot of coin-flip hands in a tournament! When you do bet it all before the flop, my only option left is to fold my marginal A-J.

For a while in the 1990s a lot of sliders reached the final tables at NLH events. Sliding all one's chips in is probably a good strategy for a weaker, inexperienced player. This way he will get lucky for a big pot or he will be eliminated, but at least the great players won't be able to slowly pick him apart. Still, for a good or great player, or someone aspiring to be a good or great player, anything that takes away your options in NLH is bad. Sliding a mountain all-in to try to win a molehill takes away all your options and is a very risky play as well. One bad move like this, and you find yourself out of options when the player behind you jumps up from his seat because he has pocket aces. It's too late now to take advantage of this new information, because you've already made your big move all-in!

Huck Seed's Advanced Theory of Suited Connectors for NLH

This suited-connectors theory is very advanced and could be dangerous to your bankroll's health. I call it "Huck Seed's" theory, but in fact I've used it myself in days past. And besides, to pigeonhole Huck Seed's great NLH play into this one theory would be unfair to Huck. Huck can play many different ways at different stages of a tournament or side game. Be that as it may, he often does play this theory successfully, as does the talented, young, up-and-coming Daniel Negreanu.

This is the theory of calling other players' raises with suited connectors, such as 6♦-7♦ or 8♣-9♣ or even 3♠-4♠. These are excellent drawing hands in NLH. Ideally, you want to call an opponent's $400 bet with a hand like 4♦-5♦ when he has another $10,000 to $20,000 left in front of him. This way, if you hit your hand, you may win that other $10,000 to $20,000. So the idea is to call a small bet from your opponent and win a large stack of chips when you hit your hand.

Suited Connectors

Here is an actual hand that I saw, between Daniel Negreanu and a two-time world champion, Johnny Chan, at the Taj Mahal in Atlantic City in the $7,500 buy-in championship event in 1999. With the blinds at $400–$800 and more than $12,000 in front of him, Johnny opened the pot for $2,600 with A-K. Daniel called the $2,600 with 7♠-9♠, and the flop came down A♦-7♦-7♣. (Daniel flopped trip sevens!) Johnny bet out small ($2,000) on the flop, and Daniel raised small ($3,000). After studying things for a while, Johnny moved all-in and Daniel quickly said, "I call." Daniel wound up busting Johnny out on this hand; and Johnny, shocked, said to me a few minutes later when I approached to offer sympathy, "Can you believe this kid?" Here is a case where Daniel invested $2,600 to win more than $12,000 if he hit. The suited connectors worked like a charm.

The downside of playing like this, of course, is that you will put yourself in a lot of untenable situations. What are you going to do when the flop comes down 2-3-8 and you have 8♣-9♣? You have flopped top pair, which is fairly powerful, but what happens when your opponent has J-J in the hole? Answer: you may lose a lot of chips! In fact, if you're not careful, you can lose all your chips in this situation.

You can thus expect to have some severe chip swings when you play poker like this. When I watched Daniel use this approach in the world championship event in 2001, his chips were up to $450,000 (and the chip lead) and then down to $70,000 and then up to $700,000 (and the chip lead again!) and then down to $170,000! Up and down, up and down, so it went with Daniel at this WSOP. He is a great NLH player, but these kinds of swings just can't be good.

Let's return to the example above for a moment. Why was Johnny shocked by Daniel's play in this example hand? Because Daniel risked almost 20 percent of his own chips before the flop with 7♠-9♠. This was just too high a percentage of his chips to risk with this hand. If you want to play this way, try not to risk more than 7 percent of your chips before the flop with these suited connector hands.

Playing the suited connectors requires an excellent read of

your opponents, so that you don't get yourself into trouble when you hit some of these hands halfway. Before you try this approach, make sure that you're reading your opponents almost perfectly. I would never recommend this theory to any novice or intermediate-level player!

When Suited Connectors Don't Work

In the main event at the WSOP of 2001, I made a raise of $3,000 with K♦-J♦ and Daniel called me with 6♦-5♦. The flop was 10♦-7♠-2♥, and I checked and then Daniel checked. The next card off was 9♦, for 10♦-7♠-2♥-9♦, so that I now had a straight and a flush draw. Any diamond would make me a flush, and any queen or eight would make me a straight. I decided that I needed to make a big bet with this draw, since Daniel had checked the flop and I thought he was weak, so I bet out $10,000.

Meanwhile, Daniel had also turned a straight and a flush draw. Any diamond made him a flush, and an eight made him a straight. Little did he know that the diamond made me a higher flush and the eight made me a higher straight! Anyway, he called the $10,000 bet, not knowing that he really didn't want to hit his hand, because it would cost him another $20,000 if he did! The last card was a "blank" 3♣, and now I checked and Daniel checked also, thinking that I was strong. I said, "You win it, I missed." He said, "No, you got it." At that point, I knew that my king high was good, and I flipped it faceup and collected the pot. Daniel said, "Whew, it's a good thing I missed my hand!" as he showed me his hole cards.

Why didn't I try to bluff Daniel on the end? For the same reason that he didn't try to bluff me on the end: we usually call each other when we have anything! And if he had tried to bluff me on the last round of betting, I might have just raised him if I noticed any weakness at all in his bet on the end.

This example illustrates another problem with suited connectors. You might just end up drawing to the lower straight or flush and wind up losing all your chips when you hit it!

Superadvanced "Megalomaniac" NLH Theory: Playing with Nothing

Some great NLH players like to call an opponent's raise with *any* two cards, because they think they can outplay the raiser later on in the hand. Again, I'll single out Daniel Negreanu as a player who uses this strategy. (Sorry, Danny.) In many NLH tournaments I've watched Daniel apply this strategy, knowing full well what he was doing! The key to the strategy lies in recognizing who the preflop raiser is. If the preflop raiser is a weak player (if you're new to the game, it's more fair to call you "inexperienced" than "weak"), look out for Daniel, because he'll be coming at you!

Many weaker or inexperienced players don't know how to bet or how to disguise their actions when they hit or miss the flop. They may, for example, jump out of their seats or bet in a very confident manner when they hit a flop. Conversely, they may telegraph their actions when they miss the flop, by betting with doubt or uncertainty written all over their faces. If they do hit, then Daniel folds (unless one of those "goofball" 6-8 off-suit hands of his actually hits). If they miss their hand, then Daniel bluffs them out and wins the pot. Of course, Daniel occasionally hurts his opponents or himself in a big pot when both he and his opponent hit the flop.

I give Daniel Negreanu and Huck Seed a lot of credit for being able to use this strategy successfully. Of course, if you ever travel the poker-tournament trails, you will see other top players, such as Layne Flack, Ted Forrest, Men Nguyen, and Amir Vahedi, using this dangerous strategy to good effect. But it is a bit too risky for my taste; I just don't like to be always putting a lot of pressure on myself to "read" my opponents and then fold my hands after I hit them on the flop. (Hitting a flop and then folding your hand because you read your opponent as being strong is a hard thing to do.) But someone who uses this theory well can accumulate a lot of chips very quickly!

Dave "Devilfish" Ulliott's Theory of NLH

The Devilfish is a great PLH and NLH player from Hull, in the United Kingdom. He has won PLH and NLH titles in the United States and Europe. Devilfish thrives on coming into a pot raising with almost anything before the flop. He may raise with 4-7 off suit or 2-5 off suit. He will almost always bet out at you on the flop, whether he misses the flop or hits it. This gives all the others a chance to fold their hands and gives Devilfish his second chance to win the pot with a bet or raise. (His first chance was before the flop with a raise.) He is very good at reading players, and that's one thing that all tough NLH strategies have in common. They all consider reading the other players well an essential ingredient.

If you do hit something and call Devilfish on the flop, then the pot has only just begun. If he thinks you'll fold your hand before risking a big bet on fourth street, then he'll bet big on fourth street, trying to bluff you. If he feels you'll fold your hand for an all-in bet, then he'll risk his whole tournament and bet it all. Likewise, he'll bet all your chips when he feels he has the best hand. This constant power-play pressure is also used by Men "The Master" Nguyen, Erik Seidel, Layne Flack, John Bonetti, and many other successful NLH tournament players. I used to use this approach myself, but once my opponents took to calling me down consistently, I began showing them only big hands. If they're going to call you, be ready to bust them.

If Devilfish wins a few pots before the flop, a few pots on the flop, and a few pots on the end with a bluff, he'll be way ahead of the game. This is a good theory of NLH play, but if used wrongly it can be disastrous for the player who is applying it. You can bluff at the wrong times and lose a lot of chips very quickly. As with all good NLH theories, if you use this one well you'll accumulate a lot of chips quickly, but if you use it badly you'll cough them up just as quickly.

Develop Your Own Style

What tactics should *you* adopt? My advice is to take a little bit from here and a little bit from there, and concoct your own style of NLH play. Some people try to play like me or Huck Seed or other great NLH players, such as T. J. Cloutier. This is usually a mistake, because those who attempt it are getting away from their own strengths, and they aren't far enough along in their own poker development to do all the things—simultaneously—

that the great NLH players do. As you continue to develop your own style, get rid of the tendencies that don't work and add some of the traits that you see in the great players or read about here, but do it slowly! Make sure that a change in a move or a style works for you before you commit yourself to it for an extended period. Above all else, make sure that you're enjoying yourself when you play NLH. Otherwise, what's the point? Only a few players can count on making money over the long haul in this game, so you had better enjoy the journey!

To learn more about where and when the major NLH and PLH tournaments are played, go to philhellmuth.com or any one of these other sites: CardPlayer.com, PokerPages.com, and LiveAction Poker.com.

Chapter 7

Limit Hold'em
Tournament Strategy

I still love poker tournaments, even after playing in more than 900 of them in the 1990s alone; I enjoy every one that I play in. The event that really fires me up, though, is the World Series of Poker (WSOP). The WSOP is where legends and champions are made; it is the poker world's world championship. (Appendix 2 talks about playing in a WSOP tournament.)

In golf there are four major tournaments, but in poker the series of events constituting the WSOP carries so much prestige that it is in effect the U.S. Open, the Masters, the British Open, and the PGA all rolled into one!

With 643 players putting up $10,000 each for the WSOP championship event of 2002, creating a prize pool of $6.43 million, the money alone almost matches the prestige of winning the event. The investment banker Robert Varkonyi took home the first prize of $2 million; the second-place finisher, Julian Gardener, had to settle for only $1 million! For a lot of players, this is life-changing money, and so it isn't surprising that a lot of poker players covet the money more than the title. I'm not one of them: I love the title more than the money! The title brings with it a lifetime of recognition and prestige. The winner is forever called a world champion of poker, and his or her picture will go up on the Wall of Champions forever (at both of the Horseshoe Casinos in Las Vegas and Tunica, Mississippi). You can see the Wall of Champions at PokerPages.com.

In 1970 Las Vegas Benny Binion started the WSOP, at his Horseshoe Casino, and called it poker's world championships. It has been poker's world championship ever since, and it has grown in stature and popularity each year.

When you win the WSOP, you are no longer just a poker player but rather a world champion. This distinction is nice, as my wife found out when she searched for residency programs back in the early 1990s. When asked about her husband's occupation, she would say, "He's a world champion of poker." I'm sure that this sounded more interesting and prestigious than, "He's a professional poker player" or "He plays poker for a living!"

Every year in late April, the best poker players in the world (and a lot of wannabes) gather at the Horseshoe Casino in Las Vegas for roughly 25 to 33 WSOP events (the precise number changes from year to year), culminating in the "big one." The "big one" is the $10,000 buy-in Championship Event that ESPN, the Discovery Channel, the Travel Channel, and other television networks show up to cover every year. The lowest buy-in event at the WSOP currently is set at $1,500. If you plan to attend the WSOP and play every event, make sure that you bring $100,000 with you! These 30 days (the "big one" alone is five days long) are undoubtedly the most exciting in poker, every year, and by

far the most lucrative. For more about the WSOP and other prestigious poker events, go to Appendix 3.

All champion poker players have to start somewhere,
though. Learning to win limit Hold'em poker tournaments was
very difficult for me. Even though I was already a world champion of poker and had won many big no-limit Hold'em events by
the time I was 26 years old, I still hadn't even made my first final
table (which is usually the final nine players) in a limit Hold'em
tournament.

If you were a pro and I told you this, you would think it
was really odd. How could I win so many no-limit Hold'em
events but consistently have trouble making the final nine in limit
Hold'em events? After a while, I began to realize that the way I
was playing my hands was holding me back, so I did what I had
never done before in poker: I studied a couple of other players to
see what they were doing differently from me. Remember this the
next time you start to blame your lack of success on bad luck:
even a world champion was willing to admit he had things left to
learn.

With no-limit, I could see what everyone else was doing
wrong in the late 1980s. For some reason, the right way to play
no-limit just seemed obvious and easy to me. Of course, I also
did my fair share of playing no-limit Hold'em badly, but at least
I knew when I was playing badly. (Moreover, that had to do with
emotional issues, which I discuss elsewhere in the book.)

In this chapter you will learn:

▮ Aggressive play is right in limit Hold'em tournaments.
▮ Tight play is right in limit Hold'em tournaments.

▌ Stealing blinds helps you survive *late* in limit Hold'em events.

▌ To win, steal more blinds at the money-cutoff line.

▌ Survive and thrive.

▌ Bring your big guns to a war!

▌ How to trap in limit Hold'em tourneys.

▌ Playing satellites improves your game.

Aggressive Play Helps in Limit Hold'em Events

One day after I was eliminated from a limit Hold'em event, I sought out Jack Keller, who at the time was really hot in limit Hold'em tournaments, and watched him play for a couple of hours. It was obvious to me that Jack was doing a number of things I hadn't been doing. He simply tried to win every pot that he played. Jack never just called someone else's raise before the flop: he always either threw his hand away or three-bet it.

This was quite different from my old strategy. I used to just call when I had a small pair, hoping that others would call as well, and that I would win a big pot when I finally hit my set. Jack, however, always three-bet before the flop, even with only a small pair, and continued to play his hand aggressively from that point on in the hand. The percentage of pots that he won was much higher than the percentage of pots that I had won, for three reasons.

First, Jack's constant three-betting before the flop helped him win more pots by eliminating more opponents preflop. When you start with fewer opponents before the flop, you'll win more pots.

Second, Jack would play his hand pretty hard on the flop and win a lot of pots if his opponents had, say, king-high when an ace hit the board.

Third, Jack would just plain try to bluff you out if he thought he could.

This aggressive play of Hold'em hands is something I've already preached to you in earlier chapters of this book. Once I began using this system, I couldn't believe the results I achieved. I made five final tables in a row playing limit Hold'em this way, and eventually, in the 1990s, I won two world championships in limit Hold'em.

Tight Play Helps in Limit Hold'em Events, Especially Early

Tight play is also an important factor in success at tournaments. The really tight players tend to be around en masse fairly late in limit Hold'em events. These players tend to play almost as tight as the "top ten only" strategy (which I discuss in Chapter 3). Notice that I said these players were around, and not that they were winning the events. Although there are usually a ton of supertight players left late in a limit Hold'em event, they usually don't win the event or even make the final table. I believe that supertight play helps you last in limit Hold'em events, but you need to be able to change speeds at the right time if you're going to win some of them.

The right strategy against a group of supertight players differs from the right strategy against a group of average players. In fact, Jack Keller's three-betting preflop with every hand that he plays is more successful against a supertight player who will fold his hand right away if he misses it. Which tight player is going to win the pot when Jack three-bets his 5-5 into his 7-7? For example, when the flop comes A-J-2, then Jack can win pretty easily with a bet on the flop. Although supertight play will help you last, you will need to change your tactics at some point in order to win.

Therefore, I recommend playing the "top ten only" strategy for the first five or six hours of any Hold'em event while the weaker players are weeded out. After the first few hours of playing this strategy, it is time to switch tactics a bit.

Stealing the Blinds Helps You Survive Late in Limit Hold'em Events

At some point after the first five or six hours, it's time to start stealing the blinds from the supertight players who are still alive in the tournament. But be wary of stealing the blinds from the looser players or the champion players, because they will probably defend with skill. Stay aware also of the person who keeps stealing your blinds, because at some point you will have to make a stand against that player.

If you take a close look around your table about six hours into the event, every time you enter one of these events, after a while you will develop the ability to see into the future a little bit. For example, there will probably be someone at your table who is playing way too loose but nonetheless is still alive. You may worry that this player may continue to be lucky, but chances are that he will bust himself out sooner rather than later, because of his reckless play. There will also be a player at your table whom you will recognize as being very tight, and you can figure that he or she will probably be around very late in the tournament, although probably low on chips.

You may even be able to see that the loose player is the one who may be your ticket to lasting another few hours yourself. Six or so hours into the event, with your blind-stealing working well, you need to make sure that you're still in a very tight mode of play. Surviving at this point in the tournament is the name of the game. But make sure that you're stealing blinds from the super-tight players. (Don't worry; you will know who they are.)

Steal Blinds at the Money-Cutoff Line

When you start to reach the money-cutoff stage (when, say, there are 19 players left, and the tournament pays only 18 spots), make sure that you have your priorities straight. As the other players begin to play even tighter, in order to last until the final 27 or 18 players, you need to understand that making the money isn't your objective at this point. You are here to finish in the top three and make the big money.

One phenomenon you will observe is that when there are 28 players left in an event paying 27 places, the players will all play even tighter, in order to be sure they "make the money." This is the time to be sure you're stealing every blind you can steal! If no one is going to put up a fight, then make sure you grab all this "free money"! So what if you are eliminated in the "stink hole" (often called the "bubble")? In other words, so what if you finish twenty-eighth when the event is paying only 27 spots! Does twenty-seventh place change your life at all? If it does, then just do what everyone does and play supertight. Just be warned that I will be there picking up your blinds every round.

This strategy—"steal while they're in survival mode"—has helped me (and many other players) accumulate chips that become important when I'm later trying to advance into the final rounds and win the tournament. But you have to be a little careful with it. Enough players have learned about the strategy to defend the blinds with aggression of their own. Not everyone will go into a shell. You have to know your players and pick your spots.

Survive and Thrive

Once you're in the money, things and people change. It's important that you take note of just what these changes are. If your opponents are playing too tight, steal their blinds. If they're playing too loose, you play a little bit tighter.

When you're in the money, you should still be waiting for some really high-quality hands before you get too involved in any pot. Remember that the limits are high, and you should be thinking about playing very tight, because at high limits losing one big pot can be devastating. If you can get away with stealing some blinds, do it; but with the limits way up there, every hand will cause a major swing in your chip count. So it's better just to sit back and watch the action and continue to survive. And when you do pick up a top ten hand, you'll be taking your shot at the pot with some power.

Sometimes I just wait for a big hand in a limit Hold'em tourney and let the cards decide how long I'll be around for that day. If I catch good cards and win, then I might win the whole enchilada. If I catch good cards and lose, then at least I'm happy that I went out with some top ten hands. If I don't catch anything decent and ante myself out of the tourney, that's OK too. But if I start playing hands that I'm not supposed to play, that's the worst of all, because I shoot myself in the foot!

Bring Your Big Guns to a War!

When you have a border skirmish with someone, you don't need to bring out the heavy artillery, but when a war breaks out, you'd better bring your big guns! The same thing can be said about playing pots late in a poker tournament. You really don't need to have too much in your hand in order to try to steal the blinds from a mouse (a very cautious player). You probably won't need too much to defend your blinds against a jackal (a wildly aggressive player) either.

But when you decide to play a huge pot, then you'd better have a huge hand. I'm always looking for A-A, K-K, Q-Q, J-J, 10-10, or A-K before I get involved in a big pot. In fact, I never feel too bad after I've been eliminated late in a limit Hold'em event if I know that I lost some big pots with some big hands. Even though I hate losing a big pot late in one of these events with A-A, what more could I have asked than the chance to play a big pot with A-A? Ultimately, I feel pretty good knowing that an opponent had to put a lot of money into the pot with his Q-K or whatever against my A-A.

How to Trap with a Big Hand

I've already told two stories in Chapter 6 (John Bonetti is featured trapping Dan Harrington in one story, on page 127) about how one player trapped another with A-A in the hole. In both stories, the player who was doing the trapping came out smelling like a rose. But trapping with pocket aces or pocket kings (especially kings, because they're vulnerable to a lone ace falling on the flop) can be extremely dangerous. By "trapping" with these hands, I mean just calling one or two bets before the flop, rather than raising or reraising with your hand. By just calling preflop and trapping other players into playing their hands when they ordinarily wouldn't have done this, you're creating a bigger pot, which means you're also risking losing a big pot.

For example, suppose that someone in front of you has raised with Q-Q, and then you decide to just call (smooth-call) with your K-K before the flop. Now someone with [A♠]-[J♠] decides to call two bets with his hand, and then the board comes off [2♠]-[4♠]-[9♥]-[3♥]-[A♠]. In this case, you would have won a huge pot from the opponent who had Q-Q if you had three-bet with your hand instead of calling two bets before the flop, because the [A♠]-[J♠] would have folded before the flop and not hung around in hopes of catching a spade draw on the flop and the (for you) dreaded ace on the river. Imagine the number of bets that you would have won from the Q-Q in this scenario.

But because you decided to trap other players into the pot before the flop, you lost a big pot. Because the [A♠]-[J♠] flopped the nut flush draw, he was forced to play his hand all the way, and then he hit an ace on the end to beat you.

Despite the grim scenario that I've just presented, trapping has its place in tournament poker, lest you become too predictable. But even I can't tell you exactly where that place is. One good time to trap is when you're in late position and no one else has entered the pot yet. This is a good place to just call one bet, to see if anyone else enters the pot behind you. In this scenario, if you make it two bets to go, then you'll probably just win the blinds. But by smooth-calling, you will at a minimum force the big blind to take a free flop. Just remember that in this case you're asking for action when you have a big hand. We all know that you should be very careful what you ask for, because you may get it!

Another time when I may smooth-call with A-A or K-K is when I'm in the big blind and someone else has raised, and it's just myself and one other opponent in the pot. I smooth-call in order to trick my opponent into thinking I'm weak (that is, merely defending my mediocre blind hand), so that he will give me a lot of action the rest of the hand. Just remember that smooth-calling in limit Hold'em with big hands can work out very badly or perfectly, depending on the way the cards fall. When you smooth-call with a big hand, you really are gambling.

Play Satellites in Order to Improve Your Hold'em Game

If you want to *win* poker tournaments and not merely be satisfied with appearances at the final table, I strongly suggest that you play in satellites so that you become used to "endgame" poker play, that is, when the table is shorthanded with big stacks and big blinds. Satellites are ten-handed minitournaments where players put up one-tenth of the buy-in to a poker tournament and the last player standing (actually, the last person sitting!) wins a seat in the main event.

For example, to play a satellite for the WSOP's first $2,000 buy-in limit Hold'em event (where several hundred players are expected each year), 10 people put up $220 each, and the winner gets a seat in the $2,000 buy-in event. The seat allows the satellite winner to contend in an event that will pay more than $400,000 for first place! In this two-step process, you can run $220 into over $400,000 in two days!

Playing satellites simulates what it's like at the final table of a poker tournament. In order to win a satellite, you start out playing 10- or nine-handed and continue eliminating players until you're playing two-handed (heads up) for the seat in the tournament.

Playing in multiple satellites also improves your short-handed limit Hold'em nontournament game (in the side games). When you play nontourney Hold'em, you'll often find that the game will either end up shorthanded (five players or less) or become shorthanded for a time while you're waiting for new players to join up. If you have no experience in these short-handed game situations, either you'll have to leave a potentially profitable game (when it fills up again) or you'll probably lose money, because shorthanded play is quite different from nine-handed play. Satellites let you practice and improve your short-handed game, because you skip all the effort of getting to the "final table." You're already there, and as players start getting knocked out, you'll begin gaining experience that will help improve your shorthanded game.

Psychological Advantages in Poker Tournaments

Making sure you're consistently friendly to the other players at the table is a wise policy. If players feel that you're a "good guy" or a friend, you increase the chance (at least marginally) that they won't call you in marginal situations where they could really hurt you, situations where they might well call someone they would love to bust.

Be careful with the great players at the table. I'm not saying that you should roll over and play dead; I'm just saying that it's probably not a good idea to steal their blinds, because they'll notice that. Remember that great players usually just want to last, so if you give them respect, they'll probably give you respect. If you start to "mess with them," though, they will mess with you, because they can. Believe me, you really don't want the great players messing with you! Try to be nice to everyone (really, I do try), and make sure that you give the great players respect. Only by giving respect will you get respect.

Limit Hold'em Tournaments: Summation

When you come to a limit Hold'em tournament, be prepared to sit down and play "top ten hands only" for the first five or six hours. If you're still in action five or six hours later, it's time to make sure that you are taking advantage of the mouse players at your table by stealing their blinds when you're in late position.

At this point in the tournament, you should still be trying to survive. You don't want to play a huge pot with a weak hand; save this sort of fancy playing until you are much farther along the experience curve. Rather, you want to play huge pots with top ten hands only.

If the players at your table are too loose, then play tight and just try to survive. If you happen to pick up a few cards (and to win a limit Hold'em tournament, you are going to have to pick up a few cards), you may win a couple of big pots from the loose players at the table. If the players at your table are too tight, then make sure that you're stealing a few blinds. If you're fortunate enough to make the final table, then draw on the experience you have gained playing all those satellites and focus on working your way into the final three spots, where most of the money is. Good luck to you when you play in a limit Hold'em tournament. Make sure that you learn something, and have a good time!

Chapter 8

Omaha:
Setup and Basic Play

The structure and initial setup are almost exactly the same in Omaha as in Texas Hold'em (the strategy, as you will see, is very, very different). The differences are outlined below. If you're skipping around among the chapters and are new to poker, I strongly suggest that you read Chapter 2 before reading this one, or else some of the commentary here won't make sense.

Omaha and Hold'em

The two big differences between Hold'em and Omaha are, first, that in Omaha you receive four facedown (or "hole") cards, instead of two and, second, that in Omaha you must use two and exactly two of the four cards in your hand, along with three and exactly three of the five board (community) cards. This distinction makes switching from Hold'em to Omaha very difficult for some players, because in Hold'em you're allowed to use one, both, or neither of your hole cards in putting together your final hand.

For example, in Hold'em, if there is a flush or a straight on the board, your hand is a flush or a straight, even if your hole cards don't contribute to it in any way. Of course, it's possible for your hole cards to improve a flush or straight that is on the board: if the board shows 7-8-9-10-J, and you have a queen in your hand, then you have a queen-high straight. Or perhaps the board will be A♦-K♦-10♦-7♦-4♦, and the Q♦ in your hand makes you the best possible hand. Often a Hold'em board will come down 7-8-9-10-J, and all the active players in the hand end up splitting the pot because they all end up playing the board (no active player has a queen).

But in Omaha, that 7-8-9-10-J board does not give you a straight unless two of the four cards in your hand allow you to complete a straight. For example, if your hand is A-A-9-10, the 9-10 that looked so insignificant to you when you started the hand, compared with your fine pair of aces, now gives you the straight. Similarly, you can play the jack-high straight if you hold 7-J-X-X (7-J from your hand and 8-9-10 from the board) or 8-J-X-X (8-J from your hand and 7-9-10 from the board) or any other combination of 7 through J in your hand. With a board of 7-8-9-10-J, you would have a queen-high straight with 8-Q (8-Q from your hand and 9-10-J from the board) or 9-Q or 10-Q or J-Q as part of your four starting ("hole") cards. You would need exactly a Q-K as part of your four-card hand to make a king-high straight.

A Quick Run-Through of the Betting and Dealing Action (Minus Some Important Elements)

In limit Omaha, there are four rounds of betting. During the first and second rounds, you can bet $1X, and for the third and fourth rounds you may bet $2X. (In these particulars, the game is identical to Hold'em.) To show you what I mean by "$1X" and "$2X," if you were playing $400-$800-limit Omaha (you'd better bring $50,000 to that game!) all bets and raises would be made in $400 increments during the first two rounds, and in $800 increments during the last two rounds. In a game like that you can easily lose $4,000 in one hand.

As in Hold'em, a button and two blinds (small and big) are used (if these concepts are unfamiliar to you, you skipped Chapter 2), and after the blinds are posted, you are each dealt four cards facedown. After you've all looked at your cards, the first round of betting begins. When that round of betting is complete, the dealer turns three cards faceup in the middle of the table. These three faceup cards are community cards, available for use by everyone. As in Hold'em, these cards are commonly called the flop. After the flop, there is a second round of betting, still at $1X, and when it is complete, the dealer turns up a fourth community card, commonly called fourth street or the turn card.

Now the third round of betting begins. Remember: this is when the stakes double. After this round of betting is complete, the dealer turns up the fifth and last community card; this one is commonly called the river. Now the last round of betting pro-

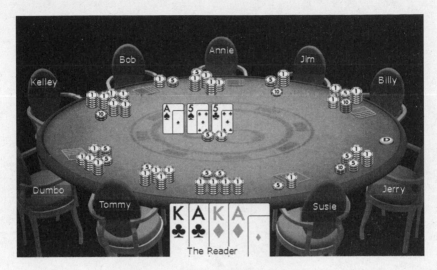

Omaha Flop

ceeds, and although the dealer is done dealing cards for this hand, his job is far from over.

After the last round of betting is complete (several players have no doubt folded by this time), the dealer helps determine who won the pot, because in Omaha, determining who won is a bit more complicated than it is in Hold'em. Since each player must use exactly two cards out of his hand, beginners (and often even experienced players) sometimes misread their hands. That's why I say the dealer's job is far from over when he has finished dealing the cards in Omaha (of course, often the dealer is wrong too).

This is also why it's a good idea for beginners and intermediates to lay their cards faceup on the table, all of them visible, at the end of each hand, even if they think they've lost. If you expose your cards at the proper time, the dealer may notice that you have a better hand than you thought, one you may have overlooked. Don't be lazy, though; don't depend on the dealer to read your hand for you. After all, you've been checking, betting, calling, or raising on the basis of your own ability to read your hand, all the way through the hand. Laying your hand down at the end is just a fail-safe move to make sure you don't accidentally overlook a winning combination.

A Quick Refresher: The Button, Blinds, Betting Order, and Betting Options

In most home poker games, the deal is passed clockwise (right to left), from person to person after each hand. Casinos furnish a professional dealer who deals every hand for you. But because betting position is important in every hand, we use the small plastic puck called the button in order to keep track of whose deal it would be if the players were passing the deck and dealing the hands themselves. The person who owns the button in any given hand has the significant advantage of being the last one to act in each round of betting, and so the dealer moves the button one spot clockwise after the end of each hand.

Before the hand begins, the player sitting directly to the left of the button posts the small blind (a bet which is usually half the size of the big blind, but which in some games may be as small as one-third of the big blind and in others as large as two-thirds of the big blind). The player to the immediate left of the small blind posts the big blind. The first card is then dealt to the player who posted the small blind, and the deal proceeds until each player has his four hole cards. The player to the left of the big blind is the first to take action; as in Hold'em, his options for the first

Omaha River

round are limited to calling (matching the big blind), raising, and folding.

A Sample Hand of Omaha

Let's now take a look at how a sample hand of Omaha might proceed. Even though a beginner should not play in a high-stakes game, let's make the example more fun by assuming we're play-ing $30- $60-limit Omaha: eight people are at the table, listed here in clockwise order:

Andy is sitting to the left of the button and thus must post the $15 small blind.
Bob is sitting on Andy's left, so he posts the $30 big blind.

Chuck, Dave, Ed, Frank, and George come next and will
act in that order.

Hal is the final player at the table, and he holds the button
for this hand.

Four cards are dealt out to each of the eight players, the first
card going to Andy in the small blind, the last card dealt to Hal
on the button (the cards are dealt one at a time). Chuck, the first
to take action, looks at his cards, sees that he has a strong starting hand, A♠-K♠-J♦-10♦, and decides to raise the existing bet
($30) to $60. (In poker slang this would often be called "making
it $60 to go.")

Dave, Ed, Frank, and George all decide to fold, but Hal,
who has 9♠-10♠-J♥-Q♣, decides to call the $60 on the button.
(Calling a raised pot, without having yet made any investment in
it, is often referred to as "calling two bets cold.") Andy, who
already has $15 in the pot because he posted the small blind,
holds K♦-K♥-2♦-9♣ and puts in $45 more to call the $60. Bob,
who has already invested $30 in the big blind, and holds A♦-4♦-
Q♥-10♥, also calls the $60 by putting in $30 more. (By the way,
I'm going to withhold, until the chapter on strategy, all comment
about whether or not these raising and calling decisions, as well
as the ones that follow, are good decisions.)

With four players still in the hand, the dealer turns up a flop
of 8♦-9♦-A♣. Let's take another look at the players' hands and
see how they fit this flop.

Andy: K♦-K♥-2♦-9♣. His pair of kings, which were never
much of a threat to win a four-way pot without improving, are
now almost certainly losing to someone who has an ace in his
hand, although because Andy can't see the other player's cards,

he can't be sure about this. Still, Andy retains some interest in the hand, because he has the K♦ and 2♦ in his hand and two diamonds have flopped. This gives him a chance to make the second-best possible flush (called the "second-nut" flush).

Bob: A♦–4♦–Q♥–10♥. Bob likes this flop a lot, because he has the "nut" (best possible) flush draw. If another diamond comes up on the turn or the river, he will make a strong hand, and, though he can't know it, he is likely to collect a number of bets from Andy, whose second-nut flush would wind up costing him a lot of money. But that's not all. Bob also has a pair of aces and an inside straight draw (often called a "gutshot" straight draw); if a jack hits the board, Bob's queen and ten will give him an 8-9-10-J-Q straight.

Chuck: A♠–K♠–J♦–10♦. This was a pretty nice starting hand, with four connected high cards and two possibilities for a flush, and Chuck has hit a *monster* draw: his J♦–10♦ gives him not merely a flush draw but also an open-ended straight-flush draw: if either Q♦ or 7♦ hits the board, Chuck is going to make a lot of money, especially from Bob, who is going to think his ace-high flush is "the nuts" until roughly the moment when Chuck reraises him for the third time. Chuck also has an open-ended straight draw—any queen or seven will give him a straight. (Unless he can make the straight flush, he'll be much better off making a straight than a flush, because his jack-high flush would lose to two other players.) Chuck also has a pair of aces with a king kicker, which at the moment is the best hand, but there is a low probability that this will win the hand, because, if he makes two pairs—aces up—then someone else will make a stronger hand. If K♣ (the only king left) hits the board, Chuck will have aces and kings, but the same king will give Andy three kings. If a jack hits the board, Bob makes a straight. If a ten hits the board, Hal makes a straight. Chuck would need two perfect cards in a row for his ace to be useful: the last two aces in the deck would give Chuck three aces, which would win *if* no one makes a straight or a flush. So he has plenty to think about, and he doesn't know what's out there facing him.

Hal: 9♠-10♠-J♥-Q♠. Hal has "hit the flop" just well enough to get into trouble. He has a pair of nines, but—more important—he has an open-ended straight draw by using his ten, jack, and queen. A seven, a ten, a jack, or a queen will give Hal a straight.

If it seems as though there are a lot of possible ways for each player to win (or lose) out there, you're right. Welcome to Omaha.

Because everyone still in the hand has a "piece" of this flop (meaning it has either improved all four of them or given them all at least some reasonable drawing possibility or other), even though those pieces are all draws rather than made hands, the betting action is likely to be anywhere from very cautious to very aggressive, depending on the playing styles of the people in the game.

Andy now has the first betting option (he "acted" first as well in the first round by posting the small blind), and because his flush draw is not a nut-flush draw, he checks. Bob, who does have the nut-flush draw, decides to bet $30. Chuck, who nearly jumped out of his seat when he saw the possibility of an open-ended straight-flush draw, pauses to think. He has a strong draw, but it is only a draw at this point, and he'd like to collect lots of bets from everyone if he hits his miracle straight flush, so he just calls. Hal and Andy also call, meaning that the pot is now $360 ($60 each before the flop and $30 each on the flop).

The turn card proves to be the 5♦, giving flushes to Andy, Bob, and Chuck. Andy, with a king-high flush, decides to bet $60 (remember, the stakes have now doubled). Bob, who knows he has the best hand at the moment and would like to either drive out anyone who might have three of a kind or at least make it expensive for such a player to draw, raises it to $120.

Chuck has a jack-high flush, but the bet and then the raise have him concerned. Still, the chance that his jack-high flush might be the winner, combined with the hope that he might hit a miracle card for his straight flush, entices him to call the $120.

Hal's open-ended straight draw has not improved, and everyone else seems very happy to see a third diamond on the board. Hal decides that he might be "drawing dead"—that is, he could hit his ideal card and still lose—so he folds.

Andy considers a reraise but remembers the old saying that "if it's possible in Omaha, it will probably happen," so he decides just to call. With another $360 going into the pot on the turn, the pot now totals $720.

The river produces the 5♥, putting a pair on the board and thus making flushes vulnerable to full houses (or even four of a kind). Andy checks, Bob bets $60, and Chuck decides that his jack-high flush is probably no good. (Before the last card, Chuck wasn't sure that his flush was good, but now, with a full house possible, he is really convinced that he is beat.) If he felt he could contest the pot for just $60, he might call, but he figures there's a chance Andy could be thinking about check-raising. Chuck folds.

Andy isn't thrilled with his hand, but there is now $780 in the pot, and he doesn't have the problem Chuck had—needing to worry that he might have to invest still more money to find out if his hand is the winner. So Andy calls (he calls $60 to try to win $780).

Bob's ace-high flush wins the pot, a surprise ending to most Omaha players who hold a flush on the turn and then see the board pair on the river. Bob rakes in the $840 pot and breathes a sigh of relief. Chuck silently curses his "bad luck" in having failed to make his straight flush but simultaneously congratulates himself for saving $60 on the end with his losing hand. Andy reminds himself for the thirty-seventh time this month about the danger of drawing to non-nut flushes in limit Omaha, and the dealer slides the button over to Andy, who will get to act last on the next hand.

You've now had a brief introduction to how and when cards get dealt in Omaha, and you have a sense of how a hand proceeds. The much more difficult part—*why* you should check, bet, call, raise, or fold at each juncture—will be addressed in Chapter 9.

Omaha Eight or Better: Setup and Basic Play

The structure of Omaha eight or better (O8B) is exactly like the structure of limit Omaha high. The betting is exactly the same, and the dealing is exactly the same, with one major distinction. In O8B, sometimes (when a low hand "qualifies") the pot is split at the end between the best high hand and the best low hand (more later about this in the section on Omaha high-low-split strategy). So figuring out who won what (high or low, if a low is possible) at the end of the hand, with all the players' hands faceup, can take a moment.

Today, O8B is rapidly becoming one of the most popular games in the world. Almost anywhere that a poker game is played, from Austria to Russia to the cyberworld, you will find an O8B game being spread (dealt). By contrast, it is very difficult to find a game of limit Omaha high anywhere. O8B just has so many possibilities. So many hands are playable, and the pots can get so big, that players seem to enjoy playing this game. I know I love it! O8B may well become most popular at your local game, if only you introduce it.

Rather than take you through any O8B sample hands here, I suggest that you turn to the section on O8B strategy (Chapter 9), where all will be made clear to you, eventually!

Pot-Limit Omaha: Setup and Basic Play

The structure of pot-limit Omaha (PLO) is exactly the same as that of limit Omaha, with one key distinction. The dealing is exactly the same, but in PLO you can bet the size of the pot when it is your turn to act. This makes for some very big bets and very big pots. PLO is the only game in which you can bet all your chips with the best possible hand on the flop or turn and be an underdog to win the pot. I'm going to take you through a sample hand in which exactly that happened to me.

Pot-Limit Omaha: Sample Hand

While I was playing in a PLO game in Tunica, Mississippi,
the following hand came up. The blinds were $25–$50, and I
called $50 with K-K-7-4 in P1. P2 called, and then P3 raised the
size of the pot ($25SB + $50BB + $50me + $50P2 + $50P3 =
$225), making it $275 to go. (SB is the small blind, BB the big
blind.) The button, small blind, big blind, I (P1), and P2 all called
the $275. With six players putting in $275 each, the pot had
$1,650 in it already, and we hadn't even seen the flop yet. With a
flop of 4♦-10♦-K♠, I was a very happy camper. I had flopped the
best possible hand! Now BB bet out $1,650, and I said, "Raise it
the pot." The math is easy because after calling the BB's $1,650
bet, I could raise 3 × $1,650 more. So I called $1,650 and raised
it $4,950, making it $6,600 to call me. By betting the maximum
here, I was trying to protect my very strong hand with a very
strong bet.

Now P2 said, "I'm all-in for $12,000." I thought, "Fantas-
tic! He has three tens, and I have him in bad shape this hand."
The action got back to the BB bettor, and he began to study for
quite some time. Now it seemed to me that the BB player had the
three tens. What the heck was going on here? Finally, the BB
folded his hand, and then I quickly called the $12,000 bet. I
proudly flipped my hand up, saying, "I have the best possible
hand." P2 responded, "OK, but you're an underdog to win the
pot." What? How could this be so? He then proceeded to flip up
his hand, A♦-Q♠-J♥-6♦. He had flopped the best possible flush
draw and needed a nine, jack, queen, or ace to make a straight.
Indeed he was the favorite to win this hand, but it was pretty
close. If the board paired, then he couldn't win because I would

make a full house or four kings. But if the board didn't pair, and a diamond, a nine, jack, queen, or ace came, then I would lose the pot.

I said, "Do you want to just deal the cards, or make a save so that we don't leave $26,000 to chance?" He said, "I'll split the pot with you." I said, "Let's just deal one card and then we'll talk" because I was thinking or hoping that the board would pair right away. He said, "Split the pot or deal both cards, final offer." I said, "OK, we'll split it, then." They did deal out the cards for posterity, and the first card was the harmless $5\spadesuit$, but the last card was $8\diamondsuit$, which would have made P2 the best possible hand (the ace high flush). Good split, Phil, you just saved $13K!

Omaha, in all its variations, is a game of great skill. I will teach you basic, intermediate, and some advanced strategies for both PLO and O8B in Chapters 9 and 10.

Chapter 9

Omaha Eight or Better (High-Low Split) Strategy

Omaha eight or better (O8B) is the world's second most popular poker game right now. If you walk into any card room on the West Coast of the United States, you will find people playing O8B. Check out any card room in Los Angeles (like the Commerce Casino) or in Las Vegas (like the Bellagio), and you'll find many different O8B limits being played. One reason for the popularity of O8B is that you are initially dealt four hole cards instead of two, therefore players find a lot more hands to play than one finds in Hold'em. The game thus generates a lot more action and plays a lot bigger than limit Hold'em. O8B, then, is a little bit more like the games people play at home with their friends. And even though there are no wild cards in O8B, it seems to have the feel of wild cards and lots of action. Lots of action equals big pots.

O8B is a high-low-split game. When you start to scoop pots (win both high and low), the money comes in quickly and in large quantities. In other words, this is the best poker game to get lucky in for a little while. Another reason why people love this game is that not even the experts seem to have a perfect understanding of a proper playing strategy for it. In fact, O8B strategy is still debated among the world's best poker players, and everyone seems to have a different opinion about which hands are playable before the flop! In no other poker game do the top pros disagree so widely on strategy.

What does "high-low-split game" mean? It means that half of each pot is awarded to the best high hand, and half of the pot is awarded to the best low hand, if there is a qualifying low (and as the name implies, your low must be at least an eight low to qualify). If there is no qualifying low, the whole pot goes to the high hand.

In this chapter you will learn:

▌ How to qualify a low hand in O8B.
▌ The importance of having A-2 as part of your four-card starting hand in O8B.
▌ A list of the best starting hands in O8B.
▌ Preflop theory for beginners.
▌ Fourth street theory for beginners.
▌ River theory for beginners.
▌ "Miami" John Cernuto's "three-wheel-card" theory.
▌ Scotty Nguyen's "A-2 or fold" theory.
▌ Ted Forrest's O8B experiment.
▌ Phil's unsuccessful O8B theory.

Let's get to how you play this game. Be forewarned that it is a very difficult game to learn, but learning it is definitely worth the time needed to work your way through this chapter. (It may help you to reread Chapter 8.)

Qualifying a Low Hand in O8B

Refer to the Stud 8/b chart on page 316. These will be the same qualifying low hands for O8B. You need to have at least an eight low (no card higher than an eight) in order to have a chance at the low half of the pot; that's the bad news. The good news is that straights and flushes do not count against you for low. An eight low means you have five low cards, the highest of them an eight, and no two of those five cards paired. A seven low means five low cards seven or less. A six low means five cards six or less. A five low, called a "wheel," is 5-4-3-2-A. This is the best possible low, and at the same time it counts as a straight for high. (Aces swing in this game, meaning that an ace is both the lowest possible card and the highest possible card.) A wheel is one of the most desirable hands you can make when you play O8B.

For further understanding of a qualified low hand, let's look at all the possible "qualified" lows (those you might want to bet on), from the worst possible eight low (8-7-6-5-4) to the best possible low (A-2-3-4-5).

All this qualifying low stuff sounds a lot more complicated than it really is. You won't have to memorize this in order to understand whether you have a qualified low or not. Rather, if three unpaired cards eight or under are on the board, then the best possible low is easy to figure out. Say that the board shows

K-8-6-Q-7 (the last community card has been dealt); what is the best possible low hand? Just figure out what would be the lowest two nonpaired low cards someone could have in his hand (to be added to the three cards on board), and you have the best possible low. (See pages 290–291 in the Razz section for a more detailed explanation of how to determine the low.) In this case an ace and a deuce are the lowest possible nonpaired cards to the 8-7-6 on board (first take the three lowest cards from the board), so the 8-7-6-2-A is the best possible low hand and the 8-7-6-3-A is the next-best possible low hand. You just take the lowest three cards on the board and add the next two best low cards (whether in your hand or in someone else's) to come up with the best possible low hand. For a board of 2-5-7-Q-K, just throw in A-3 for the best possible low hand (A-2-3-5-7) and A-4 for the second-best possible low hand (A-2-4-5-7).

I hope I'm not scaring you away from O8B by making the determination of the best low hand seem too complicated! It really isn't. The five lowest cards win. It is really that simple. The only complicated part is figuring out what those are, under the structure of taking exactly two cards from your hand and three from the board. So an 8-7-3-2-A is a worse low than an 8-6-5-4-3, which is worse than an 8-6-5-4-A, and so on. If you want to be scared away from this game, there are a lot better reasons than this one! Once you understand how to figure out which low hand beats which, you will discover that it really is easier than my explanation makes it seem.

By the way, this is a fantastic game for you to introduce into your home poker game. After the players in your private game get over the complexity of determining what hand wins the pot, they'll have a lot of fun playing this game. O8B promotes action and big pots, and all sorts of different hands can win a pot or two in this game.

When No Low Hand Is Possible; and When Two Players Share the Same Low

Remember that the low hand gets only half of the pot (if it qualifies). This means that if no one in the pot makes a low, the entire pot is awarded to the best high hand. And if the board is such that there *is* no possible low, the pot will be awarded to the high only. For example, if the board is 6-6-7-7-9, then no low is possible. This outcome arises because there are not three unpaired cards eight or under on the board. Likewise, if the board is 4-4-5-5-4 no low is possible. Even though there are five low cards on the board, only two of them are unpaired, just one of the fours and one of the fives. Confused? Don't feel bad about it: lots of experienced Omaha players get confused in this situation too. It's easy to see that no low is possible when the board looks like 9-10-J-Q-K; it's when the board is full of low cards that it's easy to get confused when you're new at this.

To avoid confusion, look at it this way: you can use only two cards from your hand, so if the board is the 4-4-5-5-4, which three allow you to make a low? The 4-4-5? The 4-5-5? The 4-4-4? None of these combinations will work to make a low. So a board of 2-3-5-9-J or A-6-K-Q-4 or 3-2-Q-Q-A all potentially qualify while boards like 3-3-4-4-3 or Q-K-A-5-J or 2-3-2-Q-K or 8-8-7-7-Q don't qualify, no matter what your hand holds.

Back to the More Usual Low Hands

Let's take a look at some best possible low hands, on the basis of a few sample boards. Why do we need to figure out what the best possible low hands are in O8B? Because when we conclude that we hold the best possible low hand, then we should be putting in as many raises as we can. When we have the best possible low hand, then of course we will usually win at least half of the pot, and we want our half to be as big as possible.

There are some situations in which you may want to stop raising on the end when you have the best possible low, primarily when there are only three players left, you have only a low, and the betting indicates that you're probably up against at least one other player with the same low. If that turns out to be the case, you'll win only one-quarter of the pot (this is called "getting quartered"), and thus you'll lose a small percentage of your own last bets and raises, but don't worry too much about this uncommon outcome yet.

Adding Two Cards from a Hand to Make the Four Best Possible Low Hands

With a board of 2-3-5-6-8, what is the best possible low hand? How about adding an A-4 to that board? If you do, you make a wheel, the best possible low hand in the game, 5-4-3-2-A. What is the second-best possible low hand with that board? By using an A-2, A-3, A-5, or A-6 from your hand, you'll make a 6-5-3-2-A low. Remember that you must use two cards from your hand and three from the board. So add the A-2 from your hand to the 6-5-3 from the board; with the A-3 from your hand, add the 2-5-6 from the board; with the A-5 from your hand, use the 2-3-6 from the board; with the A-6 from your hand, use the 2-3-5 from the board. Note that in this case the A-2, A-3, A-5, and A-6 all combine with the board cards to make the same 6-5-3-2-A low. Make sure that you see this remarkable outcome clearly before you move on to the next paragraph.

What is the third-best possible low hand with this board? The 6-5-4-3-2 low is possible (a "straight six"). You can make a straight six by using a 2-4, 3-4, 4-5, or 4-6 from your hand. What is the fourth-best possible low hand with this board? The 7-5-3-2-A low is possible, when you use an A-7 from your hand. To make the fifth-best low, add a 7-4 from your hand to make a 7-5-4-3-2 low.

Are you getting the hang of this stuff about qualified lows yet? Let's try three more examples.

No Low Is Possible

With a board of K-Q-J-4-3, what is the best possible low hand? No qualified low hand is possible with this board.

A Lot of Times You Can Just Add A-2 to the Three Lowest Cards on the Board

With a board of K-4-Q-6-7, what is the best possible low hand? Add A-2 and you have 7-6-4-2-A. Add A-3 and you have the next-best possible low, 7-6-4-3-A. Add 2-3 and you have the third-best possible low, 7-6-4-3-2. Add A-5 and you have the fourth-best possible low, 7-6-5-4-A.

Adding A-2 Works Again

With a board of 3-5-Q-8-7, what is the best possible low hand? Add A-2 for 7-5-3-2-A. Add A-4 for the second-best possible low hand, 7-5-4-3-A. Add 2-4 for the third-best possible low, 7-5-4-3-2. Add A-6 for the fourth-best-possible low, 7-6-5-3-A.

OK, I hope you're now beginning to see the light. First, you need the three lowest cards eight or lower on the board, and then you just figure out what two cards from your hand you need to add in order to make the best possible low hand.

Remember: You Have to Use Exactly Two Cards from Your Hand

It is crucial that you remember this rule. I have often seen people misread their hands because they've forgotten it. They might think, for example, that if the board reads 2♥-3♠-4♣-5♦-K♣ and they have A♠-7♦-J♣-10♦ in their hand, then they have a wheel. They sometimes misread their hands, thinking they can use the 2-3-4-5 from the board combined with the ace from the hand for a five low. In reality, they have a seven low—the A-7 from the hand combined with the 2-3-4 from the board (7-4-3-2-A). Hold'em players who are switching over to Omaha often make this sort of miscalculation.

Remember that you may use two cards for high and two different down cards for low in the same hand. Of course, you may also use the same two cards for high *and* low if you choose.

Using Two Down Cards for High and the Other Two for Low

If you have A-2-J-Q in your hand (this is a pretty good start-ing hand) and a board of 4-5-8-J-Q, your low hand will be 8-5-4-2-A, or the best possible low hand in this case. For low, you use the A-2 from your hand and the 8-5-4 from the board. Your high hand will be Q-Q-J-J-8, or top two pair of queens and jacks, using the Q-J from your hand and the Q-J-8 from the board. In this example you're using A-2 for low and Q-J for high.

Using the Same Two Down Cards for Both High and Low

If you have a hand of A♥-3♥-4♥-5♣ and a board of 5♥-6♥-8♦-10♠-K♥, then you use A♥-3♥ for the second-best possible low hand of 8-6-5-3-A. (A-2 would make the best possible low in this case.) For high you would also use A♥-3♥, for A♥-3♥-5♥-6♥-K♥, the nut (best possible) flush. As you can see from this example, it's possible to use the same two cards from your hand for both high and low. Having the best possible high hand and the second-best possible low hand in the same hand is a stunning sensation. You may well scoop both the high and the low halves of the pot with this hand.

Using One Card Twice: Once for High and Once for Low

If you have a hand of A♥-4♦-7♦-J♣, and the board shows 2♦-5♦-7♣-Q♦-K♣, then you would use the A-4 from your hand for the second-best possible low hand of 7-5-4-2-A. You would use the A-7 portion of your hand for a high hand of A-7-7-Q-K, or just a pair of sevens with A-K-Q kickers. This hand is a lot weaker than the previous example, with one pair of sevens serving as your high hand and the second-best low working as your low hand. But it's not bad: an excellent shot at low and an outside shot at high.

When Only a High Hand Is Available

With a board showing 2♥-3♦-J♠-Q♥-K♦, the best possible high hand is A-10, which makes 10-J-Q-K-A (an ace high straight). There are no pairs on board; thus there are no fours of a kind or full houses. There isn't three to a suit on the board; thus there are no flushes. So a straight is the best possible high hand, with A-10 being best and 9-10 being second-best. The third-best possible high hand is three kings, followed by all the three-of-a-kind hands. Next we have top two pair, made with K-Q out of the hand. Anyway, you get the idea.

The Importance of A-2 in Your Starting Hand

Now that we've covered how to qualify a low, from combinations of board and hand, and what the best possible low hands are, given certain boards, let's move on to a more complete picture of O8B. We'll turn now to the problem of assessing starting hands.

A few poker professionals believe there is only one two-card combination you could have in your hand that is so promising you would not have to look at your other two hole cards before deciding to play. This combination is A-2. In other words, a lot of top players believe that any hand containing A-2 is playable, regardless of what the other two cards in the hand are. Of course, I would never recommend not looking at the other two cards (although I sometimes don't look). In poker, it's always a good idea to know what your whole hand is!

The importance of starting with an A-2 among the four cards in your hand cannot be underestimated. Some professionals consider it more important than starting with A-A! Often the board will come down with a combination of three low cards of three through eight (like 3-4-5, 4-6-8, 4-5-7, or 3-7-8). When any of these combinations of three through eight hit the board, the best possible low hand is made with the A-2 in your hand. The majority of low boards require that you have an A-2 in your hand to make the nut (best possible) low. That is, most of the time when there is a low-qualified board, A-2 from someone's hand will make the best possible low. This is why most premium O8B hands contain A-2. Of course, with a board of 2-4-7-J-J, A-3 is the best possible low.

When you have A-2 in your hand, you're hoping to guarantee yourself half the pot by winning the low side and to get lucky somehow, some way, and win the high half as well. Perhaps you will win the high half with a full house, a flush, a straight, trips, two pair, one pair, or even ace high! In 2001, in the World Championships of Omaha (the $5,000 buy-in O8B tournament at the WSOP), I busted out the poker legend T. J. Cloutier at the final table when my A-J high beat his A-6 high! T. J. started with A-2-5-6, and I started with A-2-5-J. The board brought 3-7-3-3-K, and I won the pot with my A-J and the board of 3-3-3. He had A-

6-3-3-3 for high, and there was no low on the board! I went on to finish second to another world champion, Scotty Nguyen, even though I had Scotty $490,000 to $60,000 in chips at one point. I simply ran into a really unlucky stretch of cards at that point, although Scotty is considered by many to be one of the best O8B players in the world today. Don't feel too bad for me, though, because second place did pay more than $100,000.

The Rank of Starting Hands in O8B

The best possible starting hand in O8B is A-A-2-3, with the A-2 and the A-3 pairs each of the same suit. So A♥-A♠-2♥-3♠ is as good as it gets in O8B for a starting hand. Any A-A-2-3 with just one suited pair is the next-best possible hand, followed by A-A-2-3 with no suits. Why is this hand so strong? First, you're starting with the best possible pair (A-A); second, you have the nut-flush possibility when you're suited to the ace; and, third, you already have three wheel cards that offer the best possible low combination (A-2), the second-best possible low combination (A-3), and the third-best possible low combination (2-3). So this is an incredibly powerful hand, because you have so many great low possibilities and high possibilities at the same time. This is a hand that's easy to scoop the pot with, and hands that have strong scooping potential are highly prized in high-low-split games.

The next-best possible starting hand in my book is A-A-2-4, followed by A-A-2-5, and so on, all the way down to A-A-2-K. The reason why A-A-2-x is such a big hand is that you will often make the best possible low hand with it, and the A-A can hold up for high as well, especially when there is another pair on the board, like 10-4-5-7-7. After A-A-2-x, I prefer A-A-3-x, but some other pros like A-2-3-4. The argument for A-A-3-x is that you have the best possible pair, the second-best possible low card combination, and, if you're suited, the best possible flush draw. The argument for the A-2-3-4 is that you have all the low draws covered. In most cases where the board qualifies for low, you will have the nut low. What you think is more important—having all the lows covered or having high features—will determine which of these hands you like better. But there are good arguments either way. In any case, they are both very powerful starting hands in O8B.

After A-A-3-x and A-2-3-4 comes A-2-3-x. With A-2-3-x you will win a piece of the pot more than 40 percent of the time. Many top pros really want to have four wheel cards in a hand, even when that hand doesn't contain both an ace and deuce, like A-3-4-5 or 2-3-4-5.

Here is my list of O8B hands (the first 10 on the list are "premium," and the next eight I'll call "strong"), in order from best playable hand to worst playable hand. Again, this is the list of the playable hands. Suited hands are better than unsuited hands.

This is my list of the most powerful playable hands in O8B. Hands like Q♦-K♦-Q♠-K♠ are right on the edge of being playable (I'm playing them). I will almost always play two big pairs double-suited. But I'm not interested in hands like 8♠-9♠-8♥-9♥, since the pairs aren't high enough to win on their own merit. Moreover, when you do flop a set with a hand like this, your set will almost never be the highest available three of a kind on the board. Generally, when there is an eight or a nine on the board there will be overcards out there also. In Omaha, whenever there

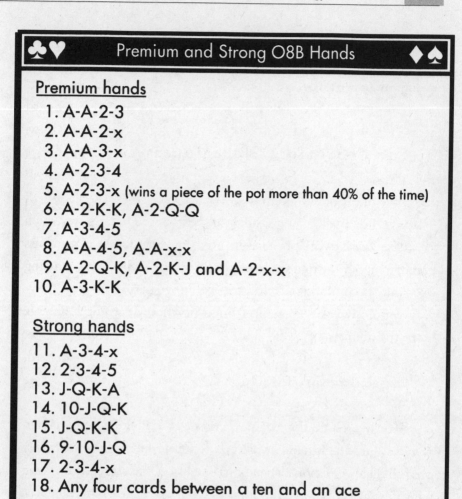

Premium and Strong O8B Hands

Premium hands

1. A-A-2-3
2. A-A-2-x
3. A-A-3-x
4. A-2-3-4
5. A-2-3-x (wins a piece of the pot more than 40% of the time)
6. A-2-K-K, A-2-Q-Q
7. A-3-4-5
8. A-A-4-5, A-A-x-x
9. A-2-Q-K, A-2-K-J and A-2-x-x
10. A-3-K-K

Strong hands

11. A-3-4-x
12. 2-3-4-5
13. J-Q-K-A
14. 10-J-Q-K
15. J-Q-K-K
16. 9-10-J-Q
17. 2-3-4-x
18. Any four cards between a ten and an ace

Premium and Strong O8B hands

are overcards there is a good possibility of an overset, so you want to stay away from hands like this. But these drawbacks do not apply to A-A, K-K, or Q-Q.

Preflop Theory for O8B Beginners

Tight Play

As is my usual practice in advising beginners in a poker game, I encourage tight play before the flop. That means playing only the "premium hands" on the list above before the flop. This way you'll always be playing from a position of strength as you learn the nuances of O8B.

Raising before the Flop

The biggest preflop decision you need to make, after whether or not to play your hand at all, is whether to limp into the betting or raise. This decision depends not only on the strength of your hand but also on what the level of your opponents' play is and how many opponents you're likely to face.

If you're playing at home with relatively inexperienced people, then it's OK to go ahead and raise with these types of hands every time, without attempting any deception. If you're playing in a casino with experienced people, you need to use deception to help shape the way your opponents act before the flop. Obviously, if you raise in early position, there will be fewer experienced opponents remaining in the pot to take the flop with you. If you just call before the flop, then you can expect more players to call one bet and take the flop with you. This is a key point, because when you have one of the top ten hands from my list (the premium hands), then you want a lot of opponents taking the flop along with you, so that you can win a big pot when you hit your hand.

For example, if you're in early to middle position with a premium hand that contains A-2, a useful play is to just call before the flop. (Don't raise yet!) This accomplishes two things: it allows your opponents to limp into the pot for just one bet behind you with their weaker low hands (A-3 and worse), while at the same time concealing the strength of your hand (concealing the possibility that it contains A-2). Once your opponents flop with the second- and third-best low draws or hands, they will usually continue to play for the big-money streets, when you will have them crushed with the best possible low hand! Again, just call with these premium hands, so as to trap your opponents and build a big pot for yourself when you make your hand.

By just calling and keeping the pot small, you will also limit your losses when you miss the board completely, as happens when all high cards hit the board or when the wrong low cards hit and counterfeit (ruin) your low hand. When you limp into the betting with a hand like A-2-3-8 and the flop is 6-7-8, you can win more money by having trapped all the A-3 and worse hands into playing with you. And when the flop is 10-10-J, you can get off your hand cheaply.

If you have one of these premium hands on the button or in the blinds, then things are different. In this case, it's OK to go ahead and make it two bets to go (raise), because you won't be driving anyone out of the pot. (No one who already called one bet will now fold his hand for one more bet.)

Ideally, when you have one of these premium hands, you

want to build a huge pot before the flop and keep all your opponents *in* before the flop. However, this is very tough to do. So in
early and middle position, just call with the premium hands, to
keep more players in the pot. In late position or in the blinds,
raise it, to get more money into the pot.

With hands numbers 11 through 18 on the list (strong
hands) you aren't looking to build any huge pots, because these
hands aren't really of the same caliber as the top ten hands. With
these strong hands you want to take a flop and hope that you hit
the flop well. With the premium hands (numbers 1 through 10)
it's very easy to flop a winning hand, but with the strong hands
this won't happen as often. Therefore, although you need to see
a flop with these hands, you don't need to build a pot with them
before the flop.

Beginners' Theory for Strong Flops and Weak Flops

While you're playing the premium hands (top ten) and strong
hands (11–18), you'll hit great flops and terrible flops and
somewhere-in-between flops. First, let's take a look at a bunch of
examples of what to do with good to great flops. Second, we'll
look at what you should do with the marginal to terrible flops.

Great Flops

When you have the luxury of a great flop, your only decision is whether or not you should ram and jam the flop (put in as
many raises as you can) or slow-play the flop (let other players

into the pot by acting weak and therefore capturing additional money from many different players).

Suppose you have A♦–2♠–3♦–8♣ and the flop is 4♦–5♦–8♠. In this situation you have flopped the best possible low, and it is uncounterfeitable, meaning that it cannot lose the low pot no matter which other low cards come up on the next two board cards. Even if the last two cards pair the ace, deuce, or three, you will still make the best possible low by using your backup cards. You have also flopped a powerful wrap straight draw (4-5 from the board wrapped with an A, 2, 3, or 6 on one of the next two cards will make you a straight), the ace-high flush draw, and a pair of eights! Wow, what a flop for your hand! Now what do you do? Do you start betting, raising, and reraising right now, or do you just call to lure in your opponents?

The argument for raising now is that you want to drive out high hands like two pair or trips so that your pair of eights might win the high side of the pot while your A-2 wins the low half. The much stronger argument here is for just calling with this hand on the flop. After all, you have the low half of the pot "locked up" unless someone else also has A-2, in which case you would get one-quarter of the whole pot (one-half of the low half; sometimes the low can even be split into three, in which case your take would amount to one-sixth of the pot). And you have a great chance to win the high side if a diamond (flush) or an ace, deuce, three, or six comes up to make you a straight. My vote is that you slow-play this hand on the flop and try to keep as many players in the pot as possible. Someone with a worse flush draw will call one bet as well, which is great for you if the flush does come.

Suppose that you have A-3-K-K and the flop is K-4-4. You have flopped kings full of fours. Normally, when you flop the top full house you would generally want to play it fast (bet and raise every possible time) to prevent someone from hitting the "back-door" low, catching two perfect cards on fourth street and the river, such as 6-7. When this happens you end up giving up half of the pot unnecessarily. In the case of A-3-K-K, however, you have a strong low hand as well as the top full house. If you slow-play it, someone who stays in may hit a card that keeps him in the pot, not knowing that he has no hope of winning the low side (he is drawing dead). On the other hand, if an opponent has exactly one four in his hand, then your playing the hand fast may prove to be best, because with trips he might be willing to put in several bets on the flop but only a few on the turn. In that case you would be costing yourself money by slow-playing. But given that you really cost yourself money only when your opponent has exactly a four, slow-playing the hand has to be considered the preferred choice, so as to squeeze more money out of a great situation.

Good Flops: Protecting Your Hand

When you have a good flop rather than one of the monster flops we've just discussed, you will most often want to ram and jam your hand on the flop, in order to build the pot—both in case you win both ways and also to drive out some opponents who might otherwise draw to a better hand. When you drive out hands that might otherwise draw to a better high or low than you, that's called protecting your hand.

Suppose you have a hand of A♣-2♠-4♠-6♠ and the flop is 5♦-6♣-7♦. In this case you have flopped the best possible low hand (A-2), a straight draw, and a pair of sixes. This is a very good flop for you. With this flop you should be thinking, "OK, nice flop. I need to ram and jam it and try to drive out any A-3 in case a two comes off and the A-3 beats my low hand. I also need to ram and jam it in case someone else has A-2 and my pair of sixes is better than his high hand" (in which case you would win the high side with your pair of sixes and one-half of the low side with your A-2, which would yield you "three quarters"). By ramming and jamming you might make a higher pair fold, thus making sure you get three quarters against another A-2. You also want to ram and jam it in case an eight comes off the deck later (which would give you an eight-high straight), to protect your straight draw, your raise having driven out higher straight draws like the 9-10 or 9-6. Of course, you would love to see a three come off the deck and make you a straight, or a six to make you three sixes.

The verdict here, then, is that you ram and jam, for a lot of different reasons, including the possibility of making your pair of sixes good (if you can raise everyone else out and the other A-2 can't beat your sixes); clearing out a higher straight draw in case an eight comes; clearing out an A-3, which could beat you if a deuce came off; and just building a big pot in case you win half or all of it.

Good Flops: Keep 'Em In

Suppose your hand is A♠-2♠-5♠-J♥ and the flop is 4♠-6♠-Q♦. In this case you have flopped the best low draw (A-2) and the best high draw (an ace-high-flush draw), and a three makes you a straight. If you have this hand, you're thinking, "Another great flop for me. I want to keep the other hands in, but I also want to build a big pot." Therefore, you'll probably bet if you're the first to act, and then just call if someone raises you, as opposed to check-raising and thus making it two bets for your opponents to call. Although it's true that you would like to get rid of any A-3 hand in case a deuce falls on one of the next two cards (where an A-3 would beat your second-best A-5), it's also true that you don't have a high hand right now, just a high draw. Therefore, you want to keep the players in the pot by betting into them but trying to make sure that it's always just one bet to them.

When you have a marginal flop, you usually either pump it or dump it, depending on whether or not you think you have a chance to win both the high and the low.

Pump it or dump it simply means that you will raise or fold on the flop. If you think that your marginal hand is the best hand, then you should pump it. If you think it's the second-best hand, dump it.

Marginal Flops: Pump It or Dump It

Suppose you have A♥-3♥-4♥-Q♠ and the flop is K♥-Q♠-7♦. This is the kind of flop that I like to bet out into and then decide what I really want to do later, on the basis of my opponent's betting and emotional response. Sometimes, that one bet will win the whole pot for me; at other times it will get raised and reraised and I'll be forced to fold my hand. If someone else bets out and there are players behind me yet to act, I'll fold my hand right there. After all, this is a pretty weak flop for me. I have only second pair.

If someone bets and everyone else folds, then I'll probably fold my hand right there, too. Sometimes I'll call in this position to see if a low card (to give me a low draw), a heart (to give me a flush draw), an ace (to give me two pair aces up), or a queen (to give me three queens) comes up. A three or a four would make me two pair and a low draw, but those cards may get me into trouble, because now I have to call all the way with my two pair! My thought process with this flop is, "Most of the time I want to win it with one bet, and I'll fold my hand if someone else bets."

When a Pair Hits the Board

Suppose you have 9-10-J-K and the flop is Q-Q-J. This is a situation in which you're looking to win the pot with one bet on the flop. With a pair on the board in O8B I'm not looking to invest any money drawing to a straight when my opponent may well have a full house already! It's much more likely in Omaha than in a two-card game like Hold'em that someone has at least trip queens and is drawing to a full house. Worse yet—and here the hand illustrates an important way for you to start looking at the game and seeing how you can read your opponents—the cards that you need for your straight (ace, king, ten, nine) are cards that someone would probably be holding in his hand if his hand contained a queen. So even when he has only trips, when you make your straight you are in grave danger of his filling up (making a full house) at the same time. When your opponents all hold four cards instead of just two, pairs on the board become much more dangerous.

When the flop is bad for your hand, most of the time you will need to fold your hand right away. This can be a bit frustrating when, for example, you finally pick up A-2-3-10 and the flop comes down Q-Q-K! You've been waiting and watching everyone else win big pots with A-2-3-x, and now you lose with your

A-2-3-x. Just remember that playing poker well includes folding your strong preflop hands when they miss. Don't chase after bad boards just because your starting hand was strong!

Bad Flops—Fold

If you have A-2-3-9 when the flop comes down K-Q-10, it's time to fold, period. You have no pair and no draw.

Suppose you have A♦-2♦-3♠-7♥ and the flop is K♠-Q♦-8♣. With this flop, it will be hard for you to win the high side of the pot unless you hit two running diamonds. Accordingly, it's best to fold your hand on the flop if someone bets into you and you still have opponents behind you. You could call one bet with this hand if you're the last person to call that bet on the flop and the pot is very large. This is so only because when you pick up the backdoor low draw (a low draw that you need two low cards in a row to make) or the flush draw on the turn, you will usually have the uncounterfeitable nut-low draw or the nut-flush draw. But never call a bet on the flop for a backdoor draw unless it's the nut backdoor draw and the pot is already very large.

Playing O8B Hands on Fourth Street for Beginners

Playing O8B hands on fourth street can be tricky. If you have the best possible hand one way (whether low or high) on fourth street, then you usually want to raise at that point, on the chance that you can drive from the pot someone who has you beat for the other direction or is drawing to make a hand that can beat you in either direction. So ram and jam when you have the best possible hand in one direction on fourth street. If you're drawing low and have no chance to win the high side of the pot, you may have to fold your hand, depending on the action and your draw. Similarly, if you're drawing to the high side of the pot and there is already a low hand possible on the board, you'll sometimes have to fold your hand in this situation as well. In O8B the game is to win the whole pot!

Drawing Low on Fourth Street, with No High Draw

Suppose you have A-2-4-J and the board is Q-7-8-Q. If it's two big bets to you to go, then in most cases you should fold your hand, unless the pot is huge as a result of all the raising before the flop and on the flop. Why pay two bets to try to win half of the pot? Of course, you can almost always call one bet if you have the best low draw on fourth street.

Drawing to a High Hand on Fourth Street with a Low Possible

Suppose you have $A\spadesuit$–$K\spadesuit$–$Q\spadesuit$–$10\clubsuit$ and the board is $2\spadesuit$–$4\spadesuit$–$9\spadesuit$–$6\clubsuit$. Even though you have an ace-high diamond flush draw, I wouldn't call even one bet on fourth street, because you figure to be drawing to just half of the pot. I might call one bet if no one was behind me who could raise the pot, but except for this one case, I'm looking to fold my hand on fourth street for one bet. This illustrates an important philosophical approach to poker. Look at my language here—I'm "looking to fold." Most beginning players are looking for an excuse to stay in the pot, any pot. More seasoned players are often looking for a reason to get out of the pot.

Jamming with the Best High Hand on Fourth Street

Suppose you have A♣-K♠-J♣-10♦ and the board is 2♣-4♣-J♠-7♣. In this case you have the best possible high hand and you should jam the pot, for two reasons. The first reason is to protect your hand by raising out people who have two pair and could make a full house. The second reason is that you want to try to bluff out the low hands and get one-on-one with another high hand, so that you can win the whole pot.

Jamming with the Best Low Hand on Fourth Street

Suppose you have A-3-4-9 and the board is 2-7-8-9. In this case you have the best possible low hand and the top pair on the board with nines. You want to jam with this hand, to eliminate any high hands that might beat a pair of nines. By doing this you could end up winning the whole pot when, say, A-4-5-8 calls you down. You could scoop the high side as well when an ace, three, four, or nine hits on the last card if you can get rid of a hand like top two pair of nines and eights. The player holding nines and eights would have a tough call if I raised this hand on fourth street.

Jamming with the Best Possible Hand Both Ways on Fourth Street

Suppose your hand is A♦-3♠-4♠-7♠ and the board is 2♦-6♠-7♦-K♦. You now have the best high hand with your ace-high flush and also the best low hand. At this point it's tempting to just call someone else's bet if he bets into you in order to trap other players into calling you down. But if you call just one bet, someone may call with two pair or a set and you may end up losing half of the pot if the board pairs. Think about it: on fourth street you have the whole pot won! (OK, someone else may have your low hand tied.) Why wouldn't you want to protect your high hand by raising the pot at this point?

Smooth-Calling with the Best Possible Low Hand

Suppose you have A-3-4-10 and the board is 2-7-J-8. You now have the best possible low hand, but no high hand at all. The fact that you cannot lose the low side of the pot no matter what card comes off, and that you have no high hand, makes smooth-calling with this hand essential. Since you can't lose the low hand or win the high hand (even an ace probably won't win high for you on the last card), it's time to build up your half of the pot by keeping as many other players in the hand as possible.

Get Rid of the Low Draws

Suppose you have A-3-4-K and the board is A-A-5-K. You have the best possible high hand, aces full of kings. No low hand is possible yet, and you're winning the whole pot. You need to jam with this hand in order to eliminate any possible low draw that either ties you or beats you (3-4, 2-4, or 2-3), so that you can win the whole pot.

Beginners' Strategy for Playing on the River

If you have the best possible hand in one direction and a chance to win in the other direction as well, then jam on the end in order to eliminate players, so that you have a better chance to win the whole pot. If you have the luxury of having the best possible high and low hands at the same time, you need to figure out if calling someone else's bet will win more money for you than raising would. If calling will allow two other players to enter the pot, whereas raising would eliminate them, then it's correct to call instead of raise. If only one other player is yet to act behind you, then it's always right to raise, because even if that opponent folds you will still get an extra bet from the original bettor. And the player behind you might call anyway. But if you have the second- or third-best hand in one direction, you may have to fold it on the last round of betting.

Jamming with the Best Hand with a Chance for It All

Suppose your hand is A♦-3♠-4♦-Q♠ and the board is 2♦-6♠-K♥-7♦-Q♣. In this case you have the best possible low hand and a pair of queens for your high hand. In this situation, you would want to jam the pot to try to bluff out the high side and win both the low side (with A-2-3-6-7) and the high side (with A-K-Q-Q-7).

This will work sometimes when another player with a strong low (perhaps he even has you tied for low) bets out on the end and you raise and eliminate the player who had kings or better for high. Since you will win at least half of the pot, it's worth a shot.

To Raise on the River with the Best Possible Hand?

Suppose you have A♦–2♦–4♥–Q♥ and the board is 3♦–K♦– 7♠–5♦–Q♣. In this case, you have both the best possible high hand (with the nut diamond flush) and the best possible low hand (with A-2-3-5-7). What do you do now? I always bet out one bet with this hand when it's my turn to act, to try to win one bet from each of my opponents. When someone else bets into me on the end, I try to figure out whether raising this player makes any sense. If someone bets into me and there are four players behind me, I'll probably just call, to try to get other callers from behind. If someone bets out into me and there is only one player behind me, I'll always raise to try to get the bettor to call me. (If the other player behind me calls two bets, that's a nice unexpected bonus.)

Folding the Second-Best Low on the End

Suppose now that you have A-3-5-J and the board is 4-7-8-Q-K. You now have the second-best possible low hand and next to nothing for your high hand. What do you do when it's two bets to you to call on the end? You can hope there will be some indication that one player has A-2, or does not (by the way he played his hand earlier), and you can then decide on the basis of that surmise. Keep in mind, however, that you're considering calling two big bets in order to win half of the pot. Folding your hand now isn't a bad idea at all for two bets.

Folding a Strong High Hand on the End

Suppose you have A-3-Q-Q and the board is Q♠-4♦-5♣-J♥-3♥. If there was a ton of betting and raising happening on the flop, it will be very hard for you to call one bet on the end. I hear you saying, "But, Phil, there's a lot of money in this pot! Of course I need to call one bet on the end. I have top set." To which I respond, "What do you think they were jamming it with on the flop? There was no flush draw, and you were the one with the three queens. If they put in a lot of action, on the flop, in this hand, almost certainly at least one player has A-2 in his hand. If one of them does have that in his hand, then he just made a wheel on the river!" In fact, that was the only card you really didn't want to see on the end, right? If you call one bet here, you may not even lose to an A-2; you might lose to another straight, the 2-6 or the 6-7. Although calling one bet here isn't a terrible play, because the pot odds are big, you will almost certainly do better in the long run by folding your hand in this situation. It is never wrong for you to fold when you can't even imagine a hand that your opponent could have that doesn't beat you.

Miami John Cernuto's "Three-Wheel-Card" Theory

In 1997, while I was working on improving my O8B game, I decided that I had better ask someone whom I respected for some advice on how to play the game. So I sought out "Miami" John Cernuto because I really had a lot of respect for his O8B game. I asked John for some advice on O8B, and this is what he told me: "Phil, you give me some advice on no limit Hold'em, and I'll give you some advice on O8B." I said—and this is a true story— "John, I'll give you $500 for twenty minutes of advice." He said, "Deal." And then he proceeded to tell me the theory of "three wheel cards" in your starting four-card hand in O8B. Since I did pay John $500 for this theory, I present it here to you!

This theory involves playing any starting hand that includes some combination of three cards from among A-2-3-4-5. Hands like 2-4-5-x or A-4-5-x or 2-3-4-x are now all playable for one bet before the flop. I have applied this theory with mostly good results for more than four years now. As long as I used some discretion, it generally won me a lot of money. But when I called three bets before the flop with 3♠-4♥-5♦-J♠ (the worst of the three-wheel-card hands), I didn't do so well!

When we begin to add weaker hands to the mix of hands that you should play before the flop, we need to point out that more skillful reading is needed. Playing these types of hands can put you in harm's way if you're not careful.

The 2♦-4♠-5♦-K♣, for example, can be in a lot of trouble when the flop comes down 6♠-7♠-K♥. In this case, you have a really bad low draw with your 2-4, top pair of kings with no kicker (one pair of kings with a five kicker), and an open-ended straight draw (4-5-6-7) that is drawing to the low end of the straight if an eight hits (still, an eight is a good card). Although this hand is very weak, it is just enough of a hand to warrant your calling one bet, because of its two-way potential. But it's important to realize that it's a trouble hand unless you make the nut straight (and even that might lose to a flush). If there is a lot of betting and raising on this flop, then you're probably up against a better low draw, a better high hand, and a better high draw (a flush draw). So some reading ability is required, which means we're into the discussion of intermediate play.

In general, you can call one bet before the flop with any three-wheel hand, but be prepared to throw your hand away even when you have a decent flop, in some cases. Keep in mind that your opponents will often have hands that include A-2, A-3, or 2-3. So use some discretion when playing these kinds of hands on the flop. Ask yourself, "Is my low draw good enough to continue on in this hand or not? Can I win the high side *and* the low side of the pot with this flop?"

Folding a Three-Wheel Hand on the Flop

Here's an example. Suppose you have 2♣-4♣-5♥-Q♠. Say that you have called along with two other players before the flop, and the flop is 4♦-6♠-7♦. You have flopped a weak low, a pair of fours, and a bad straight draw (you still need a trey or an eight, neither of which would give you the nuts). This is a decent flop for you, but if it's bet and raised into you at this point, you need to fold your hand. Your chances of winning the whole pot are minimal, while your chances of losing both sides of the pot are excellent. Even someone with a weak hand like A-5-7-K has you scooped with a weak low and a pair of sevens for high. He even has a better straight draw than you do!

Hitting the Flop

Suppose you have 2-3-4-7 and the flop is A-5-6. You have flopped the best possible low and a wrap straight draw! You cannot lose the low no matter what comes up on the next two cards (you have an "uncounterfeitable low"). This is a huge flop for your hand. Any deuce, three, four, seven, or eight makes you a straight, which will probably allow you to scoop the pot (win high and low). A deuce is particularly good, because it makes you a wheel while at the same time counterfeiting any other 2-3 that might be out there. At this point you should be ramming and jamming the pot, both to build a big pot and to drive out anyone with two pair, in case you hit your straight (you don't want him making a full house).

Calling a raise with one of the weaker three-wheel-card hands, such as 3-4-5-10, just isn't a winning play unless you're in the big blind. I'll raise it up myself when I'm in steal position with a weaker hand like this one, when no one else has entered the pot yet, because then I have a chance to win the blinds if everyone else folds.

My final caution: be careful when you play these hands. Use discretion when you decide how much you play them for and whom you play them against. Don't get yourself trapped "sucking wind," trying to make a bad low or drawing to half of the pot with a weak draw.

Never Leave Home without an Ace!

In disagreement with Miami John Cernuto's theory (remember, I said pros really disagree about this game), another old friend of mine, "Big Al" Emerson, once told me, "In O8B never leave home without an ace." Al gave me this gem of advice right before an O8B tournament at the Bicycle Club in Los Angeles. I went on to win the event and the $50,000 first prize that day.

Whereas Miami John advocates playing any three wheel cards, even if they don't include an ace, Big Al suggests quite the opposite. In contrast to Miami John's rather loose advice, Big Al is saying, "Play tight!" If you always play only hands that contain an ace, then you will almost never be sucking wind with the second- or third-best low draw. The best possible low almost always requires an ace out of your hand, unless you're lucky enough to have an ace hit the flop. So having an ace in your hand can be a good foundation.

If you were to play all three-wheel-card hands you would be getting into a lot of trouble with hands like 3-4-5-x. Likewise, if you were to fold all hands that don't contain an ace, you would be folding hands like [K♠]-[K♦]-[2♠]-[3♦] and [K♠]-[K♦]-[Q♠]-[J♦], which are pretty good hands to play. You'd also end up folding your strong three-wheel-card hands out of the blinds, which would be another losing strategy.

I confess to using the words "always" and "never" myself, but in general, advice that uses one of those two words is too inflexible. Usually, there are exceptions to any rule. If I use the words "always" or "never" with you, it's because I'm trying to keep things simple, and I'm afraid of confusing you by giving you too much information at once.

Scotty Nguyen Told Me to Play Only A-2 in O8B

In a world championship O8B event at the World Series of Poker in 1996, I asked Scotty Nguyen for some advice on how to play O8B. He suggested a very restrictive strategy: "Bro," he said, "only play hands that include A-2 and you'll be all right." I said, "Are you serious? What about A-A or four high cards in a row, like 9-10-J-Q?" Scotty said, "Trust me, bro." I did trust him, and that day I made it all the way to the final table and eventually wound up finishing in fourth place playing only A-2!

Now that I know what I know about O8B, I would never use that strategy again, but the fact that it worked all that day was pretty remarkable. To me, it shows the power of the A-2. Clearly, I had some good luck along the way that day. Playing only A-2 is just too tight and predictable a way to play O8B in a tournament or a side game, but it can be a viable strategy occasionally. Now I always play A-A and four high cards in a row above an eight, in both tournaments and side games, and so does Scotty.

Ted Forrest's Loose O8B Experiment

Ted Forrest is widely regarded as one of the best poker players in the world today. A few years ago, Ted tried a little experiment with O8B that had him playing *every hand* before the flop, to see if he could still end up winning money. Obviously, he was trying out the loosest strategy of all. Ted tried this experiment in some of the biggest poker games in the world, in both Los Angeles and Las Vegas. In other words, he tried it against some tough competition. So for more than one month Ted played every hand of O8B, except those that included three of a kind (6-6-6-J). Amazingly, he actually managed to make money playing almost every hand before the flop.

Of course, Ted is a superstar poker player, but still, to end up winning money while playing every hand before the flop for a month seems unbelievable to me! Since I knew that Ted had tried this experiment, I asked him about it later, and he replied, "Playing every hand before the flop certainly isn't the best way to play the game. To win the most money possible, you need to play a lot fewer hands." I think the fact that Ted could play every hand before the flop, for one month, shows us how much luck there is in this game—and what a great player Ted is. What it really tells me is that he must have played all these hands extremely well on the other three betting rounds.

So here we have Ted Forrest's experiment, which stands in stark contrast to the theory "play the A-2 hands only." The supertight "A-2 only" theory worked for me for a day in a world championship event (and has worked well for me at other times as well), and yet Ted managed to play the superloose theory and win money. Playing every hand and playing only a very few hands can both win money.

Well, then, do I guess that no matter how many hands you play before the flop, you'll win money? Not exactly—keep in mind that you aren't Ted Forrest or Phil Hellmuth. Bear in mind, also, that O8B is a fairly new game, and I suspect that Ted couldn't win money while playing every hand for even two weeks in today's high-limit games. The point of all of this is that different styles can work in O8B, but if you play any style that has you playing close to half of all the hands, I'll bet you won't end up winning any money—at least beyond a few very lucky weekends.

My (Unsuccessful) Theory of O8B

In 1998, I tried an experiment in O8B that ended up flopping pretty badly. For one year I played all hands that included three cards between a nine and an ace before the flop. Hands like 9-10-J-x, 10-K-A-x, 9-Q-A-x, and J-Q-K-x were all playable for me that year. The theory behind playing these high-pot hands was that when I won, I tended to win the whole pot. I didn't play high pairs in my hand like Q-Q-5-7 or K-K-9-4, because it was too hard to flop trips. Of course, I also played all the powerful hands on the list above. Using this theory, I immediately started winning a lot of money playing O8B. For the first month, I was more than $40,000 ahead playing this way, but over the next eleven months I lost more than $140,000. About then, I realized that this theory definitely isn't a winning one.

I hope I have taught you this much at least: many different strategies can work in O8B! Somewhere between Scotty's supertight "A-2 only" theory and Ted Forrest's crazy "play every hand" experiment there is a perfectly balanced style that no one has yet discovered. Even one of my two editors for this chapter, Annie

Duke, and I disagree about the order of the most powerful hands in O8B. (She's probably right as far as side games go, and I'm probably right as far as tournaments go.) Maybe there's someone out there who's learned how to play O8B perfectly, but I doubt that he or she could prove it!

Chapter 10

Pot-Limit Omaha: Beginners' and Intermediate Strategy

Pot-limit Omaha (PLO) is the number one game in Europe right now. It's played in Paris at the Aviation Club de France on the Champs-Élysées. It's played in Vienna at the Concorde Card Casino and the Casinos Austria. It's played in Amsterdam at the Casinos Holland–Amsterdam. It's played in London, in Ireland, and all over the United Kingdom. In fact, at every stop along the European poker tour, including Russia, Finland, Slovenia, Spain, and Germany, PLO is the number one side game. PLO is a game of great skill, bluffing, mathematics, and heart. In PLO, one or two good "reads" will often make the difference between winning and losing for any given session. If you make one good call against someone attempting to bluff, or one successful bluff yourself, it can make a huge difference in your results. Do you have the guts to make a huge bet on the end with nothing? Do you have the guts to call a huge bet on the end with a weak hand? If you do, then PLO is the game for you!

PLO is dealt just like limit Omaha, with everyone receiving four cards facedown to start off the action. Recall also that in Omaha, your final hand must be built from exactly two cards from your hole cards and exactly three from the board's up cards. But in PLO, you can bet the size of the pot on any of the four rounds of betting. This makes for some pretty big pots! In fact, one pot can make or break your whole night. In PLO you must protect your hand by making pot-size bets and forcing your opponents to fold when you have the best hand (or so you've persuaded them). In any pot-limit game, the idea is to put all your money into the pot (up to the total already in the pot) when you are a huge favorite to win the pot. ("All" is much more possible in pot-limit than in limit.) Ideally, in pot-limit poker, you put in a small amount of money with the worst hand and a "big ol'" pile of money when you have the best hand! For example, you could call a small preflop raise with Q♣-Q♦-8♠-9♠, have a great flop like 2♣-7♦-Q♥ (where you have flopped the best possible hand), and then put a huge amount of money into the pot with your three queens.

In this chapter you will learn:

- What you're looking to make in PLO—the best possible hand.
- The best beginners' strategy for PLO.
- The best starting hands for PLO.
- What hands to avoid in PLO.
- How to play A-A-x-x in PLO.
- How to play strong hands in PLO.
- Mathematics for PLO on fourth street.
- How to bet the size of the pot to protect your hand.

■ How to bet the pot when you're bluffing.

■ How to play the last round of betting in PLO.

In PLO, You're Looking to Make the Best Possible Hand

When the big money flies into a PLO pot, expect to see the best possible hand from your opponent. When you make a straight with 7-8 as part of your hand and a board of 9♠-10♥-J♠, you'll probably have to fold your hand! I can hear you out there right now as you read this, saying, "What, throw away a made straight? It's the third-best possible hand for this flop. How can I fold it?" When the big money goes in at this point, your jack-high straight is worth about as much as that stratosphere stock in a company that went bankrupt in 1998! In fact, it's worth even less, because at least you can use your stock certificates to paper the walls! In Hold'em, I would put in a lot of money with this hand, but this is Omaha, and it's far too easy for your opponent to have Q-K or 8-Q in his hand for a higher straight.

In fact, when the big money clatters into a PLO pot, barring unusual circumstances you will have to fold your second-nut flush as well. King-high flushes have cost weak players their entire bankrolls more times than you would believe possible. I played a PLO pot against a player named Blair Rodman in (I think) 1992 that illustrates just how easy it is to fold a strong PLO hand for a big bet on the last round of betting.

With a flop of 3♦-7♣-Q♠, Blair and I started building a small pot. I had 7♠-6♦-4♦-4♠, and Blair had at least A♦-8♦ in his hand (he showed them to me on the end when he folded his hand). I then flopped an inside-straight-flush draw (3♦-4♦-6♦-7♦), and Blair had at least an ace-high flush draw. The fourth card was 2♣ and the last card was 5♦, so that the final board was 3♦-7♦-6♠-2♣-5♦. The miracle had hit. I had caught 5♦ and made a straight flush! Even better, Blair now bet out the size of the pot into me.

Yippee—now it was time to raise just enough to keep Blair in the pot with me. I knew with certainty that he would call me if he had the ace-high diamond flush. He bet out $150, and now I raised $325. Without even thinking twice about it, Blair threw his hand away and said, "What do you take me for? I know how to throw away a big hand." Then he showed me A♦-8♦, which was the ace-high flush.

Although Blair did make a great fold at this point, what hand could I possibly be raising him with right here? I certainly wouldn't raise him in PLO with a king-high flush after he bet the size of the pot into me. He had A♦ in his hand, so he knew that I had either a straight flush or a bluff. It seemed unlikely that I would raise him on a pure bluff, so he decided that I had the straight flush, and he was right.

When you're playing PLO, look to have the best possible hand before you put in the big money. Of course, sometimes someone will try to bluff you on the end, and many, perhaps most, great players would have called that $325 raise (because it took a straight flush to beat Blair's hand), but in general you should be ready to fold a lot of second-best possible hands in PLO. You will have put a lot of money into the pot—and be tempted to go once more into the breach—but that last bet is likely to exceed all the preceding bets.

Investing a Toothpick to Win a Lumberyard

An old principle in poker is "Invest a toothpick to win a lumber yard." In other words, you can risk $1,000 in a pot-limit game and win perhaps $50,000 or more. In pot-limit poker this progression can be realized very quickly. For example, if you put $1,000 into a three-way-action pot and win it, you have $3,000. Put the $3,000 into a four-way-action pot and win, and now you have $12,000. Put the $12,000 into a single-opponent pot and win, and now you have $24,000. You might then bust someone who has only $10,000 in chips in front of him, and now you have $34,000. One more double up and you have $68,000! In pot-limit poker, a $1,000 investment is only five pots away from realizing $68,000 (or much more—after all, in this example, I slowed down the action considerably after reaching $24,000).

I had a run like this, a phenomenal comeback, in 2001 at the World Series of Poker (WSOP) in the $10,000-buy-in world championship event. On the first day my $10,000 had been driven down to around $700, but by the end of the fourth day I had roughly $1,050,000 in front of me! I had turned $700 into more than $1 million in three days! Unfortunately for me, the last day was the most disappointing poker day of my life, and I wound up in fifth place at the finish. My consolation was $305,000 for fifth place, which helped me manage my suffering.

Andy Glazer saw a player at the WSOP of 2000 turn a single $100 tournament chip into $80,000 in tournament chips before he got caught up in the seeming invincibility of his comeback and fell back. It happens.

The toothpick principle can also be applied to the individual pots that you play. If you call someone's $70 raise before the flop, then you have a chance to win all the rest of the chips in front of that player if you win the pot. Of course, you can also bust yourself, a little bit at a time, by playing weak hands before the flop. So you need to walk a fine line in order to be a successful PLO player.

Stories about stirring comebacks and startling PLO pots could fill a book, but right now we're just trying to get you started on the game, so now is the time to talk about the strength of starting hands in PLO. I'll list the hands in order of power from highest to lowest. Then I'll talk about each hand on the list and what makes it a strong hand. But first, a refresher on the workings of the pot.

What It Means to Bet the Pot

Just as in Hold'em and basic Omaha, there are small and big blinds to be attended to, before the first cards are dealt; they might be $5 and $10, which means the pot holds $15 before the first-round betting begins. If the first player to act bets $10, matching the blind, his bet is considered a call, and succeeding players can continue to call $10. If a player wants to raise, his raise can be anything between the minimum raise (a $10 raise, double the size of the big blind, is permitted) and the amount already in the pot. To do the latter, the player announces, "I raise the size of the pot." He announces this so that the dealer (or himself, or another player) will count the pot and tell him how much he can raise it.

For example, suppose that three players were to call $10,

and another player on the button announces, "Raise the size of the pot." He can make it $65 total: $15 (the blinds) + $30 (three calls) + $10 (the raiser's call) = $55, so he can make it $55 (pot-size raise) + $10 (the raiser's call) = $65.

If two of the players who called before the flop call the raise, how much is in the pot before the flop? Well, the other two players will have to call a $55 raise (they already have $10 in there), so that's three players with $65 in the pot ($195) + $15 (in blinds) + $10 (from the player who called $10, but not the $55 raise) = $220 (in the pot). With a $220 pot, someone can bet $220 on the flop.

You can see how a pot can escalate very quickly in PLO. A very modest $5–$10 blind structure can be very deceptive. (It would be a good idea for you to reread Chapter 8, on the setup and basic play in Omaha.)

The Best Beginners' Strategy for PLO

Unfortunately, there is no quick and easy way for me to describe how best to play PLO. It's full of nuances, and I recommend that you try to absorb this whole chapter before imagining that you understand the game. Having said that, I will nonetheless attempt to lay out a beginners' strategy for PLO.

As for starting hands, I recommend that you play only three of the possible pairs before the flop: aces, kings, and queens. This way, when you flop a set (make three of a kind) on the flop, you'll usually have the highest set. Sometimes, you'll catch someone with a lower three of a kind and win all his chips. You should also otherwise stick to the starting hands on the top of my list (my list of the most powerful hands in PLO is on page 236). High and medium "wraps" (four cards in a row) work extremely well in PLO. So be very selective with your starting hands.

Make pot-sized bets in PLO when you do have a strong flop. To bet less than the size of the pot is a mistake, unless you have a hand that can't be outdrawn, and there aren't many of those! Charge your opponents the maximum if they want to try to outdraw you in a big pot.

Read the sections below on how to play A-A-x-x in PLO. This is a very important hand, since A-A-x-x can range from being the best possible starting hand in PLO to being a somewhat weaker one. But I will bet all my money before the flop with A-A-x-x even if the side cards are weak! (I did say I would put in *all* my money *before the flop* with this hand, and risk my whole tournament or side game stake with it, because this hand is a mathematical favorite over any other.)

Learn to count the number of possible winning cards that you have when you're drawing (either on the flop or on fourth street). Math is important in this game! If there are 13 or more winning cards ("outs" or "wins") for you out there, you can call a pot-size bet, even on fourth street. (I have written a lot more on the 13-wins principle and how to count them up ahead in the discussion of Phil's flaw.)

So the best strategy once again is to play tightly and very aggressively. Haven't we heard that before somewhere? Perhaps in discussions of just about any form of poker in existence? The added kickers peculiar to PLO are that you have to make some tough folds; you have to understand and use some basic mathematics; and once you advance to the expert level you don't have to play quite so tightly before the flop. Don't worry too much about the math, though. My fifth-grader is doing the same math that you'll need to do at the table, although his teacher does let him use pencil and paper.

The Best Starting Hands for PLO

The best possible starting hand is A-A-K-K double-suited (like A♦-A♠-K♦-K♠). This hand can flop three aces (trip aces) or three kings, two different ace-high flushes, a straight, or some combination of those. The next-best possible starting hand is A-A-J-10 double-suited. In fact, no less a player than T. J. Cloutier considers it the best PLO starting hand. He feels the possible extra straights it allows are worth giving up the extra trips (three of a kind) and extra full-house possibilities.

But I wouldn't get caught up in trying to decide which of these starting hands is the best. You're going to play all of them about the same before the flop, and after the flop you'll know whether you have something you can push or not.

In any case, the top of the list of best hands in PLO is dominated by hands that include A-A as two of the four starting cards. In fact, you will always want to put all your money in before the flop (if possible) with any kind of A-A-x-x hand. When you have A-A-x-x in PLO, you're always a favorite against any other opening hand, unless some opponent also has A-A-x-x. In multiway pots, you would like the x-x to have a little oomph in it when you're putting all your money in preflop, because even though "dry aces" (poker slang for a hand like A♠-A♦-6♣-9♥) are a favorite over any individual hand, except a better A-A-x-x hand, they can easily be a collective underdog against multiple

♣♥ Best Starting Hands in Pot-Limit Omaha ♦♠			
1. A-A-K-K	double suited	14. K-K-A-J	preferably suited
2. A-A-J-10	double suited	15. K-K-A-10	preferably suited
3. A-A-Q-Q	double suited	16. K-K-Q-J	preferably suited
4. A-A-J-J	double suited	17. K-K-Q-10	preferably suited
5. A-A-10-10	double suited	18. K-K-J-10	preferably suited
6. A-A-9-9	double suited	19. Q-Q-10-10	preferably suited
7. A-A-x-x	(x)=any card	20. Q-Q-A-K	preferably suited
8. 8-9-10-J	double suited	21. Q-Q-A-J	preferably suited
9. K-K-Q-Q	preferably suited	22. Q-Q-A-10	preferably suited
10. K-K-J-J	preferably suited	23. Q-Q-K-J	preferably suited
11. K-Q-J-10	double suited	24. Q-Q-K-10	preferably suited
12. K-K-10-10	double suited	25. Q-Q-J-10	preferably suited
13. K-K-A-Q	preferably suited	26. Q-Q-J-9	preferably suited

Best Starting Hands in Pot-Limit Omaha

opponents. (Whether or not it has the oomph, I'm putting all my money in with it before the flop.)

After any of the A-A-x-x hands, the most powerful starting hand is 8-9-10-J double-suited. This seemingly modest hand wins an unbelievable number of pots! You can make a lot of straights with this kind of hand, and you'd generally prefer to make the straights, which can be nut hands, rather than the flushes, which won't be. When you make a flush with a hand like this, it is a pretty average flush; and as I've repeatedly said, you want to make the best possible hand in PLO. When you have four cards in a row double-suited and above a six like 10♣-J♠-Q♣-K♠ or 7♦-8♥-9♦-10♥, you have a very powerful drawing hand.

Of course, all the above are also very nice hands when they *aren't* suited. Next on our list of hands is K-K-x-x, where the x-x is Q-Q, J-J, 10-10, A-Q, A-J, A-10, Q-J, Q-10, or J-10 (preferably suited). Next on our list comes Q-Q-x-x, where the x-x is J-J, 10-10, A-K, A-J, A-10, K-J, K-10, J-10, or J-9 (preferably suited).

The Most Dangerous Starting Hands in PLO

The hands that I want to examine right now are hands that appear strong but will get you into a lot of trouble in PLO. Four cards in a row double-suited that are lower than an 8 can often be "trouble" hands. These lower "wraps," like 2♠-3♠-4♥-5♥, play very poorly in PLO. Flops like 6-7-8 are terrible for the lower wraps, because they usually make the lower side of the straight (in PLO, you want to make the best possible hand, or the high side, not the low side, of the straight).

Wraps like 3-4-5-6 double-suited at first glance seem strong, since you can make a number of straights and flushes with them, but they're really dangerous hands. Most times that you make a straight with this hand, a higher straight is possible (you really need perfect flop to make the high side of the straight with these low-wrap trouble hands, a flop like A-2-3 or 2-3-4 or 3-4-7), and every time that you make a flush with this hand a higher flush is possible. Playing hands like this before the flop is a natural setup for losing money in big chunks.

The Danger of Small Wraps

Suppose that you play 4-5-6-7 and the flop comes down 8-2-9. Now you have flopped a "wrap straight draw," with which you can hit a five, a six, a seven, or a ten to make your straight. A wrap straight draw is usually a pretty big hand in PLO. But in this case, a six, a seven, or a ten will also make you the second-best straight. If an opponent has 7-8-10-J in his hand, then you're drawing to only a five to win the pot. If your opponent has an 8-10-J-Q in his hand, then you can win only if you hit a five or a six. So your wrap straight draw is in bad shape against anyone with a higher wrap. You might do better to think of it as a "warped" straight draw. The really bad thing about this example is that it will be very tempting for you to call a lot of money to try to hit your hand, only to go broke to a higher straight when you do hit it!

Small Flush Draws

Suppose that you have 3♦-4♦-5♠-6♠ and the flop comes down Q♠-10♠-4♠. In this case, you have flopped a six-high flush (I say six-high because you have the 6♠-5♠ in your hand to complete the Q♠-10♠-6♠-5♠-4♠ flush). You should bet out on the flop to discover if your hand is any good, but you can't put very much money in the pot after that one bet on the flop. Your hand is just too weak.

Beware of Pairs Under Nines

Some other dangerous hands are pairs of nines or under. To an amateur PLO player, it may seem as if having a pair is a good thing, but these are precisely the kinds of hands that break you more often than not. When you have a hand like 4-6-8-8, and the flop is K-J-8, it is very hard to fold your hand. If your opponent has J-J-x-x or K-K-x-x, then you can win only if you hit the last eight in the deck. You're drawing to one card in the whole deck to win the pot—it doesn't get any worse than that in poker. Even if you're not up against a higher set, your hand is vulnerable to players who hold top two pair (which can make a higher full house) or have straight or flush draws. In fact, you're only a slight favorite over someone with a wrap straight draw, holding, say, 9-10-Q-A in his hand, and the board is K-J-8. So beware of bottom set in PLO.

As another example, suppose you have 4-5-5-6 and the flop is J-10-5. In this case, you have flopped a set of fives. This is a hand that's very hard for even an intermediate player to fold. If someone puts all his chips in against you, the best you can hope for is that he has two pair, jacks and tens. If he has a higher set, you're really dead in this hand! If he has a high wrap straight draw (say Q-K-A in his hand, which means that he can make a straight with a nine, a queen, a king, or an ace), you're less than a 3-to-2 favorite to win the pot. You might even have two opponents, one with two pair, jacks and tens, and the other with a wrap straight draw. If this is the case, then you're an underdog to win the pot.

Recently, I was punished for playing a small pair in PLO. I had 4♠-4♦-K♠-10♣ in late position and three players had already called the opening blind bet. I pondered for a moment whether or not I should call before the flop. I finally said to myself, "I'll call in case I flop a huge hand." The flop was [2♦]-[4♠]-[J♦], and now the big blind (Sam Grizzle) bet out the full $500 into the $500 pot. I had flopped the second-best possible hand, so I went ahead and raised it $1,500 more. Sam Grizzle now reraised me his last $4,000. I called his all-in bet quickly, thinking that I had the best hand, but Sam showed me three jacks.

Yikes—that was the only hand I didn't want to see. I was hoping that he had a set of deuces, two pair, a wrap straight draw, a flush draw, or something along those lines. I was now drawing to one card in the deck, but Sam hit a fourth jack on the turn and I couldn't win no matter what the last card was. The small $100 call (the blinds were $50–$100) before the flop was what sealed my fate in this pot. That $100 decision ended up costing me another $6,000. If only I had read my own advice and folded my small pair before the flop.

Playing A-A-x-x before the Flop in PLO

When you have A-A-x-x before the flop in PLO, you would like to put all your money in the pot before the flop whenever possible, ideally as a second raise that knocks out any "hitchhikers" and gets you heads-up. Before the flop, any A-A-x-x is a favorite to win the pot over any other individual hand in PLO. So when you have the chance, go for it. But you will rarely be able to put all your chips in before the flop. Unless everyone is playing with stacks that are relatively small for the blind structure, it usually takes a little longer to build a big pot in PLO: the giant bets tend to go in after the flop, when the hands are better-defined—for example, something like top set against a wrap with a flush draw.

All-in with A-A-x-x before the Flop

Suppose you have $A\diamond$-$A\heartsuit$-$5\spadesuit$-$9\clubsuit$ in the big blind, with the blinds at $5–$10. You have $450 in front of you to start the hand, $10 of it in the big blind already. So the pot holds $15 and the first two players to act call $10 each, making it $35. The button then calls the $10 and raises the size of the pot—the raiser is the third player to call $10 ($30) and the two blinds are together worth $15, so he can call the $10 and raise it $45, making it $55 to go—and the small blind calls the $55 to go. Now you say, "I raise the size of the pot." You announce this out loud (verbal declarations stand in poker) partly so that the dealer or other players can tell you how much you can make it to go. (There is always someone at the table who is really sharp and fast to say, "Fine, you can make it $x to go.") In this case, two players have put in $55 each (the button and the small blind) and the two prior players had put in $10 each and you will have to call the $55 before you raise the size of the pot. So we have $55 + $55 + $55 + $10 + $10, which equals $185. So you call the $55 and raise it $185, making it $240 to go. Whew! The math isn't all that complicated once you get used to it, and the dealer and other players are always there to help. Now that you have invested $240 of your chips before the flop, it's time to bet the other $210 on the flop no matter what cards come up, in order to protect your hand. That's one of the nice things about starting with A-A-x-x. You can miss the flop entirely and still have a hand that can win.

Raising with A-A-x-x before the Flop

Suppose you have [A♦]-[A♥]-[10♥]-[4♥] on the button, with the blinds at $5–$10. Now three people call the $10 in front of you. You could then raise it to $65 to go, a $55 raise: five players (including yourself and the big blind) have $10 each in this pot so far, and the small blind was $5. Or you could just call the $10. Let's look at two different theories about raising before the flop.

If You Raise before the Flop with A-A-x-x, Bet the Flop

If you raise your [A♦]-[A♥]-[10♥]-[4♥] (I would), then you'll also have to bet after most flops. You'll bet when it comes K-7-2, Q-7-5, K-10-4, 2-4-9, and most other flops as well. Of course, if you raise it $50 and the flop comes down 8-9-10 with no heart draw—the kind of flop that has probably hit your opponents—you can check and then fold if they make a big bet. A-A-x-x isn't a very powerful hand *after* the flop in PLO. Although it's the best possible hand before the flop, after the flop it can easily be beaten. Still, you never know what kinds of hands your opponents have, so you'll have to bet out on most flops to try to win the pot. But be ready to fold if someone raises you on the flop and all you have is one pair of aces.

Don't Raise the Pot with A-A-x-x before the Flop; Reraise

Some players do not like to raise the pot before the flop with A-A-x-x for the following reasons:

1. They're hoping that someone else will raise the pot *for* them and then they can reraise. This gets more money into the pot before the flop, when they do have the best possible hand (and the math is working for them).

2. By not raising, they trap other players into the pot ($10 isn't much to call), hoping for a great flop. For example, if the flop comes A-J-4, they may bust someone with a set of jacks or a set of fours.

3. If the flop does come down 8-9-10, then they have lost only the $10 call before the flop.

4. The first raise often isn't large enough to drive everyone out. In fact, very often the opposite is true: the first raise often entices players into the pot. This leaves you in the somewhat difficult position after the flop, since the other players will know, roughly, where you are, but you don't have much information about where they are. A reraise, however, will narrow the field and protect your hand.

Summing up, one strong point of this theory of reraising is that you can pile in a lot of money when you have the best possible hand before the flop. Another strong point is that you lose the minimum when you have a bad flop for A-A-x-x in an unraised pot ($10 in our example). The bad side is that you won't win as many pots with your A-A-x-x hand.

Playing Big Pocket Pairs in PLO

When you have a hand like K-K-x-x or Q-Q-x-x or J-J-x-x or 10-10-x-x, you want to take a cheap flop. These big pairs are good hands to call small bets with before the flop, in anticipation of hitting your big set. That's about all they're good for in PLO. When you have one of these hands, you're hoping that the pre-flop betting will be light, that you'll flop the big set, and that someone else will give you all his money with a smaller set.

Playing Strong Hands before the Flop—Putting in a Small Raise

When you have a hand like 10♠-J♠-Q♥-K♦, one theory says go ahead and make a small raise before the flop in order to build up the pot before the flop. With a hand like this you don't want to drive the other players out, because you may have a great flop like 4-10-J (top two pair and a straight draw); or 8-9-10 (the best possible hand with a draw to improve it; a jack or a queen makes your straight even higher); or K-K-2 (three kings); or 2-9-10 (the high wrap straight draw). You want to keep all the players in, but you want eventually to get more money in the pot as well. The best way to accomplish these goals is to raise a small amount of money before the flop. And if one of your opponents has the A-A-x-x hand, he won't be able to reraise you too much before the flop. (If you make a big raise, the A-A-x-x will be able to make a big reraise; but if you make a small raise, the A-A-x-x will be able to make only a small reraise.)

With Strong PLO Flops, Bet Hard to Protect Your Hand or Bluff

You will find yourself in more than a few situations where you will want to put all your money in on the flop, if possible.

The first situation arises when you flop the best possible hand. This could happen when you hold 6-7-x-x and the flop is 3♦-4♦-5♠, when you have 10-10-x-x in your hand and the flop is 4♣-5♣-10♦, or when you have A♦-4♦-x-x and the flop is 7♦-8♦-K♦. It could happen when the flop is 5-4-4 and you have 5-5-x-x in your hand (it's not four of a kind, but it's good enough for me to bet it all). In all these cases you want to bet out the size of the pot in order to protect your hand. By betting cheap, you are giving someone a cheap chance to outdraw your hand. All these hands can lose if you don't bet them hard. Even the 5-5-5-4-4 (fives full) full house hand can lose if you let someone holding a pair of sixes or higher take a card and hit his pair for a bigger full house. For example, if a jack comes off and a player still in the hand already had a pair of jacks, he now has J-J-J-4-4 (jacks full). Imagine that: you could win the pot with a bet on the flop (no one was going to call), but because you didn't bet, you're now going to lose all your chips!

The second situation in which you want to bet out big and move all-in if possible arises when you flop a big drawing hand. When you have 8♦-9♠ 10♦-J♣ and the flop is 7♣-8♣-2♥, you have flopped the top pair and the best wrap straight draw possible (you make the best hand if a six, a nine, a ten, or a jack comes off the deck), and no flush draw is possible. This is a hand that you can play for all your chips on the flop. Another hand that you can play for a bunch of chips is one where you flop both a set and a high flush draw, even if you think that your opponent has made a straight. With a hand of 9♦-9♠-K♠-2♥ and a flop of 8♠-9♥-10♠, you have flopped a set of nines and a king-high flush draw. You are a favorite against an opponent with J-Q-x-x (a made straight) in his hand. You can make a full house or a flush with two cards still to come in this spot. And when you pile in your chips raising, you will probably bluff out an opponent who has the second-best possible straight.

The third situation that will allow you to bet all your money on the flop arises when you have top set and you suspect that your opponent has a weak straight. With a flop of 4♦-5♠-7♣ and a hand of 7-7-x-x, you have top set. If your opponent has 6-8-x-x in his hand, you're a 2-to-1 underdog to pair the board and win the pot (on the flop). But if your opponent has 3-6-x-x, you may be able to make him fold his hand on the flop by betting huge amounts of money.

The fourth situation involves bluffing with the best flush draw. If the flop is 4♣-6♣-J♦ and you hold A♣-5♣-Q♦-9♥, then you have flopped the ace-high flush draw. By betting a huge amount of money or raising someone a huge amount of money with this hand on the flop, you might be able to bluff out someone who holds two pair. When the bluff works, you'll win the pot right there. When the bluff doesn't work, you may still win the pot if you hit your flush. It's also possible that your opponent has a wrap straight draw and a weaker flush draw. In this case, you can win the pot with your A-Q high when harmless cards come off, or even with one pair if you hit it.

In these four situations, you can bet all or most of your money or at least the size of the pot on the flop, in an attempt to win the pot right there with your strong draw or strong hand.

Playing your strong draws and your strong hands the same way will confuse the other players, and they will never know if you're drawing or already have the made hand.

Mathematics in PLO on Fourth Street

Phil's Flaw

For more than a few years I played PLO very badly, in the sense that I wasn't seeing one basic mathematical principle of the game. I can't believe that I missed it all those years, but no one was coaching me on how to play the game (and I wasn't smart enough to read a book, as you're doing now). After playing PLO for more than seven years, I finally learned something while watching "Houston Sammy" play one day. Sammy is considered the best PLO player in the world, and one day in a big game in Tunica, Mississippi, I watched him get involved in a big pot.

Sammy had 6-8-9-J in his hand, nothing suited, and the board came down 5-7-K. Sammy had flopped the nut wrap straight draw (all the straight cards that he could hit would make him the best possible hand). A car dealer from Dallas had been killing the big PLO game for a couple of weeks and had won more than $500,000. The car dealer bet out $2,000 and Sammy just called with his wrap straight draw. Now the third player in the game check-raised the pot to make it $8,000 to go. The car dealer hesitated and then called the bet. Now Sammy called the $6,000 raise as well. The next card was a jack, and the third player bet out $24,000 into the pot. The car dealer folded his hand, and Sammy called $18,000 of the bet all-in (Sammy had a right to call $18,000, if that's all he had left). Later, I asked Sammy why he hadn't moved all-in on the flop, and he said, "Well, Phil, I didn't want to have the board pair on fourth street and be drawing dead against my opponent's full house. I knew that I would have to call a pot-size bet if the board didn't pair, because I had a wrap draw. With my wrap draw I would have at least 13 wins, which meant I would have to call a pot-size bet on fourth street."

Then it finally hit me why I hadn't been doing better in PLO side games in the past. You see, I never understood that with 13 possible wins I had to call a pot-size bet! If I have 13 wins with one card to come, this means that my opponent has roughly 29 wins. In the hand Sammy played, I say roughly 29 wins because I know that 13 cards will win for him, four more are on the board, two of his opponent's four cards are probably pair cards (like K-7 or K-K or 7-7), and there are four more in my hand. Therefore, we add Sammy's 13 wins to the eight cards that we can see (his hand and the four on the board) and the other two that we assume are in the opponent's hand. This adds up to 23 cards out of 52 cards in the deck, so the other 29 cards win for the opponent. If you're still confused about 29 wins versus 13 wins, note that an example is coming right up. This means that I'm roughly a 2½-to-1 underdog to win the pot. When someone bets the size of the pot, then I'm getting laid exactly 2-to-1 on my call (if the bet is $2,000 into a $2,000 pot, I can call $2,000 to win $4,000). And I'll get to bet out on the end if I make my hand and win still more money if I'm called. The fact that I can bet out on the end after hitting my hand and perhaps get called by my opponent adds "implied odds" in favor of my calling here. It all suddenly made sense to me, but why hadn't I seen this simple mathematical principle earlier in my career? Any pro reading this is probably saying, "Duh, Phil, how could you not see that right away?" One major reason that I had been losing at PLO was that I didn't understand the basic math in the game! I wasn't making the calls I was supposed to make.

As for what happened to Sammy in this pot, he and his opponent agreed to deal the last card twice. (Sometimes, players in big PLO pots choose to deal the final card twice—for half of the pot each time—in order to lower the luck factor in the hand.) Sammy hit an eight for the straight to win on the first card, and the other player won it on the second card when a ten came up. So they split the pot.

Calling Because of the Math on Fourth Street

Suppose that you have A♥-5♥-7♦-9♠ in your hand and the flop has come down 2♥-4♥-8♠. You have now flopped the ace-high flush draw and a straight draw as well. You can hit either a three or a six for a straight, although the three will make you the second-best straight. On the flop, you bet out $340 and two opponents call you. The next card off is Q♣, for a board of 2♥-4♥-8♠-Q♣. You decide to check, and then the first player bets out the size of the pot, $1,360 (4 × $340), and the second player folds. What do you do?

Well, let's count up the number of cards you can win with. The 3♥, 6♥, 7♥, 9♥, 10♥, J♥, or K♥ would make us the best possible hand (an ace-high flush, or in the case of 6♥ a straight flush). We can also win with the 6♣, 6♠, or 6♦, they too would make us the best possible hand (an eight high straight). We can also probably win with 3♣, 3♠, or 3♦, which would make us a wheel (A-2-3-4-5 straight) or the second-best possible hand. So we have 13 possible winning cards and the rest are losers. If we know of eight cards—our four and the four on the board—and assume that our opponent has two more pair cards in his hand, then we know that there are 42 cards left in the deck.

We win with 13 of the remaining 42 and lose with the other 29, so we're roughly a 2½-to-1 underdog, but the pot is laying us only 2 to 1. Remember that your opponent's bet is $1,360, and that the pot is $1,360 as well. So you can call his $1,360 to win the $2,720 ($1,360 bet and $1,360 in the pot). But you also have to factor in the implied odds that you can bet out if you hit your hand in this spot and maybe also get called. The implied odds are enough to make this call possible for you. So you can call here in this spot. Congratulations on jumping ahead in the learning curve. It took me six years to learn as much!

Math in PLO Forces You to Fold

Suppose now that you have A♠-7♠-8♦-J♣ and the flop is 4♠-6♠-Q♣. You have flopped the nut flush draw and a belly buster (inside) straight draw (you need a five for a straight). You raise an opponent's bet on the flop and he calls. Now 2♣ comes off for 4♠-6♠-Q♣-2♣, and your opponent bets out the size of the pot. You count your "outs" and see that 3♠, 5♠, 8♠, 9♠, 10♠, J♠, or K♠ would all make you the nut flush. In addition, you can make the nut straight with 5♣, 5♥, or 5♦. So you have 10 outs out of 44 available cards. (If you assume that your opponent has two pair cards in his hand, then there are 42 "unknown" cards left. In this case you can't do that, because he may have 3-5-x-x, which makes the straight.) Thus, there are 34 losses to 10 wins, so that you're a 3.4-to-1 underdog in this case. You also know that the pot is laying you 2 to 1 when someone bets the full size of the pot. If it had been close, the implied odds would have put you over the top, but it isn't that close. You now have to fold your hand because the math just isn't there for you to call right here.

Before you consider calling a pot-size bet with your drawing hand, count the number of winning cards that you can hit. If the number of potential winners is 13 or more, you can call. If the number of winners is 12 or fewer, you should fold your hand.

Make Sure to Bet the Size of the Pot to Protect Your Hand

If you have the best possible hand on fourth street, make sure to bet the size of the pot in order to protect your hand. Remember the section on math that you've just read. Don't "price" someone else into a pot with a small bet in PLO. Make the bet that he cannot call (or at least doesn't want to call and should not call) by betting the size of the pot.

Making Big Bets with Hands That Aren't the Best Possible

Sometimes in PLO, you just need to make a pot-size bet even though you don't have the best possible hand. Often you will flop a set and then a straight card will come off that you will need to bet out into. Whether or not you should bet out the size of the pot on fourth street depends on how much action there was on the flop, and on the draw that hit. If someone has raised you the size of the pot when you bet out on fourth street, then you can assume that the raiser has hit his hand, and now you should add up the number of cards you can hit in order to win the pot. If you have trips and are very sure that your opponent has hit his straight or flush, then you'll usually have 10 cards from which to hit to make your hand (nine full house cards and one four-of-a-kind card with the four cards on the board when you have trips). For example, suppose that you have K-K-8-4, and the board is K-Q-5-9. If your opponent has a straight, then you'll need to hit a five (three left), a nine (three left), or a queen (three left), to make a full house; or a king (one left) to make four of a kind. So you have 10 possible winning cards. With 34 losing cards and 10 winning cards, it's time to fold your hand because you're a 3.4-to-1 underdog. When someone bets the pot, you're being laid only 2 to 1, so it's time to fold any hand that is a 3.4-to-1 underdog.

Betting Out with a Set into a Possible Straight

Suppose you have 10-10-K-9 and the flop has come down [4♦]-[5♦]-[10♠]. Now you bet out the size of the pot, $400, on the flop, and two players call your bet. The next card off is [7♣], for a board of [4♦]-[5♦]-[10♠]-[7♣]. What do you do now? Although the seven was a bad card for you, you should bet out the size of the pot again ($1,600) in order to protect your hand. At this point, a 3-6 or 6-8 out of your opponent's hand will beat you, by making either a seven-high straight or an eight-high straight. You make this pot-size bet in order to protect your hand from the straight and flush draws that didn't get there on the turn but are still live and might have improved when the seven appeared. If an opponent raises you the size of the pot (calls your $1,600 and raises you $4,800 more), look out, because he will almost always have the straight! If you have more than the $4,800 raise left in front of you, you need to fold your hand, because you have only 10 wins—three fours, three fives, three sevens, and one ten—of the 44 cards left in the deck: you're a 34-to-10 (3.4-to-1) underdog. The pot is laying you 2 to 1 in this case; therefore, fold.

Betting Out a Set into a Straight

Suppose now that you have Q-Q-9-J and the flop is 4♣-5♣-Q♥. On the flop someone bets out into you and you raise that person the size of the pot and get called in two places.

Because two opponents called a pot-size bet and raised on the flop, you now strongly suspect that unless someone has slipped something into the communal club soda, one opponent probably has the ace-high club draw and the other opponent probably has the wrap straight draw with 6-7-8-x in his hand. It is also possible that an opponent has a lower set than you have. However, in this case, I would be very leery of any 3, 6, 7, 8, or club coming off of the deck. I would probably check if a 6, 7, or 8 came up on fourth street.

However, if an ace or a deuce came off the deck, then I would bet out the size of the pot on fourth street even though both cards make a possible straight. Why? Because I don't think that any solid player would call a pot-size bet and raise with the low end of the straight draw. If my opponents aren't solid, or if the club soda may actually be laced with something, I have to consider the straight a more realistic threat.

If a club spikes on fourth street and an opponent bets the size of the pot into me, then I would understand that I have only 10 cards (10 cards make a full house) I could redraw with, and therefore I fold my hand. I would assume that the opponent who bet out the size of the pot into me here would have a flush, almost certainly the ace-high flush.

Knowing when to bet the pot in PLO on fourth street with a strong hand when a draw has hit is an art form. There is no magical formula for this. Just use some logic and try to make your best guess. If you're wrong, you can just fold when you're reraised. If you're right, you will probably win the pot immediately. So you're betting $X to win $X. If you're right, you win $X (the pot) with your pot-size bet. If you're wrong, you lose $X (your bet). So you will win $X or lose $X when you bet the pot on fourth street. Even money isn't a bad bet, as long as your bankroll can handle fluctuations easily.

So sometimes you need to bet the pot to protect your hand in PLO. Sometimes you will be able to read your opponents as having hit their hands, and therefore avoid making a pot-size bet on fourth street. In any case, betting the pot in PLO with a strong hand on fourth street after a draw has hit will sort out whether you have the best hand or not.

Betting or Calling Bets on the River

Calling someone's big bet on the end is all about your read of that player. What draw hit on the end—straight, flush, or full house? Was it the kind of draw that your opponent usually makes? Most of the time, when someone makes a pot-size bet on the end in PLO, it means that he has made his hand. When someone who never bluffs all of a sudden bets out big on the river when a draw hits, then you can go ahead and fold your hand! But except for some gimme situation like that, calling someone on the end when he bets big is all about heart, guts, and reading ability. It takes reading ability to see that your opponent is bluffing, heart to know that you're right, and guts to put the big money into the pot at the end calling—especially when you know that usually players don't bluff on the end in PLO. If you were to just fold your hand every time someone made a pot-size bet on the river when a draw hit, you would end up way ahead in the long run.

If you make your hand on the end, be careful not to show any emotion. Most beginning players jump right out of their seats or spill a glass of water when they hit their hand! Try to look at that last card calmly, without saying or doing anything, as it's turned up. This is a good thing to practice in front of a mirror at home. Imagine your best card coming off the deck, and see what you do while you watch yourself in the mirror. If you try any of the B-rated acting that occasionally works in your small-stakes home game ("I don't know, maybe I'll bet this hand right now . . .") against champions, they'll see right through it! By the way, acting usually doesn't work in your home game either, in PLO. The best thing to do is to be unpredictable, and the best way to do that is to occasionally bluff out a big bet on the end.

Bluffing on the End Makes Them Call You—You Have to Do It

If you never bluff, you'll rarely get called. If you bluff too often, you'll always get called. Somewhere between never bluffing and always bluffing is the right place to be. Bluffing is very important in poker. When the players know that you're capable of bluffing, you'll get called more often on the end, when you do complete your hand. But even if you do get called when you're bluffing, and lose a bundle, the bluff will pay some dividends later on!

Look for times when you know that your opponent is fairly weak: these are pretty good times to bet out with your busted draw. There will be times when you can feel your opponent's weakness when he bets, and then you have to decide if he might be too weak too call a big bluff or not.

Bluff at some pots when another draw hits, in order to disguise your bet. If you have a flush draw, and the straight card comes off, this is a good time to bluff. In this case, you are "representing" a straight, even though you really do have a busted flush draw.

If you do get away with your bluff, do *not* show your hand. Just remember whom you've bluffed and try to bluff that person again sometime soon. If you show your hand, the other players will remember what you looked like when you bluffed them, and they will use that against you later on. When you do get caught bluffing, simply say, "I have nothing" and throw your cards into the muck. Remember that when you get caught bluffing, you're likely to get called a lot more for a time afterward.

PLO: Final Thoughts

When you play PLO, remember to start with strong hands, bet the full pot size when you have a strong hand or a strong draw, make sure to use math to help decide whether you should call when you're drawing, bluff some of the time so that you're not too predictable, and be cautious when calling opponents' big bets. PLO is a game in which you want to make the best possible hand. If you remember all the above, then I like your chances in most PLO games.

Chapter 11

Seven-Card Stud: Setup and Basic Play

Seven-Card Stud is probably America's most familiar version of poker. It sometimes seems as if everyone in America knows how to play Stud, but it might be more accurate to say that everyone in America *thinks* he or she knows how to play stud! The Europeans also play a lot of Seven-Card Stud. In fact, in the biggest and most prestigious poker tournament in Europe—the European poker championships, held in Vienna—the game is Seven-Card Stud. I'm proud to say that I was the first American ever to win the European poker championships, in October 2000.

Bet Limits, and an Extra Round of Betting

In Seven-Card Stud, there are five rounds of betting, one more than in Hold'em and Omaha. But in larger higher-stakes Stud games, the betting is quite similar to that in Hold'em and Omaha:

in each hand there are two bet sizes, and the game is defined by the sizes of the bets established. For example, you might play $10–$20 Stud or $50–$100 Stud. During the first two rounds of betting, in these higher-stakes games, all bets and raises are in the smaller increment ($10 in our $10–$20 game). During the next three rounds, all bets and raises are at the higher increment ($20 in our $10–$20 game).

Despite what the high-stakes players tend to think, the bread-and-butter games, those that pay the casino's rent, are low-stakes games. In lower-stakes Stud, it is very common to run into spread limits where the betting options are broader. Probably the most common form of Stud dealt in American card rooms is 1–5 Stud, where anyone at almost any time can bet anywhere between $1 and $5 (in $1 amounts—you can't bet something like $1.47 or even $1.50). I say "almost" any time because once someone has opened a hand for, say, $3, you can't raise him $1; a raise has to be at least as large as twice the preceding bet.

Antes, Not Blinds

Seven-Card Stud is an ante game (see below for more about the right ante size for your game) and therefore has no need for the blinds that are used in the other two games. Before each hand, everyone antes an amount that is generally set at somewhere between one-tenth and one-fourth of a full bet. Just how big the ante is varies from casino to casino: you could easily find one casino dealing $5–$10 Stud with a $0.50 ante, and then walk to the casino next door and find $5–$10 Stud using a $1 ante. As I'll discuss in Chapter 12, the size of the ante weighs heavily in what kind of starting hand you should consider playable. If the antes are big, you need to be prepared to play a lot more hands than in games where the antes are small, or you will find your stack of chips disappearing just from the antes!

How a Hand Proceeds

The dealer first pulls everyone's ante into the pot, then deals out two cards to each player facedown and one card to each player faceup, one at a time—just as in Hold'em and Omaha. Everyone then starts out with three cards: two hole cards and one up card.

On the first round, the player who has been dealt the lowest up card is required to start the action by making what is called a *bring-in* bet. If there is a tie, suits are used to break the tie. The size of the bring-in bet is usually set at about a third of the lower standard bet, but it varies considerably from one casino (or kitchen) to the next. If suits do come into play in determining who must make the bring-in bet, the lowest suit is clubs, followed by diamonds, hearts, and spades, so if your up card (usually called a "door card") is [2♣], you don't have to wait to see everyone else's up cards to know you'll be making the bring-in bet.

If you have trouble remembering what suit reigns at this juncture, there is a handy little mnemonic: the letters c-d-h-s, the correct order of suits in breaking a tie, are in alphabetical order, lowest letter equaling lowest card. You needn't worry too much about this, though, because except for determining who makes the bring-in bet in Stud, suits don't matter in poker. If you have a

♣♥ Seven-Card Stud Antes, Bring-ins, and Opening Bets ♦♠			
Limit	Ante	Bring-in bet	Opening bet
$0.50-$1	dealer antes $1	$0.25	$0.50
$0 .75-$1.50	$0.25	$0.25	$0.75
$1-$2	$0.25	$0.50	$1
$1.50-$3.00	$0.50	$0.75	$1.50
$2-$4	$0.50	$0.75	$2
$3-$6	$0.75	$1.25	$3
$4-$8	$1	$2	$4
$5-$10	$1	$2	$5
$6-$12	$1	$2	$6
$8-$16	$2	$3	$8
$10-$20	$2	$4	$10
$15-$30	$3	$6	$15
$20-$40	$5	$10	$20
$30-$60	$5	$15	$30
$50-$100	$10	$20	$50
$75-$150	$25	$50	$75
$100-$200	$25	$50	$100

Seven-Card Stud Antes

royal flush in spades, and someone else has one in hearts, you split the pot.

With that issue settled, the player sitting to the left of the bring-in has three options: he can fold, call, or raise. This raise is a bit tricky, though, because although you're increasing the size of the bet, you aren't doubling it. On this first round *only*, the very first "raise" merely increases the bring-in to a full-size bet, an action that is called *completing the bet*. But again, this player need not be the one who completes the bet; he may call the bring-in bet or fold.

The action then moves on around the table, clockwise, each player having the option of folding his hand, calling the bet, or raising the bet. When this round is complete, the dealer deals another up card (now we have two up cards and two down cards) to all the players who haven't folded their hands. Now the second round of betting begins, and the action proceeds somewhat differently from what happens in the first round.

During the first round, the player holding the worst door card was required to make a small bet, of predetermined size (the bring-in bet). On the second round, and for all rounds thereafter in that hand, the player holding the *best* hand acts first, but he isn't forced to bet: he can start the action by checking. In Hold'em and Omaha, the betting position doesn't change throughout a hand. But in stud, as you can see, the player who acts first in each round of betting can and often does change the dynamics of the hand, depending on where he sits and what cards fate decides to hand out next. (After the high poker hand acts, of course, the betting proceeds in the usual clockwise direction, through the other players left in the hand.)

Note that the small bring-in bet is now gone: the smallest bet allowed in all the later rounds of the hand is either $10 (in a game of $10–$20) or $1 (in smaller games like $1–$5). If, however, anyone has made an open pair in his first two up cards (for example, he is showing two sevens), that player has an additional option. He can make the smaller $10 bet that is allowed on the second betting round, or he can go straight to the $20 bet that is normally reserved for the third betting round.

After the other players have acted on their hands and the action of the second round is complete, the dealer deals another faceup card to all the players who are still active (now they each have three faceup and two hole cards). So the third betting round begins, the player with the best (visible) hand checking or betting at the higher limit number, $20 in our $10–$20 example.

After everyone has had a chance to act on his hand and the betting is complete, the dealer deals still another faceup card (the fourth up card) to the players who are still active. Action on the fourth betting round is identical to action on the third.

When the fourth round of betting is complete, the dealer deals the last card, this time *facedown,* to the players remaining in the hand. Again, the best hand showing (who is the same player as in the preceding round, because the last card is dealt facedown) must either check or bet.

After the betting is complete, the pot is awarded to the best poker hand. Usually the bettor will say, "I have aces up" or "I have nothing," and then the caller or callers will say, "I can beat it" or "Good hand."

The basic differences between Stud and Hold'em are as follows:

1. There are no community cards in Stud.
2. There is an ante in Stud.
3. There are five rounds of betting in Stud, but just four in Hold'em.
4. In Stud, whatever player has the best board (his up cards) begins the round of action, except for the first round of betting, in which case the lowest card acts with a bring-in bet; in Hold'em the player to the left of the button always acts first.

5. Stud is the most popular game on the East Coast today; Hold'em is the most popular game everywhere else in America.

6. To play Stud well, you have to try to remember the folded up cards (did someone fold a four earlier that you need to make three fours?). In Hold'em, recall, there are no cards to remember; you can always look at the cards in your own hand and the cards on the board.

7. Casino Stud games, in which seven cards are dealt to each player, are limited to a maximum of eight players. In Hold'em, more cards are dealt—nine or ten, depending on the casino.

A Sample Hand of Seven-Card Stud

Let's take a look at a high-stakes hand of Seven-Card Stud (Stud) at Trump's Taj Mahal Casino in Atlantic City. If you plan on playing in this regular game in Atlantic City, you'd better bring $50,000 with you for a couple of days' worth of play.

Annie Duke is in seat one (S1), to the left of the dealer.
Berman (Lyle) is in seat two (S2), left of Annie.
Then two poker legends and members of the Poker Hall of Fame—"Chip" Reese (S3) and Doyle Brunson (S4).
Ed is next (S5), then Farhad (S6).
George "the Greek" is in S7.
Hellmuth (Phil—me) is in S8, on the right of the dealer.

Seven-Card Stud Setup

The game is $400–$800 Stud, with a $100 ante and a $200 bring-in bet. The dealer deals out two down cards and one up card, starting with one card down to Annie on the dealer's left, and finishing with one up card to Hellmuth on the dealer's right. Now the players all have two down cards and one up card. Ed is dealt 2♥ and puts in the $200 bring-in bet. Farhad completes the bet to $400 to go with 10♣ up, and then George folds. Hellmuth calls $400 with J♠ as an up card and A♣–K♥ as hole cards. Annie, Berman, and Chip fold their hands. Doyle raises it to $800 to go with Q♠ showing, and Ed folds. Farhad calls $400 more ($800 total) with his 10♣ up card, and Hellmuth calls $400 more ($800 total) with his J♠ up card. With Hellmuth's call, the action is complete and the dealer pulls the bets—which are in the pot, in front of the players—into the middle of the pot, and then deals three up cards to Doyle, Farhad, and Hellmuth.

Doyle hits [8♥], for a board of [Q♠]-[8♥]. Farhad catches [10♠], for a board of [10♣]-[10♠] (an open pair). Hellmuth catches [4♥], for a board of [J♣]-[4♥]. Since Farhad has now hit an open pair, he has the option of betting either $400 or $800. (The only time a player may bet $800 on the second round of betting in a $400–$800 game is when he makes an open pair on the fourth card.) Farhad chooses to bet $800, and Hellmuth, who has hit nothing, opts for an early exit and folds his hand. In fact, this was an easy fold for Hellmuth, who is facing an $800 bet and an opponent with at least a pair of tens (and probably two pair or even three tens). Doyle decides to call the $800 bet, and this completes the second round of betting; now the dealer pulls the $800 bets into the middle of the pot.

Now Doyle catches [2♣], for a board of [Q♠]-[8♥]-[2♣]. Farhad catches [3♣], for a board of [10♣]-[10♠]-[3♣]. Farhad still has the high hand on the board, so it is up to him to make the first action, and he decides to bet $800. Doyle calls the $800, and the bets are dragged into the middle of the table. The next cards are [8♠] for Doyle, and a board of [Q♠]-[8♥]-[2♣]-[8♠]; and [9♥] for Farhad, giving him a board of [10♣]-[10♠]-[3♣]-[9♥]. Now Farhad decides to check, because he has two pair, tens and sevens (his hole cards are 7–7) and he fears that Doyle has a higher two pair, queens and eights. Doyle decides to bet $800 with his hand because he believes that his two pair, of jacks and eights (*jacks up*), are better than whatever Farhad has (Doyle's hole cards are J-J). Farhad calls the $800, just in case his *tens up* (two pair, the high one being tens) are good or he catches a ten or a seven on the last card to make a full house. On the end, Farhad *checks in the dark* (he checks

Seven-Card Stud Board

before he looks at his last card) and Doyle says, "I *bet in the dark*" (he bets without looking at his last card). Farhad then looks at the last card, , and thinks for a moment. He decides that Doyle might not have his tens up beat (besides which, he caught one of the queens that Doyle is representing), so he calls the $800 last bet. Doyle then says, "Jacks up," and Farhad says, "That's good." Farhad briefly inspects Doyle's hand to make sure he has what he said he had, and then throws his own cards in facedown. By the way, because Farhad throws in his cards facedown, no one will ever really know what he had. That's pretty standard when you lose a pot—you throw away your hand facedown, and say, "Nice hand" or "You got it" or something similar.

So this is just another hand at the Taj Mahal, where you will find high-limit Stud games ($200–$400 games and above) being spread every weekend.

Two Other Stud Games

Two other forms of Seven-Card Stud are also popular, and I will be giving you some basic strategy for them in Chapters 13 and 14. These are Seven-Card Stud Low (Razz) and Seven-Card Stud High-Low Split ("Stud Eight or Better"). These games are dealt in exactly the same way as Seven-Card Stud. The only differences lie in who makes the bring-in bet and who bets first during the hand.

Betting Structure for Razz (Seven-Card Stud Low)

The betting structure in Razz is identical to that in Seven-Card Stud, with two exceptions: the bring-in bet is made by the player showing the highest card, not the lowest card; and the action on later rounds is started by the player who shows the lowest hand, not the highest hand.

In Razz, you try to make the best low hand; the best low hand possible is 5-4-3-2-A, followed by 6-4-3-2-A.

Betting Structure Seven-Card Stud Eight or Better

Seven-Card Stud Eight or Better is dealt exactly like basic Seven-Card Stud, with the same low-card bring-in bet and the high board (the up cards) betting first each time. The betting structure is exactly the same, but the strategy is dramatically different, as we will learn in Chapter 14.

There Is No Positional Advantage in Dealing Stud or Its Variants

One interesting point about these Seven-Card Stud games is that it really doesn't matter who deals: there is no positional advantage. The fact that the low up card (or the high up card, depending on the variant played) pays the bring-in bet means that there is no preset positional advantage in dealing the cards. Whoever acts first or last in a Stud hand is totally dependent on the luck of the cards.

In Hold'em and Omaha, there is an advantage to dealing because you have the chance to act last, after all the others have made their statements. This is why we use a button in Hold'em and Omaha but have no need of such a device in Stud.

Chapter 12

Seven-Card Stud:
Basic and Intermediate Strategy

My play in Seven-Card Stud tournaments has improved dramatically in the last few years, and the results have increased my love of the game. My fascination hit a new high when I became the first American to win the European poker championships, in October 2000. The event, called the Poker EM, is a Seven-Card Stud tournament held in Vienna every October. The Poker EM is the second-largest and most prestigious poker event held in Europe. Only the Poker Million title is more coveted (this is a $10,000 no-limit Hold'em event, held in London, that guarantees £1 million—about $1.5 million—for first place).

Seven-Card Stud is a game of memory, deception, and skill. In this chapter, I'll give you my strategy for survival, the basic elements that you'll need to learn before you enter a card room and play Stud.

After reading this chapter, you may find that you know more about Stud than most of your opponents at the local card club. Because many players have grown up playing Stud, they've never seen fit to read about it, even though they may have devoured books and articles about Hold'em or Omaha. In fact, the lower the stakes you play, the more likely you are to have an advantage over the table, merely because you have read and understood this chapter! Of course, understanding something in theory and applying your theoretical understanding to a game situation are two different animals. I'll show you the most important elements of strategy and tactics, but then it will be up to you to make use of those elements to win a few hands and collect a few dollars. (You might want to reread Chapter 11 before proceeding further here.)

The most important thing that *anyone* in poker—Stud or other forms—can learn is that patience is a virtue. More bad plays are made and more money is lost in poker for lack of patience than for any other single reason. I will teach you which three-card starting hands to play, and which hands patience and wisdom tell you to fold. Proper selection of starting hands is the single most important thing to learn in Seven-Card Stud.

When you're watching people winning big pots with hands that wise old heads say they shouldn't have played, it's rather hard to sit back and throw away those same hands, just because the math supports that decision. If I teach you not to play (2-2) 4, and you see your pal across the table win a big pot with the (2-2) 4, you'll be tempted to think, "That hand works, so let me play it too." You may even win a hand if you try it, but do not be fooled by short-term success. Eventually, bad play will catch up with you. Great poker play is as much about patience in waiting for the right starting hand as it is about anything else.

OK, what's (2-2) 4? You will recall that Seven-Card Stud

hands begin with two cards dealt facedown (your hole cards) and one faceup. To convey that for particular hands, I will use the convention of placing the hole cards in parentheses. Thus (2-2) 4 means that this player has a pair of deuces in the hole and his first up card is a four. The first up card has its own special name: it is usually called a player's "door card."

In this chapter you will learn:

- What the most powerful starting hands are in Seven-Card Stud.
- Why some hands are more powerful starting hands than others.
- Which hands you should (and should not) be playing in game situations.
- Slow-playing your strong hands as an alternative to jamming them on the first round of betting.
- Paying attention to what cards are on the board and how that can affect the strength of your hand and your read of an opponent.

My goal here is to help you understand when you should play certain hands and why. I will not attempt to treat every possible situation in Seven-Card Stud; that would take a full book, perhaps more than one. Instead, I will try to teach you how you can use your own common sense in order to determine which hands you should play and why you should play them—and, conversely, which hands you should fold and why you should fold them.

Beginners' Strategy: The Number One Thing to Know about Stud

In a nutshell, the key to winning money at Seven-Card Stud is to start with the best three-card starting hand. That sounds pretty simple, doesn't it? And in most circumstances it is pretty simple, although in many others an alert player will spot situations that make effective selection of a starting hand not quite so black-and-white.

Sometimes starting with the best hand means realizing that you should throw away a pair of kings. At other times it may mean making it three bets with a pair of nines! If you can always start with the best hand—whatever's best for the circumstances of the moment—then you'll do well at Seven-Card Stud. But what *is* the best hand? Is it (9-9) 4 or is it (J♠-Q♠) K♠? Most experts would quickly say that the second hand (three high cards in an open-end straight-flush draw) is far more desirable, even though a pair of nines is stronger at the moment. You need to keep in mind that we are examining Seven-Card Stud, not Three-Card Stud. You must, in analyzing the strength of starting hands, consider not merely their strength at the starting gate but their potential for developing into a strong hand later.

So you can't simply look at starting Stud hands in a vacuum. You need to take a look around at the other cards in sight (each of your opponents has one faceup), to gain a better idea of how good or bad your chances of improving are. (Perhaps your three-card starting flush is weak because a bunch of your flush cards are faceup on board.) Later in the chapter, we'll look at different scenarios where, for example, you'll fold your pair of jacks or three-bet it, depending on what the action has been in front of you.

To build on the principle of the best starting hand, let's add the idea that you need to jam with it (put in some raises) in order to give yourself the best chance for this hand to win the pot. Jamming the pot with the best hand in Stud is a time-honored tradition! Jamming will often clear the field right away (because you've made it so expensive to call), giving you fewer opponents and therefore a better chance to win the pot.

What Are the Most Powerful Starting Hands in Stud?

In Texas Hold'em, you will recall, I presented a list of the top ten hands. But in Seven-Card Stud, things are different. The most powerful starting hand in Seven-Card Stud is three aces, which I will be indicating as (A-A) A, followed by (K-K) K, (Q-Q) Q, (J-J) J, and so on; when you start with three of a kind in Stud, you are said, in poker slang, to be "rolled-up."

The next most powerful hand is a pair of concealed aces, such as (A-A) 5, followed by one concealed ace and one unconcealed ace, such as (A-5) A. The reason that the concealed aces (or indeed any concealed pairs) are more powerful than the unconcealed aces is that the concealed pair is more deceptive: no one will think you have a hand as powerful as aces.

Next on my list of powerful hands is a pair of kings—first concealed, followed by unconcealed. Then we have a pair of queens, pair of jacks, pair of tens, and (A-K) Q suited ("suited" means that all three of your cards are in the same suit). The poker legend John Bonetti ranks (A-K) Q suited ahead of (J-J) 10. So our list of powerful starting hands begins with rolled-up trips (three of a kind), moves on to high pairs, and then moves on to high suited connectors like J♠-Q♠-K♠. All these are premium starting hands in Seven-Card Stud.

The premium starting hands, then, are:

1. Three of a kind or "rolled-up" trips, beginning with (A-A) A, then (K-K) K, and so on.
2. High pairs, concealed or unconcealed, starting with aces and moving down to jacks.
3. High suited connectors, such as (A♦-K♦) Q♦ and (J♣-Q♣) K♣.

Strong and medium strength starting hands are:

4. Medium-rank pairs like 8-8 through 10-10 and medium suited connectors, such as 10♠-J♠-Q♠.
5. High suited semiconnectors, such as 10♣-J♣-K♣ or 9♥-J♥-K♥.

Now that you understand what the most powerful Stud hands look like, let's move on down the list and compare a couple of the more modest hands to help you think about which hands are more powerful. Which would you rather have, (10♣-J♣) Q♣ or (8♣-8♣) Q♦? That's close, but give me (10♣-J♣) Q♣. If you understand why I prefer the first hand, you'll have come a long way toward starting to think like a good Seven-Card Stud player, rather than remaining someone who has simply memorized a list of starting hands.

The hand (10♣-J♣) Q♣ contains three overcards above the eights of the other hand. This means that if I hit a ten, jack, or queen (and unless I see more sitting around the table, nine of these are still available: three tens, three jacks, and three queens), I will be a pretty strong favorite to win this hand. By contrast, the hand (8♣-8♠) Q♦ has an equal chance to catch one of the three remaining queens, and a chance to catch one of the two remaining eights to make trips. But take note that I'm comparing these two hands "in a vacuum," not taking into account the visible queen in the hand with the concealed eights.

The contrast between the two doesn't end there, though. Although much of the strength of the hand (10♣-J♣) Q♣ does come from the high cards that can make high pairs, I could also catch cards that could make me a flush or a straight or even a straight flush. If I look around the table and don't see many nines or kings (the cards that would give me an open-end straight draw), the hand's potential grows stronger. It grows stronger still if I don't see many eights or aces (the cards that would complete the straight if I caught a nine or king). But what I'm really keeping my eyes open for are clubs (a flush beats a straight, after all). There are 10 clubs left in the deck after we take my three out of consideration. If no one else has a club for a door card, my chances of making a flush have improved. But if I see four other players who show a club, I can consider my chance of making a flush rather remote.

All this might seem tedious or technical, but if you're not prepared to analyze hands to this extent, you won't ever be serious about Stud. Besides, it will take only a dozen seconds to assimilate all this information.

Here's another comparison for you. Which hand would you

prefer, (5♥-6♥) 7♥ or (9♣-9♦) 10♠? If you've pondered categories 4 and 5 above, you already have your answer, because a medium pair like nines makes category 4, but a low straight flush isn't listed. I agree: give me the pair of nines (9♣-9♦) 10♠, because the straight flush cards are all lower than the pair of nines. Most of the value in the hand (5♥-6♥) 7♥ comes from the potential for straight and flush, and although it looks pretty, the hand is still a long way from making a straight or flush.

How about (10♥-J♠) Q♦ versus (2-2) 7? I'll take (10♥-J♠) Q♦, even though it's not suited, because I could make a straight or a pair of tens, jacks, or queens; and even if none of that happens, I could still beat a measly pair of twos with some random event like hitting a three on fourth street and then another three on fifth street.

Although you may feel that when it comes to getting good starting cards, you're more or less at the mercy of Lady Luck, you should realize that you can make your starting hand seem a bit more powerful than it actually is through aggression, or weaken it through passivity. The hand that's doing the betting always has the edge, because the other hand may fold rather than contest its bet.

Weaker Seven-Card Stud Starting Hands

The weaker Stud hands are the small pairs 2-2 through 7-7 and three low-rank—or even medium-rank—consecutive cards, like (8♣-9♠) 10♦). These hands are usually unplayable, unless you're the first raiser in the pot.

Beginning and Intermediate Strategy: Play It Until the Bets Are Double

We need to talk now about the conditions under which you can play some of those weaker hands. The safest way to play Seven-Card Stud is just to stick to the best starting hands, but it's sometimes reasonable to play some other hands too. There are some hands that many of us like to "take two cards off" with. In other words, many top Stud players will play a speculative hand for the first two rounds of betting, and then throw it away if they don't improve it by then. Many of us will call two small bets on the first and second rounds of betting, and then throw our hand away for the big bet on the third round of betting (fifth street) if we don't improve our start by then. Any concealed pocket pair can be played that way.

For example, I might call one bet in a multiway pot with (6-6) 9, trying to hit a six for hidden trips. I figure that it will cost me one bet on the first round of betting and one bet on the second round of betting; but if I hit my hand I can win three big bets, perhaps more, on the next three rounds of betting. With (6-6) 9, I can hit a six for that very well disguised hand of trips, or perhaps I will hit a seven and an eight, which will give me a pair and an open-ended straight draw. If I hold the latter, which would look like (6-6) 9-7-8, I'm very interested in continuing if the cards I need are live (not all burned on other players' up cards). If I haven't seen too many sixes, fives, or tens folded (or still sitting out there in view), I'm playing on, unless someone else has a board that looks too strong. In fact, I will probably jam it at this point in the hand, in order to test my opponents and see if they all fold their hands right now. You never know when a well-timed raise will win a pot.

Another good hand to take two cards off with is (A-4) 4. Your starting hand in this case is a small pair with an ace kicker. If you do manage to hit the ace or the four, you will wind up with a powerful hand, either aces up or trips. A small pair with a queen or a king kicker is also playable, for similar reasons, but make sure that your kicker is larger than your opponent's pair. For example, (5-K) 5 isn't very attractive if you think you're up against aces, and (3-Q) 3 isn't appealing if it appears that your opponent has a pair of kings. In the case of a pocket pair or a pair with an ace, a king, or a queen kicker, you need hit only one nice card to put yourself in fine shape.

Another good kind of speculative hand is something like (3♦-4♦) 5♦, although you need to hit two cards to make such a hand. Be that as it may, straight-flush draws are good hands to gamble with in multiway pots as well. Do as I say, and not as I occasionally do, and don't play hands like low straight-flush draws with just one opponent! I get myself into a lot of trouble with this hand. I mean, I hate hitting the fourth flush card right away and then having to call the next three bets still drawing. It seems that when you're "flushing," everyone in the game knows it, and everyone keeps betting right on into you, charging you the maximum number of bets. This is one of those times when Lady Luck rears her head and decides whether you'll win some big pots or lose some big pots. If you hit your flush or straight draws, you may win all the chips. If you miss your draws, you're in a lot of trouble!

Beginners: What to Do with Your Hand on the First Round of Betting

It's time now for us to take a look at how different betting scenarios determine how you would act on your hand. Suppose you're playing a $4–$8 game, with the ante $1 and the bring-in $2. (I've gone over the antes, bring-ins, and betting structures for Stud in Chapter 11.)

Assume that the cards have been dealt out so that the up cards are 2, 7, K, 5, 8, Q, 9, and J, and you are the jack, with a hand of (J-7) J (a pair of jacks). Now the two is the low card, and that player must bring in the action for $2.

The Time to Throw Away Your Jacks

The seven folds, the king completes the bet to $4, and the five and the eight fold. Now the queen raises the bet $4, making it $8 to go, and the nine folds. What do you do with your pair of jacks? You throw them away (fold)! There is strong evidence that the queen has in fact a pair of queens, because he raised the king's raise. The king, too, could easily have a pair of kings. Although a pair of jacks is on my list of premium hands, you don't want to play them against a pair of queens, because you're roughly a 2-to-1 underdog against queens. If the king has a pair of kings here (and the queen has queens), then you'd be in really bad shape (a 3.2-to-1 underdog, or worse) trying to beat both a pair of kings and a pair of queens.

The Time to Reraise with Your Pair of Jacks

The seven, king, five, and eight fold; then the queen completes the bet to $4 and the nine folds. What do you do this time with your pair of jacks? You raise the bet, making it $8 to go. Since the queen is the first raiser this time, the queen could have anything, ranging from a bluff (an attempt to win the antes) to three suited cards, three straight cards, a small pocket pair, a pair of queens, or even, heaven forbid, rolled-up queens. You raise here to test the queen. What does the queen have? Is it BS, "the goods," or something in between?

Pay attention to the way the queen acts when it is his turn to act again. Does he call you reluctantly? Does he reraise you? Does he call you quickly? Try to determine, by your best read, whether he is strong or not. If he reraises you, this isn't a good sign, because he probably has your jacks beaten right now. If he just calls, try to guess what he has. Don't limit yourself in your guesses or reads: be willing to consider more than one possibility. The important point is whether he has you beaten right now or not. If you think he does have you beaten, then you should fold your hand as soon as you face a double bet. Usually that's fifth street, but remember that if someone pairs his door card it could be fourth street. Of course, if your opponents decide to give you a free card by checking, accept the gift gracefully and see what the free card brings: don't fold (as I have seen plenty of players do) simply because you know you're losing, unless someone bets.

The idea is to put money in the pot when you're a favorite, and fold when you are a clear underdog. Another beautiful thing about making your best guess about what your opponent has, by reading the way he acts, is that you will usually find out what he has anyway, and then you can adjust your guess next time. The art of determining whether people are bluffing or not is definitely something that can be learned.

The Time to Make It Three Bets to Go with Your Pair of Jacks

The seven completes the bet to $4 and the king, five, eight, and queen fold. Now the nine raises the bet $4, making it $8 to go. What do you do with your pair of jacks? You reraise the bet $4, to make it $12 to go. Unless someone has a pair larger than your jacks in the hole—for example, something like (K-K) 7—or trips, you have the best hand. (The visible king and queen folded, remember.) You raise your opponents early in order to determine if you have the best hand or not. If the seven has only a pair of sevens, then he should fold his hand right there, right now, because he shouldn't be trying to play his pair of sevens against your pair of jacks for $8 more. In the low-limit games that you'll presumably be playing in when you're starting out (even after reading my book, you should start small: nodding in agreement while you're reading is different from live play), you'll find that the pair of sevens will *not* usually fold his hand in this case, and that's good for you. Anyway, be mindful of the way your opponents act when they call or reraise you when it becomes their turn to act again. If the seven or nine reraises you, this is a pretty good indication that either he's a true megalomaniac or (more likely) that he has your pair of jacks beaten.

This scenario has shown how you should act on your hand on the first round of betting. It also gives you some basic understanding of the value of your hand and how that value changes, depending on which other hand is doing the raising and reraising. Now I want to look at other considerations that you need to think about on this round of betting. Right now let's examine slow-playing your hands in Seven-Card Stud. Then we'll see how paying attention to the other cards on the board will help you play your hand better.

Slow-Playing Your Hands in Seven-Card Stud

In 1997, I went to the Taj Mahal in Atlantic City to play in U.S. Poker Championships. While I was there, I began to play a lot of $300- to $600-limit Seven-Card Stud in the side games. These games were terrific and I was running hot, and before long I found myself ahead more than $250,000, even though the main purpose of my trip had been to play the tournament, not the side games! One thing that kept working well for me was trapping the overaggressive Stud players when I had a big hand. So when I had A-A in the pocket, I would just call the raises on the first round of betting and see what happened. Sometimes I wouldn't even put a raise in until sixth street, but usually I would start to play my hand hard on fifth street. This strategy worked like a charm for me. Imagine—I would start with (A-A) 7, and the queen next to me was so busy raising the ten next to him that he never saw me coming! I ended up involved in a lot of big pots where I had the best hand. Of course, I lost a lot of those pots because I let other opponents in by not raising them out early: I was hot, but not untouchable. Still, I would usually clear most of my opponents out of the pot when I finally put a raise in on fifth

street, because now the bets were double. So I would wait in the
weeds, slow-playing my hand, and then pounce on fifth street to
get the pot down to two players, most of the time. One reason
this strategy worked so well for me was that most Stud players
are very aggressive. They were so aggressive in Atlantic City that
they would raise the other players if they thought there was *any*
chance that they had the best hand. This would leave me heads-
up with a big pot and the best hand! That is the scenario I long
for in poker. One opponent, a big pot, and I have the better hand!

Although slow-playing is a legitimate strategy in Stud, it can
also get you into trouble. I think I might have overdone it a bit in
Atlantic City, but I was running so hot that it didn't matter—at
least on that trip. I almost never slow-play my hands when I'm
playing in a Stud tournament. I've found that this confuses the
other players too much, and then they put more bad beats on me
with their otherwise unplayable hands. In other words, I lose
more pots when I slow-play my hands, and you can't afford to
do that in tournaments. In the side games, you can afford to lose
some pots through slow-playing, because the pots you do win are
usually bigger.

Watch the Other Players' Up Cards for Information

The best Stud players in the world always know what all the up
cards are (or were, if some were folded) during any given hand.
If you have a pocket pair or a flush draw and you're thinking
about calling or raising with your hand on the first round of betting, make sure you study the other players' up cards very care-

fully before you act. If you have (7-7) 6, and you're thinking about calling an opponent's opening bet, then seeing even one seven on the board should make you fold your hand. Similarly, if you're considering calling a bet with (8♠-10♠) K♠, and you see three other spades on the board, you should know that it will be pretty hard for you to make your flush. When I have a pair of kings, I'm always paying close attention to where the aces (if any) are. I know that when I have a pair of jacks in Stud, such as (9-J) J, my opponents are likely to try to hit their small pairs with a queen, a king, or an ace kicker, so I keep a sharp eye out for these overcards!

Winning the Pot with a Draw

I like to play my drawing hands very aggressively in Seven-Card Stud. When I have four cards to the flush in the first four cards, I like to start jamming the pot in case my opponent has a hand too weak for him to call me down with. At the final table of the European Championships (the Poker EM), which I won in 2000, I was the low card up holding (A♦-7♦) 4♦. An opponent in early position raised the pot and I called his raise, because I was the bring-in bet, and it didn't cost me a full bet to call. The limits were $2,000–$4,000, and my next card was 6♦, for a hand of (A♦-7♦) 4♦, 6♦. My opponent bet another $2,000 into me, and I decided that I had better raise it (make it two bets, or $4,000, to go) in case he had a weak hand. When he called me, I paired my six, for (A♦-7♦) 4♦, 6♦, 6♠, and I bet out and he folded. Whew! His fold enabled me to win the $14,000 pot right there, without a fight.

Had I just called my opponent's bet on the second round of betting, would he have folded his hand when I paired my sixes and bet out on the third round of betting? Maybe, but maybe not, so by playing the hand correctly, I won it without having to hit my hand. If I hadn't raised, and then missed my flush and lost the hand, would I have been "unlucky" to have lost, when I had a nice hand like a four flush with a pair? No! I would have created my opportunity to lose. That's not bad luck, that's bad play. Good play enabled me to prevail without the need for luck. Make sure that you always play your flush draws very aggressively, because you'll have to play them until the end anyway. How different is it if you're betting or calling someone else's bets all the way through a hand with a flush draw? A lot! You'll win the pot if your opponent folds his hand when you're doing the betting.

Throwing Your Hand Away When Your Opponent Pairs His Door Card

Beware of an opponent pairing his door card in Seven-Card Stud (the door card is the first board card that you start with in Stud). Often, a player starts a hand with a split pair, and when he pairs his door card, he's made trips right away. If he does have trips and you have a pair whose rank is higher than his trips, you can win only if you hit your trips—but there are only two of your cards left in the deck!

In other words, look to fold your hand right away when your opponent pairs his door card. You just don't want to continue to play a hand when you feel you're an underdog by a huge margin. If my opponent pairs his door card on fourth or fifth street, I will almost always fold my hand immediately. If he pairs his door card on sixth street, then before I make my decision I check to see if I have a straight draw or a flush draw or two pair (less enticing, but still a possible call if the pot is large enough). If I have one of these draws, I will usually call my opponent's bet. If I have only one pair without any draws, I will usually fold my hand, unless I strongly believe that my opponent has a flush draw and only one pair.

Throwing Your Hand Away When Your Opponent Hits an Overpair on the Board

You've started the hand with (K-K) 7 and your opponent has started his showing a nine. Then he hits 4-A-A for a board of 9-4-A-A, and bets into you. I know that you want to call him; most amateur players do! I know that the pot is big, but if you simply have one pair of kings without any other draws, then it's time to fold your hand! I know that most of you who are reading this want to try to catch a king or even a second pair, but "the price is wrong"! The opponent with the pair of aces most likely has two pair (aces up), and in this case you can win the pot only by catching a third king! The chances of your hitting a third king are minute, so when the pair of aces bets out into you, simply fold your hand and accept the loss. Don't forget: even though his most likely hand is aces up (in which case you could win only if you hit a king, anyway), he could have trip aces and you not only could be drawing dead but could lose a fortune even if you do happen to catch the third king.

By the way, when your opponent hits an open pair of aces it is usually a good time for you to fold two pair as well. Think about it: if you call trying to make a full house, then you'll also call on the end, just in case your opponent has only one pair. So it can cost you two or three big bets to call your opponent all the way to the end. Still, you need to decide your move by your read of the situation. Perhaps you think your opponent has a pair of aces and a flush draw against your two pair, and in this case you can call him down. On the other hand, he may not have any straight or flush cards showing when he hits his open aces, and in this case it's easy to read him for two pair. But the math just isn't right for you to call with your two pair when your opponent has aces up.

Likewise, when an opponent hits a pair on the board that outranks the pair you have, it's almost always right to fold your hand. Of course, there are exceptions, such as when you have (2-A) 2-K-Q-7 (a pair of twos with three big cards), and your opponent has a board of 6-4-9-9. In this case (he didn't pair his door card), it seems likely that you'll win the pot if you hit a deuce, a queen, a king, or an ace. Another exception is when you have a straight or a flush draw along with your pair. The general rule in this case is: fold your hand if your opponent hits a bigger pair on the board than you have in your hand.

One Final Thought: Don't Fight the Math

When you decide to try to win with the worst hand in poker, we professional players call that "chasing." Chasing can be defensible if the pot is large compared with the amount you have to invest in the chase, *and* if you have enough "outs" (cards that might win for you). Even though that last sentence is true, I almost didn't want to include it here, because beginners usually chase far too often and without nearly enough reward waiting for them (that is, the pot is too small compared with the amount they invest while chasing), and I don't want to give you an excuse to make a poor play. Often, the math just isn't right for you to attempt chasing down your opponent. Trying to fight the math is a bad move in poker! Save your chips for the hand where you're the mathematical favorite, and then bet them. Seven-Card Stud can be looked at just that simply: play pots when you're a mathematical favorite, not when you're a mathematical underdog. If you can do this, then I will see you someday at the World Series of Poker!

Chapter 13

Seven-Card Stud Low (Razz) Strategy

The object of Seven-Card Stud Low, or Razz, is to make the worst hand possible! Razz is dealt just like basic Seven-Card Stud, but the object, oddly enough, is to make the lowest hand. In Razz, flushes and straights don't count against you (that is, they have no value). But pairs and trips are bad (because it is harder to make a five-card low hand with them). Aces are considered low. In Razz, the best possible low hand is 5-4-3-2-A, which is called a wheel. The second-best possible low hand is a six perfect, or 6-4-3-2-A. The chart on page 291 shows a list of the best possible low hands in order.

You will eventually figure out that it isn't that hard to discern which low hand is best in close cases. A seven-five low (7-5-x-x-x) is lower than a seven-six low (7-6-x-x-x). A seven-six-five-three low (7-6-5-3-x) is lower than a seven-six-five-four low (7-6-5-4-x). Figuring out the best low hand is just a matter of

♣ ♥ The Best Low Hands from Best to Worst ♦ ♠

1. 5-4-3-2-A	21. 7-6-5-4-3	41. 8-7-5-2-A
2. 6-4-3-2-A	22. 8-4-3-2-A	42. 8-7-5-3-A
3. 6-5-3-2-A	23. 8-5-3-2-A	43. 8-7-5-3-2
4. 6-5-4-2-A	24. 8-5-4-2-A	44. 8-7-5-4-A
5. 6-5-4-3-A	25. 8-5-4-3-A	45. 8-7-5-4-2
6. 6-5-4-3-2	26. 8-5-4-3-2	46. 8-7-5-4-3
7. 7-4-3-2-A	27. 8-6-3-2-A	47. 8-7-6-2-A
8. 7-5-3-2-A	28. 8-6-4-2-A	48. 8-7-6-3-A
9. 7-5-4-2-A	29. 8-6-4-3-A	49. 8-7-6-3-2
10. 7-5-4-3-A	30. 8-6-4-3-2	50. 8-7-6-4-A
11. 7-5-4-3-2	31. 8-6-5-2-A	51. 8-7-6-4-2
12. 7-6-3-2-A	32. 8-6-5-3-A	52. 8-7-6-4-3
13. 7-6-4-2-A	33. 8-6-5-3-2	53. 8-7-6-5-A
14. 7-6-4-3-A	34. 8-6-5-4-A	54. 8-7-6-5-2
15. 7-6-4-3-2	35. 8-6-5-4-2	55. 8-7-6-5-3
16. 7-6-5-2-A	36. 8-6-5-4-3	56. 8-7-6-5-4
17. 7-6-5-3-A	37. 8-7-3-2-A	57. 9-4-3-2-1
18. 7-6-5-3-2	38. 8-7-4-2-A	58. 9-5-3-2-1
19. 7-6-5-4-A	39. 8-7-4-3-A	
20. 7-6-5-4-2	40. 8-7-4-3-2	

The Best Low Hands

reading the low hand from the highest card to the lowest card and seeing which hand goes lower first. I once lost a $15,000 pot to the legendary Seymour Liebowitz in a low-ball event at the World Series of Poker when his 9-7-5-4-2 beat my 9-7-5-4-3 low. It came down to the fifth and final card in this case! We both had a 9-7-5-4 in our hands, but his deuce "pipped" my three (edged it out by one point in value).

Right now Razz is something of a fringe game in the poker world. In fact, most poker rooms don't even spread a Razz game these days. Although we have a Razz World Championship each year, it is among the lowest-attended events at the WSOP. Still, Razz is an important game that is played for high stakes on a daily basis in Los Angeles at the Commerce Casino. Razz is also often included in high-stakes games at the Bellagio in Las Vegas, sometimes dealt just by itself, but more commonly dealt as part of a rotation of games like HORSE (Hold'em, Omaha, Razz, Stud, and Stud Eight or Better). By the way, sometimes while playing HORSE, the players will not notice that the game has changed—for instance, when the game goes from one variation of Stud to the next—and they lose a large pot because of this! It happens to everyone, including me, more than once.

Even though many top professional players feel that Razz involves more luck and requires less skill than most other poker games, I feel that Razz demands a lot of skill. In Razz, reading your opponents well is crucial to being a great player. If you're reading your opponents well, you can make some calls or folds that other players cannot make. The reading part comes when your opponent hits what appears to be a perfect low card for him. If you read that it was, indeed, perfect for him, then you'll need to fold your hand (depending on what you caught). If you read that the card in fact paired him, then you'll be able to continue playing your hand. For example he might hit a three, for a board of (x-x) 2-3, but there is a decent chance that the card paired him, because, presumably, he is starting with all low cards in his hand.

In Razz it's important to play tight, make well-timed bluffs, and steal the antes on the first round of betting. In other words, in many ways Razz is a lot like all the other poker games in this book.

In this chapter you will learn:

▮ The Razz starting hands that you can play no matter what the cost.

▮ That the up cards in Razz determine the strength of your hand.

▮ That the up cards in Razz tell you when to make an "ante steal."

▮ Why you should jam your strong three-card starting hands.

▮ The argument for slow-playing in Razz.

▮ Which hand is favored to win after five cards.

▮ How to "represent" hands in Razz.

▮ What "board lock" is in Razz.

▮ When you should fold your hand.

▮ When to call a bet as the bring-in bettor.

The Best Playable Hands in Razz

A-2-3 is the best possible starting hand in Razz. Any combination of cards between an ace and a five (but no pairs or trips!) is considered a great starting hand in Razz. The 3-4-5 is the worst possible starting hand among any of the highly desirable ace-to-five combinations of cards, but there really isn't much difference between 3-4-5 and A-2-3. Generally any hand that contains three cards between an ace and a seven is considered playable for any number of bets on the first round of betting.

The starting requirements for a Razz hand are very easy to remember. Basically, you want to play all hands that have three cards between an ace and an eight, unless there's a lot of raising going on right away, in which case you want to start with a three-card seven or better. Three-card eights should be routinely folded when they're up against two players who appear to have better hands. The time to play a three-card eight that doesn't appear to be the best hand would be when you're heads up (one on one) in a pot; that way you're trying to outdraw just one player, instead of two. Three-card eights are good "ante-stealing" hands or even good hands to reraise an opponent with when you suspect that he's weak.

The Up Cards Will Determine the Strength of Your Hand

In Razz, there will be times when you'll fold your starting hand of (2-3) 9. There will also be times when you will reraise someone with (2-7) 10. It all depends on what you see among the starting up cards—the combination of cards (one each) that your opponents are dealt, faceup, to start the hand. When the starting up cards around the table are K, Q, J, Q, 10, and 10, your hand situation is quite different from when you're facing up cards of, say, A, 2, 3, 3, A, and 7. In the first case, the best possible starting hand out there is (A-2) 10. In the second case, the best possible starting hand is (A-2) 3, and *five players* could have starting hands consisting of an ace-to-five mix of cards! With the first "rough" board above, reraising with (2-7) 10 as a starting hand would be a good play. With the second "smooth" board above, you couldn't play even (8-6) 7 for a raise! So the up cards, in these and many other cases, determine your hand strength in Razz.

The Up Cards Sometimes Tell You What to Do

If you have the only up card below a ten to start a hand, then in effect you don't even need to look at your hole cards! This is a good automatic situation for you to raise from, and thus steal the antes, though I'd recommend that you do look at your hole cards. If your opponents see that you haven't looked at your hole cards and know that they have something reasonable in the hole themselves, they may call a bet to which they otherwise would have responded by folding.

Automatic Steal When You're the Only Low Card

Suppose that the up cards are K (the high card required to bring in the bet), J, 7 (your own up card), 10, J, and Q. The king brings it in for about one-fourth of the full bet. (We learned about bring-in bets for Stud in Chapter 11 on page 260.) Now the jack folds. Make sure that you now raise it, completing it to the full opening bet. This will probably force everyone behind you to fold. You're hoping to win everyone's ante, and it's very unlikely that anyone will call you in this situation. Because no one can call you, you always need to make this raise, even if you have K-K in the hole, in order to win the antes.

Automatic Raise When It's You versus the High Bring-In Card

Suppose that the up cards are K (the bring-in bet), 4, 7, Q, J, 6 (your up card). The king once again brings it in for about one-fourth of the full bet size and everyone else folds to you, with your six up. It doesn't matter what your hole cards are in this case, because you have to raise by completing the bet to one full-size bet, in order to win all the ante money already in the pot. In this case the king is the only card behind you, and he'll fold most of the time, allowing you to win the pot. Even if you have (A-2) 6 as a hand, you don't want to give the king a free card here. This is just an automatic raise.

Semiautomatic Raise: Stealing the Antes

Suppose now that the up cards are Q (the bring-in bet), 4, 10, J, 5 (your up card), and 3. The queen opens for about one-fourth of a full bet, and now the four, ten, and jack all fold to you. If you raise (complete the bet to one full-size bet) with your five up, and the three and the queen fold, then you've won all the ante money. This is thus a good place to raise in order to try to bluff out the three and the queen and steal the antes. You're risking one bet in order to win about two bets. The exact amount you're trying to win will vary with what the ante structure is, but at almost any normal ante structure the math says to raise and steal the blinds!

Of course, if you sense that the three has a strong hand and you don't have anything, then you can fold your hand instead. (It's amazing how many times people give away the strength of their hands in poker!) The world's greatest Razz player, Ted Forrest (who gives us a world-class tip at the end of this chapter), says that he will sometimes let his hand decide whether or not he will try a steal in this situation. If Ted has a hand that contains three low cards, like (5-7) 5 or even (5-5) 5, then he'll try to steal; but if he has (10-J) 5, he won't. His rationale is that if he has some low cards, it's a lot less likely that his lone opponent will have any.

Starting with the Best Possible Hand

Suppose that the up cards are Q (the bring-in bet), 8, 9, 10, 9, and 7 (you). When you have a three-card seven like (4-5) 7 or (A-6) 7, then you have the best hand in the field at this point. Your opponents' best possible hand is (A-2) 8, because an eight is the lowest card on the board, other than your seven. In this case, it's time to jam it up and build a nice-size pot! What's especially nice here is that although you have the best up card, your opponents won't necessarily give you credit for having a strong hand, and you stand a good chance of getting action on your raise.

Another aspect of paying close attention to what the up cards are at the start of a hand is to check for cards that protect your hand. For example, your three-card smooth eight will be a favorite over someone else's three-card seven if you look around the board and notice that your three starting cards appear in abundance. (If these cards that would pair you are already burned as other players' up cards, you won't hit any of them later.) Again, because all these "bad" cards (for you) are no longer available in the deck to hit your hand, your hand is much stronger than it would be otherwise.

It's also important to remember all the exposed up cards between an ace and a nine, so that you'll have a good idea of whether a card was likely to have made your opponent's hand, or to have paired him. For example, you might have noted that the folded up cards were 3, K, 7, 3, 8, and now you know that a three is a "joker" for your opponent (the best possible card for him to catch), because with two threes out, it is less likely that he already had one in the hole. You might even catch a three yourself that pairs you, leaving you, for example, (3-5) 7, 2, 3; but the same expectations might now win you the pot with a bet, because your opponents will notice that you caught a card that is unlikely to have paired you—in this case, it is *you* who caught what appears to be a joker.

Duplicated Cards in Your Hand

Suppose that the up cards are Q (the bring-in bet), 4, 4, 5, 8 (your card), and 7. If you have (4-5) 8 for a hand, then you're a favorite to win the pot over any three-card seven behind you who doesn't have a four in his hand. Remember that only one four and two fives are left in the deck at this point for the seven to hit, while you happily find yourself the owner of hole cards that are in short supply. Pay close attention to little things like this when you play Razz, and you'll soon learn that they aren't "little" at all. Of course, if the three-card seven keeps raising you, then he may have the last (often called the "case") four in his hand already.

Why You Should Jam It in Razz with Your Strong Hands in Three

The reason why you should jam it (raise and reraise) in Razz when you have the best starting hand is so that you can call on the next round of betting when you catch a bad card. If you're just calling in the early rounds and letting other hands into the pot right away, you may put yourself in a situation where you pretty much have to fold on the very next round of betting.

Jamming Keeps You in the Pot

Suppose that the up cards are J (the bring-in bet), 6, 7, 8, 5, and 6 (you). The jack brought it in for about one-fourth of one bet, and the first six completed the bet (raised it) to one full bet. Now the seven calls the bet and you have (A-3) 6. I recommend that you raise it here, making it two bets to go. That way you're making sure that you get to see both the fourth and the fifth cards. If you just call the bet and then the first six catches a four, the seven catches a five, and you catch a queen, it could easily happen that the 6-4 bets out and the 7-5 raises, leaving you forced to fold your (A-3) 6-Q hand. In fact, folding your hand is the correct play here, but, if you had reraised before the flop, you could now call two bets with that hand (barely). The math is much better for a call later when you have built the pot up in the first round of betting with your strong starting hand. The larger pot makes "chasing" to see if you get back into the driver's seat on fifth street more sound. Your show of strength on the first round may also let you in more cheaply on fourth street, even if you do catch a bad card and your opponents catch what are apparently good ones. (Your opponents now know that you're committed to the pot, and thus they may not charge you two bets.)

Another reason to reraise with a strong starting hand is that your opponent may have a problem with his hand. I have reraised my opponents on three cards and then watched as they threw their hands away, allowing me to win the pot uncontested. (Perhaps they all had junk like K-K in the hole!) Or it might be that a six raises and you have (3-4) 7. A reraise here makes the pot bigger and ensures that you will see a fifth card. Manipulating the size of the pot is important in Razz.

The Argument for Trapping in Razz

I don't much like trapping in Razz, but I do trap sometimes in order to throw the other players off and induce them to draw dead (with hopeless prospects). If you trap with a hand like (A-2) 5, you can sometimes get a lot of action later on in the hand when you make a very strong hand. By pretending that you're weak and just calling the other players' bets and raises on the first and second rounds of betting, you may find yourself in a great situation by the end of the hand. By the time you finally do put in your raise, they don't think that you have anything worth worrying about.

One day I was playing three-handed $800–$1,600 Razz in Los Angeles at the Commerce Casino when I saw an opportunity to trap. The low card (a ten) brought it in for $200 and the nine next door completed the bet to $800. I had (A-3) 6 and decided that it would look like a trap if I just called the $800. So I raised the bet to $1,600 to go. I was acting just as I had acted the last time I bluffed a pot (using the same mannerisms and betting pattern), and I could tell that both of my opponents thought I looked weak while they called. In fact, it looked as if the nine wanted to reraise me and make it $2,400 to go! Anyway, I caught a four for (A-3) 6-4, and both of my opponents caught perfect low cards. I decided that checking would be the perfect play, since they both thought I was weak and they had both caught perfectly. So I checked, the ten bet out, and the nine called the bet. I just called, thinking that I might be able to trap my opponents for a really big pot on the next few rounds of betting. At this point I had one of the best possible hands, but I was still sure they thought I had nothing.

The next cards brought me a queen for (A-3) 6-4-Q, and both opponents hit OK cards. I decided that betting out would confuse them, so I bet $1,600 and the 10-2-8 made it $3,200. Now the 9-7-10 called the $3,200! The fact that the 10-9-7 called was a surprise, and now I decided it was time to let the cat out of the bag. I reraised, making it $4,800 to go. They both quickly called (I had made it obvious that I had a very strong draw, but it was clear that at least for the moment the best I could have had was a queen low). The next card brought me an eight for (A-3) 6-4-Q-8. Their up cards were now 10-2-8-7 and 9-7-10-2. I bet out, and now they both just called me. I knew that the first opponent had made an eight low (but the best she could have was an eight-seven low to my eight-six low) and the second opponent had made a nine low, and that they were both drawing to beat me! This was unfortunate, because I could just as easily have caught a card that would have shut them both out and guaranteed that I would win the pot (a two, five, or seven would have done it).

But I've lost plenty of pots in situations like this one, and I knew the eight I caught was a very good card for me; at least it gave me the best hand. I could have caught another "paint" (face card) and been trailing with one card to go. On the end, I bet out without looking at my last card and the first player actually folded her eight low! Now the second player called and I said, "Eight-six low so far." He said, "Seven low." I said, "What? Let me look at my last card." I was stunned that my opponent had caught two perfect cards in a row to make a seven low! Luckily for me, I caught a seven on the last card to make a better seven low than my opponent had. I say "luckily," and certainly it was fortunate that I caught the seven, but I had put myself in position to win by drawing to a stronger hand than my opponent had been drawing to. Wow, what a nice $30,000 card the seven was!

If I had played my hand fast all the way, the pot wouldn't

have been as big as it was. My trap fooled both of my opponents and allowed me to win a much larger pot than I was "supposed" to win with this hand.

A Razz Trap Gone Awry!

I've been telling you about a hand where the trap worked perfectly, but now I need to tell you about a time when the trap cost me a huge pot! In a four-handed $600–$1,200 Razz game, the following hand came up between Johnny Chan and me. (In 2002, Johnny passed me and became the all-time leading money winner in the history of the World Series of Poker—with more than $3 million.) I had started the hand with (A-5) 4 and I simply called the $200 bring-in bet—in order to trap Johnny, who was sitting right behind me. He completed the bet to $600 with what I eventually learned was (A-A) A, a pure bluff! In other words, I was getting exactly what I wanted! I had trapped Johnny into playing (A-A) A, one of the worst possible starting hands in Razz! So I just called his $400, and now I caught a six, for (A-5) 4-6, and I checked to Johnny, who caught a seven for A-7 on the board.

I checked again, knowing that I had an extremely strong hand. Johnny bet out into me with his A-7, and I smooth-called him once again, pretending to be weak. The next card brought a five for me and a hand of (A-5) 4-6-5. Johnny caught a five as well, for A-7-5 on the board. I checked again, but now I was worried that he had a strong hand, because I judged that the five probably hadn't paired him. (I didn't think he had a five in the hole, as I had two fives myself.)

I checked again, Johnny bet out $1,200, and I just called. I was no longer thinking about trapping Johnny; I was concerned that he had a strong hand, and I was worried about whether or not I could win the pot! On sixth street I caught a queen, for a hand of (A-5) 4-6-5-Q, and Johnny caught a nine for a board of A-7-5-9. Johnny was now low, so he bet $1,200 into me, and I called. Now I was sure that Johnny had at least one good card to go with his four-card nine on board. In other words, I was sure that he had at least a nine low at this point in the hand.

My last (down) card was an ugly-looking king, for a final hand of (A-5) 4-6-5-Q (K), and Johnny bet out $1,200 into me. I didn't even consider calling the bet with my queen low, so I said, "Look at what I was trapping you with. I had a six-low draw after four cards! You're pretty lucky to win this pot. All I could make was a queen low." Johnny chuckled and showed me that he had started with three aces on a pure bluff, but on the last card he had caught a jack and bluffed into me with his jack low (A-5-7-9-J was his five-card low hand, after he discarded A-A). As it turned out, I couldn't have beaten his jack low anyway with my queen low. (He was bluffing with the best hand, something that happens more often than you might think when you make what you believe is a successful bluff.) But talk about opening the door for someone! If I had just opened the pot for $600 in the first place, then I would almost surely have won it right there on the opening bet. It's not often that (A-A) A can make a better low than (A-4) 5. It's also interesting that I was trapping Johnny in the same hand that he was trying to bluff me out on. We were both putting moves on each other. This is a case where the trap cost me a lot of money.

Who Is the Favorite after Five Cards?

One of the fascinating features of Razz is that the best drawing hand after five cards is the favorite over an *already made* nine low! This seems counterintuitive to most of us. Often in poker, we want to have the "made hand," not the drawing hand. If you have (A-3) 5-7-Q and your opponent has (A-3) 4-8-9, you are—curiously enough—a favorite to win the pot. I've seen people get confused by this and put in a bunch of raises with a made nine with two cards left to be dealt and then bemoan their bad luck later, saying, "I had the made hand; I was pretty unlucky to lose that pot." I've been tempted to say, "Not exactly, pal; you were the underdog." But I try not to correct players' perceptions, because I might be in the same position against them the next time around. So take the best drawing hand, not a made nine, with two cards to come in Razz.

Of course, with just *one* card to come the made nine is a big favorite (roughly 5 to 3) over the seven draw. With one card to come, I love having the best hand in a big Razz pot, especially if it's an eight low or better.

Representing a Hand in Razz after You Make a Hidden Pair

In Razz, when you make a hidden pair (when you make a pair with one of your down cards and no one can see it), it's important that you bet anyway. I wouldn't suggest betting out into two other opponents in this situation if they both hit perfect-looking low cards; but if you're going to call a bet anyway, then why not lead out with a bet? Certainly you should lead out if you hit a low hidden pair and your opponent catches a bad card, because you may win the whole pot right there for a single bet. Let's look at some examples of what can happen in a Razz pot when you lead out with a hidden pair.

Suppose you have raised a pot with (A-8) 5 and your opponent has called with a six showing. Now you catch an ace for (A-8) 5-A and your opponent catches a jack. If you bet out here, representing that the ace was a good card for you, your opponent may actually fold his hand right there and let you win the pot, even though you caught a card that was in reality worse than his jack.

But let's suppose now that your opponent calls you after you've bet out. Let's say that you hit another ace and your opponent catches a four, for a board of 6-J-4, while you have (A-8) 5-A-A. What do you do now? First, there is a 30 to 45 percent chance that your opponent has made a pair of hidden fours in this case. (I say 30 to 45 percent because I'm assuming that he has three cards to a seven or an eight in order to call your bet after you hit your ace on the fourth card.) So if his hole cards are some combination of A (the only one left), 2, 3, 4, 5, 7, and 8, then there are roughly six hidden pair cards and seventeen nonpair cards for him to hit. If he does make a hidden pair, then in most cases you'll win the pot by making a bet. So I advise you to bet out bluffing, even though you have trip aces in this situation!

Another reason to bet is that if you just check, your opponent will know that there's something wrong with your hand,

and he may bluff you out even though he paired up with his hand! A roughly 35 percent chance of winning the pot with a bet is good enough for me to bet out! (If you lose, so what? If you don't bet you'll lose anyway.)

Conversely, if *you* have the 6-J-4 hand, and the four didn't pair you, and it's your opponent who has the 5-A-A board, you should raise him if he bets, because he may have a really weak hand and your raise may win you the pot. By raising the 5-A-A board, you are shutting him out from catching two perfect cards in a row to beat you. In other words, if he does have the (A-8) 5-A-A hand (three aces), your raise will force him to fold his hand. And if he does have that hand and you *don't* raise, he may catch a good card on the next card and go on to beat you or even bluff you out. Razz is a very complicated game in which a well-timed raise can go far toward winning or losing any given pot.

Look for the Old "Board-Lock" Situation

A lot of times you will have your opponent "board-locked." This means you're certain that (at least at the moment) you have a better hand than he can possibly have, no matter how good his hole cards are. If you have an eight low or better and you have your opponent board-locked, then go ahead and raise as many times as he wants to raise you.

Suppose that after six cards you have (A-2) 8-5-6-9, and your opponent has a board of 8-6-J-5. You can clearly see that the best hand he could possibly have at this point is 8-6-5-2-A

low. You already have 8-6-5-2-A, so the best he can be is tied
with you at this point. Make sure to raise him as many times as
you can! He may not see that you could have him board-locked,
or he may think that his 8-6-5-3-A is better than what you have.
These situations come up in Razz when the hands are close, but
when you do have your opponent board-locked, with an eight or
better low, make sure to jam up the pot. Remember, though,
what I said earlier about the better draw being a favorite over a
made nine on fifth street.

Conversely, your opponent may have you board-locked.
When your opponent is jamming the pot against you, make
sure that he can't have you board-locked before you put in too
many bets.

When It's Time to Fold Your Hand in Razz

When I have an eight-low draw and my opponent could already
have a seven-low made, I'm going to fold my eight-low draw
most of the time. (Again, a good read allows you to play outside
this rule.) Let's see some examples.

Don't Draw Weak against Power on the Board

With a hand of (8-5) 4-2-J, and your opponent showing a
powerful board like A-3-4, you will almost always want to fold
your hand when he bets into you. The best hand that you could
make on the next card would be an eight low, whereas your
opponent may already have 5-4-3-2-A, a wheel! At minimum,

you have to figure that he has a better low draw than you have. Folding your hand here is a pretty good idea.

Suppose you catch two bad cards in a row on fourth and fifth streets and your opponent catches two good ones. It doesn't matter that you have already put in three bets each; just bow out.

Don't Try to Hit Two Perfect Cards in a Row

Don't try to "do the Ted Forrest"—hit two perfect cards in a row.

Suppose that you have (A-3) 4 to start, your opponent has a six to start, and you reraise him to start the hand. Now you catch a king, and he catches a deuce. He bets into you and you call. Now he catches an eight and you catch a queen. When he bets his 6-2-8 into you, it's time to fold your (A-3) 4-K-Q. Yes, it was a pretty starting hand, but don't call a big bet on fifth street and hope to hit a perfect card and thus pick up a draw that might or might not get there on the river! That's way too many ifs. It's time to give up and fold this hand.

Alternatively, you have four cards to a nine or worse, and your opponents are betting and raising with smooth-looking boards. Try to avoid drawing to a hand like this for a lot of bets from opponents who are clearly drawing to much stronger hands than you are.

Fold a Four-Card Nine for a Lot of Heat

Suppose you have called two bets with (A-6) 5 and now you catch a nine. Now the player showing a board of 2-3 bets out and the player showing a board of 3-5 raises, so that it's two bets to you to play your (A-6) 5-9. It's time to fold your hand, because it looks as if both of your opponents are drawing better than you are. The problem here is that if just one of them hits his hand, you'll need to catch *two* good cards in order to beat him! Another reason to fold is that you don't know that it's going to be only two bets to see the fifth card. If you do call, you may find that you now have to call a "capped" bet (maximum number of raises allowed) on fourth street if the other players decide to keep raising with their strong hands.

One World-Class Tip from Ted Forrest

This exception to playing three-card sevens is courtesy of Ted Forrest, who is the best Razz player in the world. You can fold a three-card seven when:

1. It is two bets to you, or you have called one bet and it's now two more bets to call.
2. It is a "rough" three-card seven like (6-7) 4 or (3-6) 7 or (6-7) 2. (It's called rough because if you make a seven it will be among the worst possible sevens.)
3. Some of the cards that you need to hit are on the board—for example, an ace and two fives are on the board when you have (7-4) 6.

4. It appears that two or more players have better starting hands than you.

Defending When Yours Is the High Card on the Board

When you're the high bring-in card, at the outset of the hand, there are some situations in which you should call the completion of the bet. Make sure, though, that you call the completion only if you have just one opponent in the pot and have two wheel cards in the pocket (hole).

Suppose that your hand is (4-5) K and your king is the high card on the board. Because your king is the high card on the board, you have to put in the bring-in bet, which is about one-fourth of a full bet. Suppose that everyone else folds, and now someone holding a five completes the bet and you're the only player left in the pot. You can call the other three-fourths of the bet. Of course, if you don't catch a perfect card for your hand right away, it's time to fold your hand.

Remember that if you do catch two perfect cards in a row, you should probably raise it with your draw, since the five could be hiding a weak hand. Using a well-timed raise to give other players a chance to fold their weak hands is always a great move in Razz!

Again, Razz is not a commonly spread game, but it's a good game to become familiar with. This is because mixed games (in which people play several different poker games in rotation, like the HORSE series mentioned earlier) are becoming more popular, and Razz is often included in the mix as players seek to protect themselves against specialists in Seven-Card Stud and Hold'em. Razz is a game that people can learn and become comfortable with in a fairly short time, and if you follow the advice in this chapter you should have a good lead over players who think that Razz is as simple as ABC.

Chapter 14

Seven-Card Stud
Eight or Better Strategy

Seven-Card Stud Eight or Better (which I will call Stud 8/b) is dealt just like Seven-Card Stud. Stud 8/b is a high-low split game (sometimes referred to as Seven-Card Stud High-Low Split) with an eight low qualifier. Right now Stud 8/b is frequently played in high-limit poker games all over the country. In Stud 8/b, one half of the pot goes to the high hand, and the other half goes to the low hand, *if* the low hand is an eight low or better (if it's not, the high hand takes the whole pot). In Stud 8/b, you can use any five of the seven cards that you have for high and any five of the seven cards that you have for low. There is no "declare" on the end in this game: after the last round of betting, you simply flip all seven of your cards over and use the best five low cards for low and the best five high cards for high. For example, if you have a hand of (3♦-4♦) 6♣-8♦-Q♦-A♥ (J♦), then your high hand would be a flush Q♦-J♦-8♦-4♦-3♦ and your low hand would be A-3-4-6-8. If you like, you can use the same five cards for your high hand and your low hand. For instance, you may have (2♦-3♥) 8♥-4♠-5♦-K♠ (6♠) for a hand and use the 6-5-4-3-2 for a six-low, and the same cards (6-5-4-3-2) for a six-high straight high hand. As in all the other professional games, flushes and straights do not count against you in low.

In this chapter you will learn:

▮ How to "qualify" a low hand.
▮ The premium starting hands.
▮ How to play your big pairs on the first round of betting. (Jam it!)
▮ The time to throw away a big pair.
▮ How to play your premium low-type hands on the first round of betting. (Trap!)
▮ When you should throw away your premium low-type hands.
▮ Whether or not you should trap other players with your premium hands.
▮ An advanced way to play the last round of betting.

Scooping the Pot

What the pros are trying to do when they play Stud 8/b is *scoop* the pot—that is, win the whole pot. There are three ways to scoop the pot. First, you may scoop the pot if everyone else folds. Second, you may scoop the pot by making the best high hand when no one has a qualified low hand. Third, you may scoop the pot by making the best high hand and the best qualified low hand.

Qualifying a Low Hand in Stud 8/b

The rules of the game require that you need to have at least an eight low (five cards under an eight, such as A-3-4-6-8) in order to have a chance at the low half of the pot; that's the bad news. The good news is that straights and flushes do not count against you for low. An eight low means you have five low cards, the highest of them an eight, and no two of those five cards are paired (3-5-6-7-8 is an eight low, but 2-2-4-5-8 isn't). A seven low means five low cards seven or less. A six low means five cards six or less. A five low, called a "wheel," is 5-4-3-2-A. A wheel is the best possible low, and at the same time it counts as a five-high straight for high. (Aces swing in this game, meaning that an ace is both the lowest possible card and the highest possible card.) A wheel is one of the most desirable hands you can make when you play Stud 8/b.

For further understanding of a qualified low hand, let's look at the chart on page 316 of all the possible "qualified" lows, from the best possible low (A-2-3-4-5, wheel) to the worst possible eight low (8-7-6-5-4, "straight eight").

All this stuff about qualifying low hands sounds a lot more complicated than it really is. You won't have to memorize this chart in order to understand whether you have a qualified low or not. Rather, if you have an eight or better low in five of your seven cards, then you have a qualified low, period.

I hope that I am not scaring everyone away from Stud 8/b because it seems too complicated to figure out the best low hand! It really isn't. The five lowest cards win. It is really that simple. So 8-7-3-2-A is a worse low than 8-6-5-4-3, which is worse than

All the Qualifying Low Hands for Stud 8/b ♣♥ (in order of best to worst) ♦♠

1. 5-4-3-2-A	20. 7-6-5-4-2	39. 8-7-4-3-A
2. 6-4-3-2-A	21. 7-6-5-4-3	40. 8-7-4-3-2
3. 6-5-3-2-A	22. 8-4-3-2-A	41. 8-7-5-2-A
4. 6-5-4-2-A	23. 8-5-3-2-A	42. 8-7-5-3-A
5. 6-5-4-3-A	24. 8-5-4-2-A	43. 8-7-5-3-2
6. 6-5-4-3-2	25. 8-5-4-3-A	44. 8-7-5-4-A
7. 7-4-3-2-A	26. 8-5-4-3-2	45. 8-7-5-4-2
8. 7-5-3-2-A	27. 8-6-3-2-A	46. 8-7-5-4-3
9. 7-5-4-2-A	28. 8-6-4-2-A	47. 8-7-6-2-A
10. 7-5-4-3-A	29. 8-6-4-3-A	48. 8-7-6-3-A
11. 7-5-4-3-2	30. 8-6-4-3-2	49. 8-7-6-3-2
12. 7-6-3-2-A	31. 8-6-5-2-A	50. 8-7-6-4-A
13. 7-6-4-2-A	32. 8-6-5-3-A	51. 8-7-6-4-2
14. 7-6-4-3-A	33. 8-6-5-3-2	52. 8-7-6-4-3
15. 7-6-4-3-2	34. 8-6-5-4-A	53. 8-7-6-5-A
16. 7-6-5-2-A	35. 8-6-5-4-2	54. 8-7-6-5-2
17. 7-6-5-3-A	36. 8-6-5-4-3	55. 8-7-6-5-3
18. 7-6-5-3-2	37. 8-7-3-2-A	56. 8-7-6-5-4
19. 7-6-5-4-A	38. 8-7-4-2-A	

All the Qualifying Low Hands for Stud 8/b

8-6-5-4-A, and so on. Put it like this: a six low beats a seven low, an eight-six low beats an eight-seven low, a seven-five-three low beats a seven-five-four low, a six-five-four-deuce low beats a six-five-four-three low, and a seven-six-five-three-ace low beats a seven-six-five-three-deuce low. If two people have an eight low, then look to the next card: the lowest wins. If they both have eight-six lows, then look to the next card: the lowest wins. And so on: the first guy to go lower wins. If you want to be scared away from this game, there are reasons a lot better than this one! Once you understand how to figure out which low hand beats which, you will discover that it really is easier than my explanation makes it seem.

When No Low Hand Is Possible, the Best High Hand Wins the Whole Pot

Remember that the low hand (if it qualifies) gets only half the pot. This means that if no one in the pot makes a low, the entire pot is awarded to the best high hand.

When Players Tie for High or Low

In Stud 8/b, it is very rare to see players tie for high or low, but this happens sometimes. If two players tie for low, they split the low half of the pot with the player who won high. This means that the dealer will give half the pot to the high hand (think high half of the pot), and then split the remaining half between the tied low players (think low half of the pot). In this case, the player winning high receives 50 percent of the pot, and the players splitting low receive 25 percent of the pot apiece.

I saw a hand in which two players made the same six-low hand and raised all the high hands out, only to see one of them win the high half of the pot with a pair of twos! In that case, the high half went to the pair of twos, and the low half was split between the players, so that one received three-quarters of the pot and the other one-quarter.

Go for the Low, Hoping to Luck Out and Win Both Ways

In general, the pros like to start with three low cards that can draw to a straight or a flush for high while making a low hand as well. Hands like 3-4-5 or 2-3-4 or 2-4-5 are considered pretty good starting hands, especially when they are suited, since they can in due course win both high and low. I love a situation in which I'm free-rolling to win the whole pot! *Free-rolling* means that you have one side of the pot already locked up (usually the low side) and some draws with a reasonable chance to win the other half of the pot.

A hand like (2-3) 4-A-7 with two cards to come against a hand of (K-9) K-7-8 is free-rolling. The first hand already has a low hand the other player can't beat (7-4-3-2-A), and it can also hit a five for a straight, an ace for a pair of aces, or some combination of two pair (3-4) or trip cards (7-7) to win the whole pot with the last two cards. So the first hand is free-rolling for the high side of the pot, and the opponent holding the pair of kings can win only half the pot.

I'll next list the best possible starting hands in Stud 8/b and explain what makes them powerful. Then I'll talk about how to play hands in Stud 8/b on the first round of betting, and whether or not you should trap your opponents.

The Best Starting Hands in Stud 8/b

The best possible starting hand in Stud 8/b is (A-A) A. The next-best possible starting hand is either (K-K) K or (8-8) 8. The (8-8) 8 is a very deceptive starting hand, since the other players can't be sure if you're going high or low. I would prefer it over the (K-K) K hand for this reason: with (8-8) 8 you can represent that you're going for the low hand, and then force other low draws to fold if it looks as if you've made your low. And of course three eights are not a bad bet for the high hand as well.

Some players believe that (5-5) 5 is a better starting hand than (8-8) 8, for a very logical reason: a hand that holds neither a five nor a ten can't make a straight, which means that a player who starts with three of the fives has not only a strong high hand but also a nice defense against what would otherwise be one of the most likely hands to be out there against his trips (because only one five remains for the low hands to fill a straight with). Also, when you start with a door-card five, it is easier for the other players to fear your low hand, and they may be induced to fold their own low draws. But your opponents are likely to make low trips; and trip eights (the hand that I think is equal to trip fives) will beat trips sixes or sevens (whereas trip fives won't)!

After all the *rolled-up* starting hands (poker slang in Stud for starting with three of a kind), we move on to (A-A) x (preferably, the x is anything between a two and an eight). With a pair of aces and a low card to start a hand, your prospects for scooping the pot are good. You may scoop it with two pair of aces up, aces and a low, like (A-A) 3-4-7-J-(6) for a 7-6-4-3-A low and a pair of aces for high; or with aces up and a low, like (A-A) 2-4-6-6 (3) for aces and sixes as a high and a 6-4-3-2-A for low); or even with just one pair of aces. The next best starting hand is (A-2) 3 suited. With this hand you can make a strong low hand, a flush, a straight, aces up, aces and a low, or just aces.

Next on our list of top hands are (2-3) 4 suited and all the other low suited connectors hands, such as (3-4) 5 or (6-7) 8 or (5-6) 7, including (A-x) x suited, where the x in both cases is a card below an eight. I would rather start with (A-x) x suited than the low suited connected cards mentioned above. But I think that it is pretty close between these two types of hands. In fact, to me, the power of having an ace in your suited low cards outweighs the power of having them connected.

In any case, next on the list is (A-A) x (where x is a nine or higher). One pair of aces wins a lot of pots in Stud 8/b!

Next we have any three unsuited wheel cards (five or lower), one of them an ace, such as (A♦-4♣) 5♠. Then we have three unsuited wheel cards without an ace, such as (2-4) 5.

I would rather start with three flush cards that include an ace and another wheel card (especially if the high card is on the board) than with three nonwheel non-ace straight cards (6-7) 8. I'm talking about hands like (A♦-5♦) K♦ or (A♠-3♥) Q♥ over unsuited hands like (4-5) 6 or (5-6) 7 or (6-7) 8. An ace is almost like having an extra card in this game, because it's the lowest low card and can also make the highest pair. Aces are powerful cards in Stud 8/b!

Next on the list are either three unsuited cards in a row (4♦-5♣) 6♥ or three low cards eight or below with an ace among them, such as (A-5) 6. With all of these three-in-a-row-low hands we're hoping to make both a straight and a low, and scoop the pot. With

The Premium Starting Hands in Stud 8/b

1. Trips like (A-A) A, (K-K) K, (Q-Q) Q all the way to (2-2) 2
2. (A-A) x (x = an eight or lower)
3. (A-x) x (x = five or lower) like (Ac-4c) 5c
4. Low suited connectors like (3d-4d) 5d or (6c-7c) 8c and three flush cards with an ace, all eight and under like (As-4s) 8s
5. (A-A) x (x = a nine or higher)
6. Three unsuited wheel cards with an ace like (Ad-3c) 5s
7. Three unsuited wheel cards without an ace
8. Three suited cards with one ace, one card eight and under, and a card above a nine
9. Three cards eight and under with an ace
10. Three cards in a row like (4-5) 6 and (5-6) 7

Premium Starting Hands in Stud 8/b

the three-low-cards-with-an-ace-among-them hands we're hoping to make both a pair of aces and a low, and scoop the pot.

I would consider all the hands that we've talked about up to this point premium hands.

Now let's talk about some of the other starting hands in Stud 8/b on our list, in order of powerful to weak. If pressed, I must say that I slightly prefer (6-7) 8 over (K-K) 6, although for purposes of deception I love the fact that the kings of the latter are concealed (in the hole) in this case. With (K-K) 6 you're hoping that your pair of kings or two pair of kings up scoops the pot when no one makes a qualified low hand.

Next on our list is a pair of kings, followed by three low cards all under a nine, with a one-card gap between two of them, such as (4-5) 7 or (4-6) 7 or (5-7) 8. Should these hands be rated above K-K on the list? We've already covered three wheel cards in any order, and I would say that the remaining combinations of three low cards under an eight with one gap shouldn't be listed above a pair of kings in value (because it's too hard to make a straight and win the high side of the pot with one of these hands). The last four hands that I have talked about on our list are all very close in value.

Next, I suppose that I like a pair of queens or three flush cards with two of them wheel cards.

Finally, we have small pairs with small kickers, such as (5-6) 5 or (3-3) A or (8-8) 2, and the like. These are very dangerous hands in Stud 8/b. Yes, you can make a low hand with these kinds of hands, but beware—they can get you into a lot of trouble. You might find yourself up against two opponents, one who has a better low draw than you do and one who has a better high draw than you do. I do see some value in a pair of eights and another low card, especially when you're up against a three-card-low hand. The three-card-low hand will need two perfect high cards to beat your pair of eights.

Now let's move on to talk about how you should play your three-card hand on the first round of betting.

A Solid, Safe Strategy for Beginners in Stud 8/b

The best way to play Stud 8/b as a beginner is to play only the premium hands listed in the chart on page 321, plus big pairs like queens and kings, and only the latter while making a few ante steals along the way. By sticking to these hands, you'll be a favorite in most of the hands that you're involved in. This patient strategy is very effective. Why not win money or at least hold your own while you're learning the nuances of a new game?

Beginners' Strategy after Three Cards: Trap or Not?

To trap or not to trap—that is the eternal question in poker! By trapping, I mean that you just call your chief opponent's bets and raises with a powerful starting hand in order to induce your other opponents to continue playing their weaker hands. Lately, though, I seem to have gotten away from trapping in Stud 8/b. I've been playing my powerful starting hands fast (raising and reraising) in order to try to win the antes with them right away. By doing this I'm putting in a lot of money right away in order to try to scale down the field and give myself a better chance of scooping the whole pot.

But this strategy hasn't been working too well for me. Jamming with 3-4-5 against pocket kings and clearing out the field has made it easier for the kings to call me down, and it's hard to scoop kings with 3-4-5! And jamming with 3-4-5 against A-5-6 hasn't been working too well either. But by playing your strong starting hands aggressively at the beginning of the hand, you do increase your chances of winning the pot. Is jamming the pot on the first round of betting the right way to do it? Although I think this is the right way to do it if you have a high starting hand, it may be better to trap with your powerful low hands. By trapping in Stud 8/b with a low hand, I'm putting in less money right away with my powerful hand and allowing some other, weaker hands into the pot. With a starting hand of (3-4) 5, should I simply try to win the antes right away? Well, you *should* complete the bet (make it one full bet to go, rather than just call the one-quarter-size bring-in bet), but do not reraise if someone else completes the bet too. Why not risk a small amount of money, so that if you do catch two bad cards you don't lose very much? And if you do hit some nice cards, you'll have a lot of players in there paying you off when you make your six-high straight (which will most likely win the low half *and* the high half of the pot)!

It boils down to this: trapping with powerful low hands will allow you to lose less when you catch bad cards and win more when you hit good ones. The downside is that you'll win *fewer* pots right away, in the first round of betting. I've been most successful when trapping with my low hands and playing my high hands fast.

Beginners' Strategy: Trap with the Low, Jam with the High

When you have a good high-type hand like (K-K) x, you should jam it, in order to clear out the field and allow yourself the best chance to win the pot. With high hands, you just want to win the pot, period. If you have (K-7) K and several players have already called the bring-in bet (the bring-in bet is discussed in Chapter 11) or a completion of the bring-in bet (to one full bet), then don't bother jamming the pot, because you may find yourself folding your hand on fifth street to two low hands. Jam with your kings in two- or three-handed pots; but against three or more opponents, wait to jam it until either they catch bad or you catch good.

With powerful low hands like (A-2) 5, just call someone else's bet (or raise) and keep the pot small and the field big. That way, if you hit something like J, Q to your hand, you lose the minimum. Conversely, if you hit 3, 4 to your hand (and make a wheel), you'll win the maximum, since you'll have a lot of opponents in the pot to pay you off on the last three big-bet rounds of betting. (Most of the time your wheel will win the high side of the pot as well.)

I recommend smooth-calling with premium low hands, unless a couple of players have already entered the pot, in which case you want to jam the pot right away. With this early raise, you'll deprive your hand of some of its deception value, but you'll still build a big pot. When I consider jamming a pot with a couple of callers already in the pot, I'm looking for a premium low hand on the upper half of the list, not merely a (6-7) 8 off suit.

Ideally, when you have one of the top premium starting hands in Stud 8/b, you want many opponents and many raises on the first round of betting! But you want more opponents more than you want a bigger pot, on the first round of betting.

Beginners' Strategy: The Time to Fold Your Premium Low Hands

It's time now to talk about what you should do when you catch a bad card on the fourth card of a hand in Stud 8/b. If you've started with a premium low hand (the list of premiums is on page

321) and have now caught a bad card, then in general you "buy" one more card. (Players often call this "taking one card off," meaning that you're staying in for a look at one more card, and if your hand doesn't improve significantly on the fifth card, you're out of there.)

Buying One More Card, but Not Two

Suppose you've started the hand with (A-4) 5, and now you've caught a queen. Do you call one bet in this case? Yes, you would call one bet, but calling two bets is questionable in this spot. I think it *is* OK to call two bets in this spot, especially if no one has an ace up. After all, you can hit an ace or queen for a big pair; a two or a three to give you a wheel draw; or a 6, 7, or 8 to give you a low draw. On the next round of betting, you would fold your hand if you catch a 9, 10, J, or K. It also depends on how many bets you've called on the opening round and what your opponents' boards suggest to you. If you suspect that someone has a pair of aces, or that two other players have broken into strong low draws, it's time to fold for the two bets.

Catching a Bad Card to Your Weak Premium Low Hand

Suppose you've started with (5-6) 7, and now you've caught a queen to your hand. I've already pointed out that you can "take off one card" for one bet in this case. What do you do when it's two bets to you? The (5-6) 7 is one of the weakest premium low hands on the list, because if you do make a low, it's likely to be a "rough" one. (A weak low hand is often called a "rough" low hand.) Therefore, you probably will have to fold your hand, depending on what your opponents' up cards are.

If your opponents all have high up cards, above a nine, you could call two bets, figuring that you have the only low draw and that your low cards are very live, since the other players seem to be working from high pairs in their hands.

If one of your opponents seems to be going low and has two cards under an eight, then you should fold your hand for two bets.

Calling with Your Strong Premium Hand

Suppose you've started with ($A\clubsuit$-$3\clubsuit$) $4\clubsuit$, and now you've caught the $Q\diamondsuit$ to your hand. What do you do when it's two bets to you to call? You call quickly! What do you do if it's three bets to you to call? You'd be tempted to call three bets without thinking about it, but you should take a close look at the board first.

1. First, I would be looking to see if one of my opponents has a pair of aces.
2. Second, I'd be taking note of all the other low up cards.
3. Third, I'd look to see how many clubs might be left in the deck, since I have a club flush draw with my hand.

If all three of the above findings looked bad for me, especially if I thought that someone already had a pair of aces or trips, then I'd fold my hand at this point. But because my starting hand was so strong, I'd be looking for excuses to call! If I hit a 9, 10, J, or K that wasn't a club on the next card, I'd probably fold my hand. Of course, if I had already called three bets with my hand on the round before, I might decide to call one big bet at this point in the hand if I'm fairly sure that it won't be raised. When the pot gets really big, you can justify making some calls that you wouldn't ordinarily be able to make.

In general, the time for folding with your premium low hands is after the fifth card, when the bets are now doubled. In other words, if you catch two bad cards to your low starting hand, then it's time to fold it.

Beginners' Strategy: The Time to Throw Away Your Big Pairs

There is a certain art in knowing when to throw away your high pairs in Stud 8/b. Here, I'll be talking about when it is right to fold your high pair of nines through kings. Although it's very hard to throw away a pair of aces, there are times when you need to do that as well. Remember that when you're playing a big pair (nines through kings) in Stud 8/b, you're almost always locked into playing for just half of the pot. It's possible, of course, for you to scoop the pot, but you'll almost never win the low half of the pot with a high pair (unless your other five cards make an eight low or better).

For these reasons, most big pairs don't appear on the list of premium hands. Be that as it may, learning when to fold your big pairs is something we need to examine. A dangerous time to be holding a big pair is when you're up against three opponents who appear to be going low and they all hit low cards on the fourth card. Even worse, if all three opponents catch low cards again on the next card, you'll have to throw your big pair away. (When your opponents make low hands, they will be drawing for both sides of the pot, whereas you can win only the low half. Also, there's likely to be a lot of betting and raising going on, so that you'll have to put in a lot of big bets, hoping to win only half the pot.)

It's also a dangerous time for a big pair when one of your opponents hits a running small pair on you, as when his up cards come 5-4-4. Sometimes, he'll have made hidden trips or two pair. Another folding situation for you is when your opponent hits four low cards in a row on you, such as 3-4-5-6. You'll also have to fold your big pair when two opponents hit three wheel cards each on you. Still another scary situation for a big pair arises when an opponent who has been jamming the pot hits an ace—for instance, when the up cards come 5-6-A. This is especially dangerous when there are no other aces in sight! Let's take a look at some examples.

Folding a Big Pair to Two Opponents Who Have Three Low Cards Each Up

Suppose that you have (K-8) K and your two opponents have a board of a six and a board of a five. Of course, you've read my book, so you jam it with your pair of kings right away in this hand. Let's suppose that the five raised it in "three" (the first round of betting) and you reraised it in three and now the six calls two bets. In this case you have to wonder what the six called two bets with. My guess, knowing nothing about the player, would be that the six has an ace in the hole. So if the six hits an ace at any point in this hand, I'd put my radar up and see how he's acting.

The next cards come down a jack for you, to give you (K-8) K-J; a four for the five for 5-4; and a five for the six, for 6-5. Now you need to check, since both low hands have hit low cards. (I'm still assuming that they both have low hands at this point.) Your hand is significantly weaker now that they've both hit low cards. If they both hit high cards nine and above, then you could bet out with your hand. But now the cards come down a two for you, to make (K-8) K-J-2; a three to make a 5-4-3; and a four to make 6-5-4. Now you're pretty much done with your hand. If one of your opponents makes a low hand, you're drawing to only half of the pot anyway. At this point in the hand, either opponent could have two pair, a straight, a made low, or a made low with a straight draw. Therefore, you shouldn't call even one bet with your hand. It's time to give up and fold. The good news is that you've lost only three small bets with this hand.

Folding a Big Pair to One Opponent with Four Low Straight Cards

Suppose that you've started with (Q-7) Q and your one opponent has started with a five. You raise on the first round of betting and the five calls you. Now the five catches a six for 5-6 and you catch a four for (Q-7) Q-4. You check to the 5-6, because he now has two low cards showing. If the five had caught a nine or higher, then you would have bet instead of checking.

On the next cards you caught an eight for (Q-7) Q-4-8 and the five catches a three for a 5-6-3 board. You check, and then the 5-6-3 bets out into you. You could fold your hand right here, right now, figuring that your opponent at a minimum has a draw to win the whole pot from you. After all, he must have started with something! Still, I would probably call him right now, thinking that I could still win the whole pot if he has a pair and a low draw. If my opponent now catches A, 2, 3, 4, 5, 6, or 7, on the fourth up card, you'll want to fold your hand unless you make two pair or three queens. If your opponent catches an eight or higher, then you'll call him again (and on the end). In fact, if you make two pair and he hits a bad card, you'll probably want to bet out into him, depending on how you read him at this point.

Folding a Big Pair to the Ace Up Card

Suppose you have (K-K) 10 and your two opponents have an ace and a six up. The six raises and then the ace reraises on the first round of betting. What do you do? If there is no other ace on the board, you simply fold your hand! You figure that the ace has a pair of aces, and even if he doesn't, he has a strong low hand and an ace draw with it. If there is one other ace on the board, I would still lean toward just folding my hand, for the same reasons that I mentioned above. If there are two other aces on the board, I would make it three bets to go, to try to get one-on-one with the ace and clear out any other low draws.

Folding a Big Pair: Beware of an Ace!

Suppose you have (K-K) 10 and a four has raised it and you reraise and a five behind you calls the two bets. You have to wonder what the five called two bets with, and if the five then hits an ace, you need to try to read him and decide whether or not you should fold. The five could be holding a high pair, like jacks or queens (the five is thinking you have tens, not kings, because you have a ten up), and if this is the case, then you'd be happy. Still, if the five hits an ace and the four hits a low card, you'll call one bet, but not two bets. If the five hits an ace and the four hits a high card, you'll call with your radar up.

The point of this example is that an ace is a scary card (for *your* hand) for the five to hit, and if the five does hit an ace, you're looking for an excuse to fold your hand. The perfect excuse for you to fold when the five hits an ace is that the four (the third player) breaks out into two more low cards. So you'll fold when the four breaks out into 4-8-2 and the five breaks out into 5-A-9.

As you can see from all these situations, playing big pairs in Stud 8/b can get you into a lot of trouble! If you're going to play big pairs, be sure that you fold them when you should be folding them.

Short-Handed Stud 8/b (Four Players or Fewer)

One reason I've gone over how to play big pairs in Stud 8/b is that big pairs go up in power as the number of players goes down. So a starting hand with a pair of jacks is pretty weak in an eight-handed game early in the day, but a lot more powerful in a three-handed game. As the players thin out during a game of Stud 8/b, the game becomes a lot more like Seven-Card Stud high, where the best starting pair is the favorite in each hand. It's a pretty interesting phenomenon that Stud 8/b begins to play a lot more like basic Stud as you lose players and get down to four players or fewer.

When I'm in a four-handed game of Stud 8/b, I stop trying to trap the other players with premium low hands. I just jam the pot, trying to win it as early as possible.

Making a Big Hand: Trap or Jam?

When you make a strong five-card hand in Stud 8/b, you have to decide whether or not you want to jam it in order to eliminate players, or slow-play it in order to keep more players in the pot. Often, the nature of your hand and the nature of the board will tell you what you should do.

If you make a wheel (A-2-3-4-5) and your opponents are drawing to make low hands, you don't want to drive them out. Why not let them draw at low when you have the perfect hand and they can't beat you anyway? So a wheel is an excellent trapping hand.

If you make a seven-high straight (3-4-5-6-7), you'll try to raise all the low draws right out of the pot, so that your seven low holds up for the low half of the pot. When I have a seven-high straight and the accompanying rough seven low, I'll jam the pot in order to protect my hand.

When you make a full house in Stud 8/b, you want to jam the pot in order to weed out the low draws, so that you can scoop the pot.

The concept of when to protect your hand and when to trap with your hand seems to fall along the lines of trapping when you make a strong two-way hand and protecting when you make a strong high hand. Most of the time, though, you want to jam the pot, both to protect your hand and possibly to build a bigger pot for you to scoop!

World-Class Play on the Last Round of Betting

Here is an advanced concept in Stud 8/b, one that a lot of players don't even know exists. It is something to think about in the last round of betting. The concept involves making the bluff raise with a high hand on the end. This is a play that works only on world-class players who are capable of folding their hands on the end to save one raise.

When you're obviously on a high hand in Stud 8/b and your opponent, who you suspect is going low, hits a small two pair instead of a low, then you can go ahead and raise on the end with your one-high-pair hand, because your opponent will suspect that you have a high hand which beats his high hand. Ted Forrest was able to use this play successfully for years, until some of the other high-limit players finally figured out what he was doing. (Ted wrote an amazing Hand of the Week for me describing that very play; you can read it at philhellmuth.com.) The problem with this play is that most players *won't* fold their hands on the end with two small pair in low- or mid-limit games. Therefore, this play is to be saved for occasional use in the high-limit games at the Bellagio or Commerce Casino.

Literally the Biggest Pot I Ever Saw in Stud 8/b

I remember one beautiful pot in which a well-known high-limit player named Don ("Zulu") Zewin won a $50,000 pot in a $400–$800 game ($50K pots are unheard of at this limit). Don had a hand of (2-3) 6-5-8-4 (7). Three of his opponents had high hands (aces up, trips, and a flush draw), and the other opponent had a seven-high straight made after five cards. The betting and raising going in this hand were incredible! One player had started with aces, one with trips, and so on. When Don was showing down his hand on the end, he said, "Six-high straight." The high hands all threw their hands away, and now the seven-high straight said, "Seven-high straight," and started to reach for his half of the pot. Don absentmindedly flipped up his last card— it was a seven—when he suddenly realized that he had made an eight-high straight. Don said, "Sorry, I overlooked my hand. I have an eight high straight!" The dealer, who was busy stacking this enormous pot to divide it up, and would have been stacking at least another two minutes, just pushed it all to Don in about four different strokes. All those white hundred-dollar chips, green thousand-dollar chips, and stacks of hundred-dollar bills in one enormous pot! It took Zulu more than five minutes to count all the cash and chips and determine that the pot had $54,400 in it.

Chapter 15

Poker on the Internet
and Cyber Hold'em Strategy

For centuries, poker had pretty much exactly the same form. Sure, there were subtle changes in rules and even in the card rooms where the game is played. But overall it remained fairly unchanged—that is, until the last year of the twentieth century. Then, just as with the rest of the business world, the Internet created enormous changes for poker.

Now you can learn about poker, read about poker, chat with people about poker, and, yes, even *play* poker anytime, from the comfort of your own home. The Internet has created an entirely new market for poker information and activities, and it is helping to create the fastest expansion in new players that we've ever seen.

People who were intimidated by formal poker rooms in the past now can learn the basics and risk very little money to play, with no loss of face when they make a dumb call or simply make an error. They can learn the game at their own pace, and risk virtually nothing to get some experience under their belt. (The economics of Internet games has made it possible to spread games that are much smaller than can be profitably spread in a casino, as small as a dime or quarter or even free!) And they have a chance to play and chat with people all over the world.

Jumping on the Wave

In 1998 I felt that I should have a website to generate some poker traffic—especially since I was living in the middle of web hysteria in Silicon Valley, a place where you simply tried to generate traffic and then tried to figure out how to make money. In fact, if your website had enough hits, it was almost guaranteed to be worth some money, especially in the growing and lucrative gaming market.

The name was the easy part to decide on, and so philhellmuth.com was born. Inevitably, though, I had to decide on some goals and content for my site. Eventually I came up with two "reports" that I would post on philhellmuth.com; I called them "Hand of the Week" (HOW) and "High Limit Results" (HLR).

HOW would talk about some of the great poker pots that I have played, and witnessed, including key pots in each year's world championships and other major events. I pitched HOW to *Card Player Magazine* (the industry's leading publication), and the editors loved it. I would write the HOW articles for the magazine and then archive them on my website. This launched my writing career, and the overwhelmingly positive feedback I received from readers made me think that I might have something worth offering.

The HLR articles are all written specifically for my site. They provide some insight into the biggest poker games in the world today. In HLR I write about the games played by high-limit poker players, and the $50,000-plus swings that we take in just a couple of hours! I write about the game we were playing in, who was in it, and where it was held. If you're interested, just go to philhellmuth.com and click on "Two Nines Room."

philhellmuth.com "Live" and Archived Audio Broadcasts

In an effort to drive traffic to philhellmuth.com, I dreamed of offering millions of people the chance to listen to the final table of the World Series of Poker (WSOP), the poker world's equivalent of a world championship, during a live Internet audio broadcast. A businessman friend of mine named Jeff Pulver (pulver.com) set up the site, and the first live audio broadcast of WSOP in 1999. We did it by "making it up as we went," handing Andy Glazer's old clunker of a cell phone back and forth to different players for analysis.

In 1999, we had only 1,000 hits, but in 2000 we had tens of thousands of hits for our second WSOP broadcast. Then, as people became aware that we were doing the broadcasts, the number of hits started spiking up each year thereafter. The broadcasts from 1999, 2000, and 2001 are archived at my site and at UltimateBet.com (UB), though I have to admit that I have never listened to the broadcast from the year 2001, as it was by far the most disappointing poker day of my life! In 2001, I finished in fifth place in WSOP, which was worth $305,000; but first place had been worth $1.5 million and—more importantly to me—a lot of history.

The Next Step—UltimateBet.com (UB)

Now that I had a nice-looking website up (philhellmuth.com), I felt I should look into some other web-related projects. A good friend of mine named David ("Porkchop") Wight had stopped playing poker professionally in order to run a business called Show Gear Productions. One day David told me that if I wanted to make money, I was in the wrong business—the Internet was the place to be. Finding a steady source of income sounded pretty good to me, since I knew that I could potentially lose all my money on any given day. The swings can drive a person toward insanity! As the old pros say, "Poker is a tough way to make an easy living."

David and I decided to look into starting an online poker room together, but after a few months he chose to devote all his time to his already thriving business, and I ended up consulting and promoting for UltimateBet.com, a beautiful online poker room which I believe 100 percent in and am fully committed to. I helped the software team that built UB with the poker rules, and I was also able to have some input in the concept side of the project.

For instance, the team implemented my idea of having five-handed tables available at the site. These "shorthanded" tables allow you to play a lot more pots, because the hand values are lower, so I recommend them to anyone who tends to be impatient or likes to be involved in a lot of pots.

The bottom line for online poker: you can play from the comfort of your home, office, or hotel room and get in more than twice as many hands per hour. At UB, you can even play free. And while it's not the same as playing face to face, sometimes I like it even better! I recommend that you give online poker a try before you spend any serious time in a "brick and mortar" card room. You can often find me playing small-stakes online poker at UB. Look for table "Phil Hellmuth." But pay attention to some of my hints in this chapter, because you'll need to alter your strategy a little when you make the transition.

In this chapter you will learn:

▌ Deception and reading in Cyber Hold'em.

▌ Ten-handed Cyber strategy.

▌ Five-handed Cyber strategy.

▌ Limit Hold'em two-handed (heads-up) theory.

▌ Limit Hold'em heads-up: Howard Lederer's theory.

▌ About rec.gambling.poker.com (RGP), the online "newsgroup" for poker.

▌ About UltimateBet.com, an online poker room.

▌ About philhellmuth.com, my website with my "Hand of the Week," live Internet broadcasts, pictures, and more.

▌ About CardPlayer.com, the information website for the industry-leading *Card Player Magazine*, with tournament results and more.

▌ About PokerPages.com, the website with tons of information about poker, tournaments, and much more.

Online Poker Strategy

Now it is time to move on to the strategy part of this strategy section! First, I'll talk about playing 10-handed Texas Hold'em—by far the most popular game on the Internet (especially limit Hold'em). Second, I will cover the best strategy for five-handed games. Finally, I will talk about how to play two-handed ("heads-up") Hold'em games. Most of the information that I dole out here will refer you back to certain sections that you have already read earlier in this book. For example, my section on full-game limit Hold'em for the Internet will refer you to Chapter 3 of this book and the "top ten only" strategy that I talk about there. The new information about strategy that you will read in this section will have to do with playing five-handed games and two-handed games.

If you would like online strategy for all the other poker games that I cover in this book, I recommend that you simply follow my sections on beginners' strategy for each game. Again, I would program a computer exactly like this so that it could take advantage of online players' primary weakness—they play too many hands before the flop. In other words, they have no patience! One thing is virtually certain: my sections for beginners are all filled with plenty of patience. Now you just need to use these patient strategies to crush your online opponents in the small-stakes games!

Limit Hold'em on the Internet—
Deception and Reading

Limit Hold'em is a fast-moving game for a fast-moving society, and I have noticed that online players seem to move into and out of games more quickly. Online players are often playing on their lunch break at the office, or they just have an hour to kill before dinner or before going out at night. In any case, the lineups change quickly, and so you don't have a lot of time to figure out what the other players are doing. Therefore, you need to notice which players are doing what in order to determine what type of players they are. Pay particularly close attention to the hands that they show at the end of a pot. If a player has raised a pot and then bet all the way down to the end and shows 6♦-7♣, you know that he is a jackal type. (My animal types are discussed in Chapter 3, page 33.)

You'll be able to determine what kind of players your opponents are by the number of pots they play and the type of hands they show down. If you notice that a player hasn't played a pot in a while, the early evidence suggests that he may be a mouse type. Of course, if you play at the same online room over and over again, you will start to understand from past experience what type of players the others are.

Remember, though, that the sword cuts both ways in online poker. The other players won't know anything about you except what you let them see. If you are raising a lot of pots, the other players will think that you are a jackal, especially if you show down some weaker hands. You may show some of your weaker hands at the end of the hand even if you don't win the pot, in order to convey the illusion that you are a jackal. Or you can show your strong hands faceup at the end of a hand in order to give people the impression that you are a mouse. In general, I like to show my strong starting hands faceup, to make people think I am a mouse. Then I will be able to bluff more pots in the future, because they think I always have a big hand. (In lower-limit games, however, it is pretty hard to bluff someone out on the end!) Even though you can't read other people's facial expressions, there is still plenty of information available about the way they play Hold'em. You can also confuse the other players by showing down weak or strong hands in order to give them the wrong impression about the way you play Hold'em.

Other things to watch include the amount of time a player takes to make a decision, and the number of other games a player is in. If players are in another game, they are likely to lose concentration, and you may be able to take advantage of this weakness by playing more aggressively against them. A good online "tell" is whether or not a player bets his hand right away. Sometimes you can figure out if a quick bet means a hand or a bluff. A quick bet is usually a sign of weakness, and a slow bet is usually a sign of strength. Everyone in poker is an actor, and when people bet slowly they are usually trying to say to you, "I don't know if I should bet this hand or not. Let me think. I'm pretty weak right now." At least that's what they want you to think when they bet slowly on the end. By contrast, a quick bet is meant to convey an impression of strength; they're saying, "I have a huge hand, and I'm going to bet because of this." You might not want to believe it, though!

Limit Hold'em Strategy—10-Handed Games

I am recommending that you use the "top ten only" strategy when you play online poker at a 10-handed table. The strategy of the "top ten" hands is laid out in Chapter 3 of this book. This strategy is simple, safe, and very effective. Using this strategy should allow you to build up some profits while you play online poker. If I could design a computer program to play my money online, this is the way I would program it.

The reason I recommend this slow strategy is that the online players in small-stakes poker games play so badly that the "top ten" strategy will be a big winner in the long haul. There is no need to get fancy and take big swings up and down with your money online: the patient route will smooth out the swings and produce the desired wins. Make sure that you play in games of an appropriate size for your bankroll. If you intend to risk $100 online, make sure that you play no higher than $1–$2 limit. This way you will have 50 big bets to play with, and you will give the "top ten" strategy a chance to succeed for you. With 50 big bets, you will have a decent shot at turning $100 into a lot more money over 40 hours of play using my online strategy.

However, 50 big bets are still not much money in a poker game, and 100 big bets are a much safer amount to start with. Please do not be discouraged if you lose your initial $100 playing the "top ten" strategy. Luck is a big part of poker, and although this strategy is a favorite in any online $1–$2 game, sometimes you can just get unlucky!

Limit Hold'em Strategy—Five-Handed Games

Hold'em is a very different game when you are playing it at a table where the maximum is five players. You will find that the swings you take in a five-handed game will tend to be much bigger than the swings you take at a ten-handed table. Beware of this and understand that it is just the nature of the beast! Five-hand-maximum tables don't exist right now in the "real world," probably because the casinos figure they have a limited amount of space and need to use it for full-size tables. Online casinos, of course, face no such limitation.

So this strategy can be used only online or anytime that the online game you're playing in gets down to five hands. At a five-hand-maximum table, we can now add all pairs, any A-x, and "20" (two cards that add up to 20 or more) to the mix of hands we can play before the flop. Of course, I'm not saying that you can play these additional hands all the time. For example, I wouldn't play 10-J for three bets before the flop. However, you can now call two bets with these types of hands or make it two bets yourself with them. Because you are playing more than three times as many hands before the flop in a five-handed game than in a 10-handed game, you may also find five-handed tables a lot more fun, and potentially a lot more profitable.

When you play five-handed poker it is more important to find out where you're at in a hand on the flop. I cover this concept very thoroughly in Chapter 3. Also, if you have a hand like A-K or A-Q you will end up calling your opponents down a lot

more often when you don't hit your hand, so you will naturally
be exposing yourself to more risk.

Limit Hold'em Two-Handed (Heads-Up) Theory

Heads-up poker is strategically much different from a full game.
Interestingly, some players who are jackals in a full game tend to
do very well in a heads-up game. Perhaps the reason is that they
are already used to playing many hands aggressively. Being a
tough player in a nine-handed Hold'em game requires patience,
discipline, and aggressive play. However, being a tough player in
a heads-up Hold'em game requires superaggressive play, good
reads in almost every hand, and the ability to play bad hands
well (so to speak). Notice that I didn't mention patience as an
important trait in a tough heads-up player. This is because
patient players usually don't learn how to play bad hands well.

   Knowing when to bet with bottom pair on the end because
you are certain that your opponent has ace high is an important
ability in a heads-up match. In other words, knowing if and
when you have the best hand is extremely important in heads-up
play. While this may be important in any game of poker, you'll
have to do it far more often in heads-up play.

   When you're playing against a player who bluffs out against
you all the time heads-up, I recommend that you smooth-call
with a lot of hands on the flop and on fourth street, and then
raise on the river.

Slow-Playing against a Superaggressive Player

Often, you will find yourself playing heads-up with a super-aggressive player. When this is the case, I like to slow play my hands. Suppose that I have Q-Q in the pocket and the aggressive player has raised on the button. Most of the time in this situation, I will just call him before the flop to trap him later on. Suppose that the flop is J-8-5. Now I like to check and just call again! Give him a little rope. Let's say that the next card off is a deuce for J-8-5-2. Now I check again, and if my opponent bets, now I finally raise! If I trap my opponent here, he will be less likely to try to bluff on every hand, because he knows that I am capable of trapping him again soon!

Limit Hold'em Heads-Up—Howard Lederer's Theory

Limit Hold'em is a very different game heads-up. I know of one great player, Howard Lederer (Annie Duke's older brother), who will raise every time that he has the button in heads-up Hold'em, and it seems to work well for him! Raising every hand when you have the button is a really good strategy to use against a novice. The idea is to raise every hand on the button and then bet every flop. When you do this, you're giving your opponent a chance to fold his hand every time you make a bet. You're putting pressure on him constantly and forcing him to call you down with some really weak hands. This is really hard for anyone to handle—especially since a high percentage of the time in Hold'em you don't even flop a pair! However, if you're up against a tough player, you're in trouble when you play like this.

My counterstrategy for this is simply to reraise every time I have ace high, king high, two cards above a nine, or a pair. And then I bet out at them every flop!

More Information: Rec.gambling.poker.com is the Online "Newsgroup" for Poker

If you are interested, an online poker newsgroup is located at rec.gambling.poker.com (RGP). RGP has a big voice in the poker world today, and the RGP group meets every year to play poker at the Big August Recreational Gambling Excursion (BARGE) in Las Vegas. I was the keynote speaker for BARGE in 2001, and I had a great time hanging out with the RGP regulars. Their enthusiasm for poker is very refreshing and contagious! Imagine poker games spontaneously breaking out on the floor of a room that RGP was renting or poker tournaments with teams of four players each!

Often, people will start threads involving poker strategy that are both illuminating and interesting to read, and it is always interesting to me how others think poker hands ought to be played. Other threads talk about the latest rumors concerning players and poker tournaments. (Everyone has a voice on RGP, and unfortunately some voices are a little bit too loud and negative for my taste.) One particularly useful thing you can learn from RGP is where the local poker game in your area is played and what the stakes are. Just ask! By the way, you'll find that "newbies" are always welcome at RGP.

One thing I should point out if you are going to visit RGP: not everyone who offers advice really knows what he is talking about, although people try to make it sound as if they know a lot. Be cautious about taking advice on RGP as gospel, at least until you figure out who the more trustworthy posters are.

Resources

Love it or hate it, the Internet has made an indelible mark on the poker landscape. More people are learning about poker and playing it because of the ease of access to learning tools and free or low-stakes games online. And there doesn't appear to be any turning back . . . the Internet is here to stay. I don't think it's a coincidence that tournaments and card rooms around the world are seeing record attendance; people who learn online are eager to try what they learn face to face!

You can also bet that there will be more and more opportunities to get into profitable games online. The play tends to be loose and fast, and solid players with excellent fundamentals should be able to make the games pay off. The opportunities are even better when you factor in the chance to play at multiple tables at the same time, and to do so in your favorite easy chair!

With the Internet's ease of access and its ability to grow quickly, I think it's only a matter of time before we see 10,000 people in an online tournament. I don't know about you, but I'm likely to be one of them!

Here are some resources that you might find helpful:

To Practice and Play Online

UltimateBet.com

This is the only site that I currently recommend. It's
regulated by the Kahnawake Gaming Commission and is
honest and professional. I also happen to think that UB's
game is the only one that will really let you concentrate.
It's the only place that I'd play. Period.

Poker Articles and Information

philhellmuth.com (see page 338)

CardPlayer.com: A great site that offers many of the same
resources as the magazine, but in an electronic format. You
can find many great articles written by some of the best
poker writers in the business, including Glazer and myself.
There is also information about where and when upcoming
poker tournaments are being held and results from past
tournaments. Barry and Jeff Shulman have done a great
job with this site and also with *Card Player Magazine*.

PokerPages.com: More information than you can believe
on the game of poker. If it's out there, I can usually find it
at PokerPages, including tournament results, schedules,
online articles, links, and a sharp "Online Poker School."
Tina and Mark Napolitano have done a wonderful job
with this site and they also managed to bring Mike "the
Mad Genius" Caro on to help.

Last Notes on Playing Online

The legal landscape surrounding the online gaming industry is constantly shifting and being revised as lawmakers wrestle with some of the legal challenges that online gaming poses. While many of the legal issues seem to be undecided, you should check your local laws before playing poker online for money. It may not be allowed in your area.

Rank of Hands
in Poker

The best possible hand in poker (Hold'em is a poker game!) is the royal flush. I have made only two in my career so far! Here is the rank of hands in order from strongest to weakest. There are four suits in poker—clubs, diamonds, hearts, and spades.

1. Royal flush (10♠-J♠-Q♠-K♠-A♠)—the ten through the ace, all of the same suit.

2. Straight flush—five cards in a row (straight), all in the same suit. A royal flush is simply an ace-high straight flush. The 2♣-3♣-4♣-5♣-6♣ (six-high straight flush) and 7♦-8♦-9♦-10♦-J♦ (jack-high straight flush) are straight flushes.

3. Four of a kind (quads)—having all four of a card like 6♣-6♦-6♥-6♠ (four sixes) or 8♣-8♦-8♥-8♠ (four eights) qualifies as four of a kind.

4. Full house (full boat or boat)—three of a kind and two of a kind in one hand. For example, 5♦-5♥-5♠-K♦-K♠ (fives full of kings) or J♠-J♥-J♦-2♣-2♦ (jacks full of twos) or 9♠-9♣-9♥-7♦-7♠ (nines full of sevens).

5. Flush—having five of a suit would qualify as a flush. For example, 2♠-5♠-7♠-J♠-K♠ (king-high flush) or 5♥-7♥-J♥-Q♥-A♥ (ace-high flush) or any combination of five to a suit would make a flush.

6. Straight—five cards in a row. Two examples are 3♦-4♠-5♥-6♥-7♣ (seven-high straight) and 9♥-10♠-J♥-Q♦-K♣ (king-high straight).

7. Three of a kind (trips or a set)—having three of a card, such as 4♠-4♦-4♥ (trip fours or "set of fours") or J♥-J♠-J♦ (trip jacks or "set of jacks").

8. Two pair—two of a kind twice in one hand. Examples are A♥-A♣-4♦-4♥-9♦ (aces up) or J♠-J♥-2♣-2♠-7♥ (jacks up) and 7♥-7♦-3♥-3♠-A♣ (sevens up).

9. One pair—two of a kind. Examples are A♠-A♣-9♥-6♦-3♠ (aces) and 8♥-8♠-J♠-2♣-4♥ (eights).

10. High cards—highest five cards from the top down. Examples are A♠-Q♦-6♥-4♠-2♣ (ace-queen high), A♠-J♣-6♦-5♥-3♠ (ace-jack high), and K♠-J♦-8♦-6♥-3♣ (king-jack high).

Don't be put off by these seemingly complicated rankings! Most big poker pots are won by one pair or two pair or three of a kind (trips). This ranking stuff comes very easily once you begin to play poker.

Champion of the Year Award

In late 2001, I decided to create a new award in poker, the "Champion of the Year" award. To help me establish a qualifying list of events, I polled the top 15 poker players. Players like T. J. Cloutier, the world champion Johnny Chan, John Bonetti, the world champion Huck Seed, Ted Forrest, the world champion Chris Ferguson, Annie Duke, Erik Seidel, Tony Ma, Daniel Negreanu, Men Nguyen, Layne Flack, and a few others filled out a list of what they considered the most prestigious poker tournaments. I took the average and came up with a list (Appendix 3) of the most prestigious poker tournaments. From this list, I designed the "Champion of the Year" award, which is different from the "Player of the Year" award established a couple of years earlier by *Card Player Magazine*.

I had felt that the "Player of the Year" award was based on too many tournaments, and that someone who played 300 events annually would have a huge edge over the poker champions who play only 50 to 70 events a year. The two-time world champion Johnny Chan doesn't have time to play in more than 50 tournaments each year. And many other top players—like Chris Ferguson, Ted Forrest, Annie Duke, Huck Seed, Erik Seidel, John Bonetti, and I—can't play in more than 70 events each year. Some of us have families (Annie, Erik, and I), some of us trade stocks full-time (Chris), some of us play $2,000-$4,000-limit poker four times a week (Ted and Johnny), and others just have too much going on in their lives to play in 300 poker tournaments each year. In order to give all the great poker players in the world a chance to win a major award, we now have the "Champion of the Year" award. You can track the "Champion of the Year" award at philhellmuth.com or in the back of *Card Player Magazine.*

The system I established to grant points to tournament winners is very basic. Players receive points only if they make the final table, and most of the points are given to the top three finishers. Check out philhellmuth.com for full details about the annual point distributions, and the current standings. A traveling "Champion of the Year" cup is awarded to the Champion of the Year, sort of like the Stanley Cup. (I imagine the players may drink champagne out of this cup as well!)

You will undoubtedly notice that the World Series of Poker (WSOP) dominates the list. This is because WSOP is where "millions are paid and legends are made." WSOP is to poker what the four majors are to the PGA Tour: it is the Masters, the U.S. Open, the British Open, and the PGA Championship all rolled into one! In Appendix 4, I show you what it is like to walk in and play in a WSOP event.

The Most Prestigious
Poker Tournaments

I have included below a listing of what I consider the Top 50 poker tournaments in the world. The events that are marked with an asterisk are also part of the World Poker Tour (WPT). With the advent of the WPT in 2002, poker tournaments are being taken into the American public's living rooms. Players who make the final six in any of these events also make the TV cut. The hole cards are recorded and made into a program that plays on the Travel channel and other major networks. The television exposure is nice, but the huge WPT first-place prizes make this one of the most prestigious events ever. Although the World Series of Poker (WSOP) is still the Holy Grail to us players, the WPT events (the WSOP isn't one of them, yet) are gaining. Look for the WPT in your home soon!

Phil's Top 50 Tournaments
(not listed by ranking)

Binion's World Series of Poker (WSOP) Events

1. $2,000 Limit Hold'em
2. $1,500 Omaha Hi/Lo Split
3. $2,000 No-Limit Hold'em
4. $1,500 7-Card Stud
5. $1,500 Limit Omaha
6. $1,500 7-Card Stud Hi/Lo Split
7. $1,500 Pot-Limit Omaha
8. $2,500 Gold Bracelet Heads-Up Match Play—No-Limit Hold'em
9. $1,500 Pot-Limit O8B
10. $2,000 HORSE (Hold'em, O8B, Razz, Stud, and Stud 8 or Better)
11. $2,000 Pot-Limit Hold'em
12. $2,500 7-Card Stud
13. $3,000 Limit Hold'em
14. $1,500 Razz
15. $2,500 Pot-Limit Omaha
16. $2,500 7-Card Stud Hi/Lo Split
17. $3,000 Pot-Limit Hold'em
18. $1,500 Ace to Five Draw Lowball
19. $1,500 No-Limit Hold'em
20. $2,500 Omaha Hi/Lo Split
21. $1,500 Pot-Limit Hold'em

22. $5,000 7-Card Stud
23. $2,000 S.H.O.E (Stud, Hold'em, O8B, Stud 8 or Better)
24. $5,000 Limit Hold'em
25. $1,500 Limit Hold'em Shootout
26. $5,000 Pot-Limit Omaha
27. $1,500 Limit Hold'em
28. $5,000 Omaha Hi/Lo Split
29. $3,000 No-Limit Hold'em
30. $2,000 1/2 Hold'em + 1/2 Stud
31. $5,000 No-Limit Deuce to Seven
32. $1,500 Triple Draw Lowball Ace to Five
33. $10,000 WSOP No-Limit Hold'em Main Event

World Poker Tour (WPT) Championship

34. $25,000 No-Limit Hold'em *

World Poker Open Events

35. $2,000 No-Limit Hold'em
36. $10,000 Championship Event *

World Poker Challenge

37. $5,000 Championship Event *

LA Poker Classic Events

38. $1,570 Limit Hold'em with Rebuys ($1million guarantee!)
39. $10,000 No-Limit Hold'em *

Legends of Poker

40. $5,000 Championship Event *

World Poker Final Events

41. $2,500 7-Card Stud
42. $10,000 No-Limit Hold'em *

U.S. Poker Championship

43. $4,000 7-Card Stud
44. $7,500 No-Limit Hold'em

Bellagio Tournaments

45. $10,000 Bellagio Tourney *
46. $3,000 Limit Hold'em

Ultimate Poker Classic

47. $5,000 No-Limit Hold'em Tourney *

Lucky Chances Casino Gold Rush

48. $3,000 Limit Hold'em Tourney *

The Poker EM (Vienna)

49. $3,000 European 7-Card Stud Championship

Euro Finals of Poker (Paris)

50. $10,000 European Texas Hold'em Championship

Playing in a World Series of Poker (WSOP) Tournament

All the WSOP tournaments are held at the Horseshoe Hotel and Casino (Horseshoe) in downtown Las Vegas, Nevada, at high noon. To register for a WSOP tournament, you first get a card with a registration number on it from one of the cages. This card is good for all the WSOP events that year. Then, take cash for the buy-in and fees of the tournament you wish to enter to the main cage in the tournament area. There your money will be exchanged for chips, which you then take to the registration desk. You hand over your card and chips, receive a table and seat assignment (randomly drawn by a computer), and wait for your event to begin. It is best to be in your seat by noon, as the tournament will start when the director announces, "Shuffle up and deal" (the former WSOP tournament director Jack McClelland's old line). There will be a television monitor close to your table showing you the number of players entered in the event, the number of players left in the tournament at that moment, the amount of time left in the current level, and how much money the first-place finisher will win.

As players are eliminated, the tables are combined. When nine players have been eliminated, one table is taken out of use. For example, if 450 players entered a Hold'em tournament, 50 tables would be set up for the beginning of the event. When 90 players remained, only 10 tables would be left. This consolidation continues until only the final table remains.

If you take a look around the tournament room, you'll see all manner of poker players. You'll see black men and women, white men and women, Asian men and women, Jews, Catholics, Buddhists, atheists, agnostics, rich, poor, casino owners, the Los Angeles Lakers' owners (Jerry and Frank), actors, and the biggest collection of champion poker players anywhere. Since this event is held from late April through May, you'll also see players watching the NBA playoffs on television. On the hour, every hour, the limits will rise, so the pots get bigger and bigger and the chip stacks get bigger, until you hit the final table early the next morning.

There will be breaks along the way. At 2:00 P.M. you get a half-hour lunch break. Two hours later you'll get a fifteen-minute break. Two hours after that you'll get a one-hour dinner break. And then every two hours until the end of the day, you'll get a fifteen-minute break.

Once the final table is established (nine for Hold'em), you're done for the day. The next day you get to come back and play at 2:00 P.M., under the lights and cameras, for all the money! The final table is broadcast around the casino on television monitors, and key hands are announced over a loudspeaker so that those playing in the next day's event can listen to the action. There are also bleachers set up around the final table for spectators and the media. Making a final table at WSOP is really quite a memorable event.

The goal is to become one of the final three players, where some kind of three-way deal can be made. The difference in prize money among first, second, and third place is frequently so big— say, $200,000 for first, $100,000 for second, and $50,000 for third—that the players like to make a save. (Someone might suggest, for instance, that they take $100,000 apiece and play for $50,000 for first place.) Because of the huge difference in prize money between first place and third place, deals seem to come up a lot in poker these days. If you're fortunate enough to win, then nirvana! You get a coveted gold bracelet, a ton of pictures, congratulations, a story written about the event with your name at the top of the list, and usually at least $150,000 in cash! Sounds pretty good, huh?

Final Thoughts about WSOP

You probably noticed that every WSOP tournament is on the list of the most prestigious poker tournaments. That's because the WSOP stands alone as the single most important event in poker. Having just one bracelet from the WSOP is a big deal, and not very many players have two. If you want to make history as a poker player, then the WSOP is the place to do it. In fact, the slogan of WSOP is, "Where millions are paid and legends are made."

Along with increased attendance and the increased stature of the WSOP each year, there have been three other notable changes. As of 2002, the WSOP is now a nonsmoking event—no cigarettes are allowed in the tournament room. Smokers are, however, only 50 yards away from a place where they can light up. The second change is that cell phones have been banned from the tournament room. ("Hello. Can you hold on a second? I just put in my last $100,000 on a bluff!") The third change is that CD players have been banned from the tournament room. My CD player was one of my trademarks! If you watch any video that I appear in at the WSOP, covering 1988–2000, you will see me with my headphones on, probably listening to Pearl Jam, Hootie and the Blowfish, Alanis Morissette, Snoop Doggy Dogg, the Rolling Stones, or some group of the 1980s.

If you're lucky enough to play in a WSOP event, enjoy yourself; you'll be playing with the best poker players in the world!

Phil's Glossary

A-X SUITED—(N.) Hold'em term for an ace and an under-card of the same suit, like – or –.

ACTION—(N.) Gambling or loose betting: "The action was tremendous." "I want some of that action." "Give me some action."

ADVERTISE—(V.) To make a loose play with the intent of looking like a loose player, thus inducing extra action from your opponents later.

ALL-IN—(ADV.) When all your chips are in the pot: "Jeff just moved all-in for $95,000!"

ALL-IN PROTECTION—(N.) "Anti-billionaire" rule, the concept that you cannot be "bet out of," or be eliminated from, a pot just because you run out of money on the table. For example, if the pot has $165 in it and you have only $79 left, you may call that portion of your opponent's $200 bet by putting all $79 of your chips in the pot. If you win the pot, you can win the whole $165 main pot and $79 of his $200.

AMERICAN AIRLINES—(N.) Pocket aces, A-A, in Hold'em.

ANTE—(N.) Amount of money or chips that each player puts into the pot before the cards are dealt.

BACKDOOR—(N., ADJ.) Catching two cards in a row to make a particular hand. "I made the backdoor flush and won a huge pot."

BAD BEAT—(N.) Unlucky turn of events that causes you to lose a hand. "Ouch, that was a really bad beat!"

BANKER—(N.) Player at a table who is responsible for passing out the chips and keeping track of the money and credit.

BANKROLL (BR)—(N.) Amount of money you have that you will risk on poker or any other endeavor. "Right now he has a $2,500 bankroll to work with."

BELLY BUSTER—(N., ADJ.) Straight draw in which only one card will complete your hand, otherwise known as an "inside straight draw." For example, you complete a belly buster straight when an eight is dealt to complete a 7-8-9-10-J straight.

BET—(V.) To initiate the betting after a new card is dealt. When no one has bet in front of you, and it is your turn to act, you may bet or check.

BETTING OUT, BETTING INTO—(V.) See bet.

BETTING ROUND—(N.) Betting that occurs from the time a new card is dealt until the action is complete. "I won the pot on the last betting round with a bluff!"

BETTOR—(N.) Player who first voluntarily puts money into the pot.

BIG BLIND—(N.) Blind that is two to the left of the button. The big blind always costs one betting unit. See also blind, small blind. "I folded in the big blind, but I would have won a big pot."

BIG MONEY STREETS—(N.) In limit poker, the betting rounds in which the bets are doubled. For example, in a $10–$20-limit game the big money streets are the rounds when you bet $20.

BLANK—(N.) Card that doesn't help your hand. "There were a ton of cards that made my hand, so I was disappointed to see two blanks."

BLIND—(N.) Money posted directly to the left of the button, before the cards are dealt. There are two blinds, and the small blind is generally half the size of the big blind.

BLUFF—(N.) Bet that conveys to others that you have a stronger hand than you actually have.

BOARD—(N.) Faceup cards in Hold'em, Omaha, or Stud.

BOARD-LOCKED—(ADJ.) Situation in Stud games in which one player, regardless of the cards he holds in the hole, cannot beat another.

BOAT—(N.) Full house. Sometimes referred to as a "full boat."

BRING-IN BET—(N.) Forced bet in Stud games; the bet that starts the action. The bring-in bet is usually about 25 percent of a full bet, and it is made, on the first round of betting, by the highest board card or the lowest board card, depending on the Stud variation.

BROADWAY—(N., ADJ.) Ace-high straight (10-J-Q-K-A).

BROKE—(ADJ.) See busted.

BUBBLE—(N.) Last nonpaying spot in a poker tournament. For example, nineteenth place in a tournament that pays eighteen players.

BUILDING A POT—(N.) Raising in order to increase the amount of money in the pot.

BUSTED—(ADJ., V.) To be out of money, to run out of chips in a poker tournament. "Poor Al, he's busted again." "I just busted out of the tournament."

BUTTON—(N.) Physical and symbolic designation of the person who is "dealing" and therefore last to act in the betting rounds.

BUY ANOTHER CARD—(V.) Call a bet to see the next card dealt.

BUY-IN—(N.) Amount of money you start playing with in a game, or the amount it costs to enter a poker tournament.

CALL—(V.) To match another player's bet. When someone bets, you may fold, call, or raise.

CALLING SOMEONE DOWN—(V.) Calling all of another player's bets, because you believe that you have a better hand.

CALLING STATION—(N.) Someone who calls other players too often.

CAPPED—(V., ADJ.) Used to describe a pot with the maximum number of bets allowed in a limit poker game on any given betting round. A capped pot in Las Vegas has five bets; a capped pot in Los Angeles has four bets.

CASHED—(ADJ.) Placed in the money (paying spots) in a poker tournament.

CATCHING A CARD—(V.) Having a card come that was one of the cards needed to win a pot. For example, the instance where someone needs a flush card and it comes. "I caught the perfect card on the last card."

CHASING—(V.) Trying continually to hit long shots.

CHECK—(V.) To not bet. When no one has bet yet, you also have the option not to bet, without folding your hand.

CHECK-RAISE—(V.) To check and then raise within one betting round. You may check initially and then, when it is your turn to act again, raise someone else's bet.

CHIP AND A CHAIR—(N.) Phrase used when someone has only a couple of chips left in a tournament.

COLD—(ADJ.) Used to describe a situation in which the game seems to be going poorly and you haven't been winning many pots over a period of at least an hour. "John sure was cold at the end of that tournament."

COLD CALL—(N.) Calling three or four bets without having invested any money previously in the pot. "Can you believe that he called three bets cold with that garbage?"

COMMUNITY CARD—(N.) Card that may be used by each player at the table.

COMPLETING THE BET—(V.) In Stud variations, raising the bring-in bet to one whole bet.

COWBOYS—(N.) Pair of kings, K-K, in Hold'em.

DEAD—(ADJ.) See drawing dead.

DEAL—(V.) Giving out the cards to the players and board, throughout an entire hand.

DEALER'S CHOICE—(N.) Game in which the dealer has the option of choosing the game.

DECLARE—(V.) State whether you are pursuing a high or low hand.

DOOR CARD—(N.) First faceup card in Stud games.

DOUBLE-SUITED—(ADJ.) Used to describe a situation in which your four hole cards contain two suits. Example: A♣-4♠-5♣-8♠.

DOUBLE UP—(V.) Increase your chip stack 100 percent.

DOWN CARDS—(N.) Player's private hole cards, which are dealt facedown and which only he can see. See also facedown, hole cards.

DRAW—(N.) Situation in which a player needs one card to complete a poker hand.

DRAWING DEAD—(N.) Used to describe a situation in which a player cannot win the hand, regardless of what cards come up. "I had him drawing dead that hand."

DRAWING HAND—(N.) See draw.

DRY ACES—(N.) Pair of aces with no other draws.

DUCKS—(N.) Pocket deuces, 2-2, in Hold'em.

DUMP—(V.) Fold.

EAGLE—(N.) World-class poker player. One of the "animal personalities" that I use to teach you strategy.

EARLY POSITION—(N.) One of the three positions to the immediate left of the big blind, in a Hold'em or Omaha hand.

ELEPHANT—(N.) Player who plays too many hands and calls too many bets. One of the "animal personalities" that I use to teach you poker strategy.

ENDGAME—(N.) Strategy pertaining to the last five players or fewer left in a poker tournament.

EVEN-MONEY POT—(N.) Used to describe a situation in which a player's chance of winning the pot is roughly 50 percent.

FAMILY POKER GAME (HOME-STYLE POKER)—(N.) Kind of poker game that you might play with your close friends, coworkers, or family, usually involving low stakes and wild cards.

FAST—(ADJ.) Used to describe a loose, aggressive style of play, including lots of betting and raising. This style involves playing a lot of hands. "He's the fastest player in the game."

FIFTH STREET—(N.) In Hold'em and Omaha, the final faceup card dealt and the last round of betting; in Stud games, the fifth card dealt (the third one dealt faceup).

FINAL TABLE—(N.) Final nine players remaining in a Hold'em tournament; final eight players remaining in a Stud tournament.

FLAT CALL—(N.) Instance in which a player with a very powerful hand calls instead of raising.

FLOP—(N.) First three cards dealt faceup in Hold'em. All three cards are flipped up at once, and they are community cards (all players use them). "That was a beautiful flop for my hand."

FLOP—(V.) Make a hand on the flop. "I flopped the straight and won a huge pot."

FLUSH—(N.) Five cards of the same suit, such as 5♣-7♣-8♣-J♣-K♣.

FLUSH DRAW—(N.) Situation in which a player has four cards of the same suit, thus needing only one more of that suit to make a flush hand.

FOLD—(V., N.) Concede the pot either by throwing your hand away or by a verbal declaration ("I fold").

FOUR OF A KIND—(N.) Four cards of the same rank, such as 6♣-6♠-6♥-6♦.

FOURTH STREET—(N.) In Hold'em and Omaha, the dealing of the fourth community card and the ensuing round of betting. "On fourth street, the five of diamonds came and I made a flush."

FREE CARD—(N.) Used to describe a situation in which no bets are made on any given round of betting.

FREE ROLL—(N.) Describing a situation in which you are sure to win but also have an opportunity to win a further amount. For example, in a high-low split game, being assured of winning one side of the pot already (usually the low side), but also having a chance to win the other half of the pot.

FULL RING PLAY—(N.) Playing with the maximum number of players allowed in a side (nontournament) game. Nine is usually the maximum in a Hold'em side game.

GAME THEORY—(N.) Tactics for a particular game.

GARBAGE—(N.) Weak hand. "Why do you always play that garbage?"

GET QUARTERED—(V.) Receive only 25 percent of a pot, usually in high-low games.

GOOD SHAPE—(N.) Used to describe a situation in which a player has a high probability of winning the pot. "I was in really good shape when we put all the money in the pot."

GUTSHOT—(N.) See inside straight draw.

HAND—(N.) Refers to your cards, or to the process of dealing the cards until the winning of the pot. "Boy, that hand took awhile."

HEADS-UP—(N., ADV.) Used to describe a situation in which poker is played one-on-one; mano a mano. Some people like heads-up better than a full table. "I played Freddy Bonyadi heads-up and lost $75,000!"

HIGH-SOCIETY CHIP—(N.) Poker chip worth $100. In the movie *Rounders,* Matt Damon says, "Give me three racks of high-society chips." A rack has 100 chips in it, so Matt ordered $30,000 worth of chips!

HIGH HAND—(N.) Hand that is competing for the high side of the pot. See also low hand.

HIGH STAKES—(N., ADJ.) Usually refers to poker games $75–$150 and higher.

HIT A CARD—(V.) Catch a good card or a card that wins the pot for you.

HOLD'EM—(N., ADJ.) World's most popular poker game. Each player has two cards facedown, and the players share the five community cards faceup in the middle of the table. The best five-card hand wins.

HOLE—(N.) See position.

HOLE CARDS—(N.) Player's private facedown cards that only he can see.

HOME-STYLE POKER—(N.) See family poker game.

HORSE (HORSE)—(N.) Game in which you play equal numbers of hands (or equal lengths of time) in five different games. The games are Hold'em, Omaha Eight or Better (High-Low Split), Razz (Seven-Card Low), Seven-Card Stud, and Seven-Card Stud High-Low Split (E = eight or better). HORSE is very popular in the poker community right now.

HOT—(ADJ.) Used to describe a player who is winning more than his share of pots. "Wayne Tyler sure was running hot today."

IMPLIED ODDS—(N.) Odds a player factors into his calculation of pot odds to account for being called if you complete your hand.

INSIDE STRAIGHT—(N.) See belly buster.

IN THE DARK—(ADV.) Without looking at the facedown hole cards. "Stuart Skorman bet $80 in the dark."

IN THE MONEY—(ADV.) In the paying positions in a poker tournament.

ISOLATION—(N.) Technique in which a player reraises a weaker player's bet, trying to play him heads-up (one on one) by making it expensive for any other players to call.

JACKAL—(N.) Crazy, seemingly illogical player who makes a lot of bets and raises. One of the "animal personalities" used to demonstrate examples in this book.

JAM—(V.) Bet and raise as many times as you can in a particular hand or round of betting.

JOKER—(N.) In poker parlance, refers to the perfect card. "Bonetti hit the joker again."

JUDGMENT FOLD—(N.) Folding a hand on the basis of your read of all the factors.

KICKER—(N.) Highest card with your pair.

LADIES—(N.) Pair of queens.

LATE POSITION—(N.) In Hold'em and Omaha, refers to the player on the button, and the two players to the right of the button.

LAY DOWN—(N.) Fold. "He just made a great lay down!"

LIMIT POKER—(N.) Variations of poker in which the amounts of the bets are preset, in contrast to no-limit poker, where you can bet any amount at any time.

LIMP IN—(V.) In Hold'em and Omaha, to call the big blind bet before the flop.

LION—(N.) Very tough, consistently winning poker player. One of my "animal personalities."

LIVE HAND—(N.) Hand that hasn't been folded or declared folded.

LOCK UP—(V.) To be winning, with no chance of losing.

LOOSE—(ADJ.) Style of play in which you play a lot of hands. "Here comes Ted. Man, can he play loose sometimes!"

LOW HAND—(N.) Hand that is competing for the low side of the pot.

LOW-STAKES—(N.) Usually refers to limit poker games $1–$2 and smaller.

MADE HAND—(N.) Complete hand that is a straight or better.

MAJORITY PLAY—(N.) Term used in this book to refer to certain Hold'em hands, including all pairs, A-x suited, and K-Q.

MANIAC—(N.) Loose, aggressive player who likes to raise a lot of pots. See also jackal.

MARGINAL-PLAY HAND—(N.) Somewhat weak hand that should not be played according to the odds.

MESS WITH (ANOTHER PLAYER)—(V.) Raise an opponent with a weak hand in order to give the impression that you are a wild, loose player.

MISS—(V.) Fail to complete your hand. "I can't believe that I missed my draw again!"

MONEY GAME—(N.) Nontournament game, or side game. Participants in a money game play for cash.

MONEY CUTOFF LINE—(N.) Point in a poker tournament at which a player makes money if he survives that point. In other words, twentieth place if the tournament pays twenty players deep.

MOVE ALL-IN—(V.) Put all your chips into any given pot.

MOUSE—(N.) Supertight player who always has a strong hand when he bets. One of the "animal personalities" that I use to teach you tactics.

MULTIWAY POT—(N.) Hand in which more than one opponent is involved.

NLH—(N.) No-limit Hold'em.

NO-LIMIT—(ADJ.) Variation of poker games in which players may bet as much as they want, as opposed to limit poker, where there is an established betting structure.

NO-LIMIT HOLD'EM—(N.) Often referred to as the Cadillac of poker. Players may bet any amount at any time.

NOSEBLEED—(ADJ.) Metaphor used to describe high-stakes poker in which players can lose large amounts of money very quickly. "Chip Reese is playing in the nosebleed games."

NUTS—(N.) In Hold'em and Omaha, the best possible hand given the faceup cards.

ODDS—(N.) Percentage chance that a player will win a pot.

OFF SUIT—(ADJ.) In Hold'em and Omaha, used to describe cards of different suits, like [A♠]-[Q♥].

ON THE END—(ADJ.) On the last card or last round of betting.

OMAHA—(N.) Variation of poker in which each player is dealt four facedown cards and players share five community faceup cards. Players must use exactly two from their hands and three from the faceup cards to make the best five-card hand.

OMAHA EIGHT OR BETTER (O8B)—(N.) Omaha high-low split. See Omaha.

ONLINE POKER—(N.) Poker played on the Internet.

OPEN A HAND—(V.) Be the first bettor.

OPEN-ENDED STRAIGHT DRAW—(N.) Draw in which a player can hit two different cards to complete a straight. For example, a player with 8-9-10-J has an open-ended straight draw because he will hit the straight if either a seven or a queen comes.

OUT, OUTER—(N.) Number of cards required to make a hand. If any ace is needed to win, then you have four outs ([A♣]-[A♠]-[A♦]-[A♥]). If a seven is needed to win, but you already have [7♦] in your hand, then it is a three-outer ([7♠]-[7♣]-[7♥]).

OVERCARD—(N.) Card on the board higher than the pair you have.

OVERPAIR—(N.) Pocket pair above the common cards in the middle. If the board is J-6-2, then Q-Q will be an overpair. "I swear Layne Flack always has an overpair!"

OVER THE TOP—(ADV.) Refers to situations in which a player reraises an opponent. This term is usually used in no-limit Hold'em. "I came over the top of him for all my chips."

PAINT—(N.) Face card, i.e., J-Q-K-A.

PAIR—(N.) Two of a kind, such as 4♣-4♥.

PHIL'S HAND—(N.) Pair of black nines, known as my hand because I won the WSOP with them.

PIP—(V.) Lose a pot in a very close hand.

POCKET PAIR—(N.) Pair in a player's facedown cards, such as 5♣-5♥.

POCKET ROCKETS—(N.) Pair of aces among a player's facedown cards.

POSITION—(N.) Refers to where a player is seated relative to the button. The names of the positions are, from left to right: button, small blind, big blind, 1 hole, 2 hole, 3 hole, 4 hole, 5 hole, 6 hole.

POSITIONAL ADVANTAGE—(N.) Refers to a situation in which a player sits behind an opponent in a hand, thus acting after the opponent.

POST—(V.) Put up an ante.

POT—(N.) Money gathered in the middle of the table during a hand.

POT-LIMIT—(ADJ.) Variation of poker games in which the maximum bet a player may make is the size of the pot at the time the bet is made.

POT-LIMIT OMAHA (PLO)—(N.) Variation of Omaha in which the maximum bet a player can make is the size of the pot at the time the player acts. Europe's number one poker game.

POT ODDS—(N.) Calculation of odds: the size of the pot divided by the cost of calling a bet.

POT-LIMIT HOLD'EM—(N.) In this game, a player can bet the size of the pot at any time. "There is a great pot-limit Hold'em game at Artichoke Joe's Casino on Friday nights."

PRESTO—(N.) Pair of fives among a player's facedown cards. The name was coined by an online newsgroup, rec.gambling. poker.com (RGP).

PROTECT YOUR HAND—(V.) Raise or bet to eliminate opponents and increase chances of winning with a strong hand. "Johnny Chan knows how to protect his hands."

PUCK—(N.) Button.

PUT IN A BET—(V.) Make a bet.

QUALIFY LOW—(V.) Make a low hand that is entitled to win half the pot in a high-low split game. Usually an eight-low is a qualifying low.

RABBIT HUNTING—(N.) Looking at what cards would have come up, after all players have folded their hands. This is considered bad etiquette in poker, because it slows the game down.

RACK (OF CHIPS)—(N.) Container that holds 100 chips. Sometimes players use "rack" to describe the amount won or lost. "Last night Daniel Negreanu won two racks."

RAG—(N.) Weak or unplayable card. Small community cards can be referred to with this term. "The flop was all rags."

RAISE—(V.) Add a bet to an opponent's bet.

RAM AND JAM—(V.) Raise and reraise as much as you can. "Phil Ivey sure did ram and jam that hand."

RAZZ—(N.) Another name for Seven-Card Low.

READ (AN OPPONENT)—(V.) Make your best guess at what your opponent's hand is; try to determine whether your opponent's hand is weak or strong.

REPRESENT—(V.) Pretend that and play as if you have a strong hand. "Huck Seed bet all his chips representing a flush."

RERAISE—(V.) Raise someone who has raised. "I reraised Steve and he folded his hand!"

RESTEALING—(V.) Reraising a player who you believe is making a steal (he's weak), to try to bluff him out of a hand.

RESPECT—(N.) Believing that your opponent has a good hand and acting accordingly. "I give Doyle Brunson a lot of respect when I play a hand against him."

RIVER—(N.) Round of betting that occurs after the last card is flipped up in the middle. Also, the last card flipped up. "Amarillo Slim is so darn lucky that he catches whatever he needs on the river."

RGP—(N.) Online poker newsgroup, rec.gambling.poker.com.

RIVERED IT—(V.) Made your hand on the river (last card). "John Juanda rivered the ace-high flush."

ROLLED-UP—(V.) Started a Stud hand with three of a kind (trips), such as 5♣-5♠-5♥.

ROUGH—(N.) Low hand that ranks among the worst possible low hands. For example, 8-7-6-5-2 is considered a rough eight low.

ROYAL FLUSH—(N.) A-K-Q-J-10 (ace-high straight) of the same suit.

RUSH—(V.) Term used when someone is winning pot after pot. "Alan Cunningham was on a nice rush the other day."

SATELLITES—(N.) Ten-handed minitournaments in which players put up one-tenth of the buy-in to a poker tournament and the last player standing (actually, the last person sitting!) wins a seat in the main event.

SCOOPING—(V.) Winning a whole pot in a high-low split game.

SECOND NUTS—(N.) Second-best possible hand.

SET—(N.) Three of a kind. This is a very popular word in pokerese. "At the 1999 world championships, Huck Seed flopped a set and won a $700,000 pot."

SET A TRAP—(V.) See trapped.

SEVEN-CARD STUD (STUD)—(N.) Classic American poker game, in which each player is dealt three cards to begin the hand (two down and one up). If the players stay in the hand long enough, they will have seven cards apiece, and the best poker hand will be awarded the pot.

SEVEN-CARD STUD EIGHT OR BETTER (STUD 8/B)—(N.) Dealt like Stud, but in this game half the pot is awarded to the high hand and half the pot is awarded to the low hand (if that hand is an eight low or better).

SEVEN-CARD STUD HIGH-LOW SPLIT—(N.) See Seven-Card Stud Eight or Better.

SEVEN-CARD STUD LOW (RAZZ)—(N.) Stud game in which the best low hand wins the pot (aces are considered low).

SHERIFF—(N.) Player who calls opponents down to make sure they aren't bluffing.

SHORTHANDED—(ADJ.) Refers to a game with four or fewer players in it.

SHOWING DOWN—(V.) Flipping the hands faceup after all the betting is complete.

SIDE GAME—(N.) Nontournament poker game. "David 'Chip' Reese is one of the greatest side-game players in the world."

SIX PERFECT—(N.) Refers to a 6-4-3-2-A low hand—the best possible six-low hand.

SIXTH STREET—(N.) Refers to the sixth card dealt in Stud games, and the ensuing round of betting.

SLIDER—(N.) Someone who moves all his chips into a pot frequently in no-limit Hold'em.

SLOT TOURNAMENT—(N.) Tournament in which the object is to run up your balance in a slot machine—implies that no skill is required, since slot machines involve only luck.

SLOW-PLAYING—(V.) Underbetting a strong hand, in order to lure other players into calling.

SLOW-ROLLING—(V.) Flipping the winning hand faceup, late, after someone else believes he has won the pot. Slow-rolling is considered bad etiquette in poker.

SMALL BLIND—(N.) The physical location for the small blind is just left of the button. It is usually half the size of the big blind. "Dewy Weum reraised him from the small blind and won a huge pot."

SMOOTH-CALLING—(V.) Just calling someone else's bet when you have a strong hand, in order to lure your other opponents into the pot.

SMOOTH HAND—(N.) Low hand that is one of the best of its rank. For example, a smooth seven low would be in seven-five-low, such as 7-5-4-3-A or 7-5-3-2-A.

SOLID—(ADJ.) Strategy in which you play very few hands. Has connotations of emotional control and soundness of play. "Don't play any hands against David Gray; he's as solid as a rock."

SPLIT POT—(N.) Pot divided in half in high-low split games.

STAKES—(N.) Amount of money being played for. "Lyle Berman plays high-stakes poker."

STAND—(V.) To stop letting someone bluff you out, because you're sick of it. "Russ Hamilton called him, feeling it was time to make a stand!"

STREET—(N.) Refers to one complete round of betting, including the card that was dealt preceding the betting. "Monsieur Matloubi plays fifth street really well."

STEAL THE BLINDS—(V.) In Hold'em on the first round of betting, to make a raise trying to make the blind hands fold, thus winning the pot immediately. "Men 'the Master' Nguyen kept stealing my blinds today."

STRAIGHT—(N.) Five cards in a row, such as A-2-3-4-5 or 7-8-9-10-J.

STRAIGHT DRAW—(N.) Refers to a situation in which you need two different cards that will make you a straight. For example, if you have 4-5-6-7, then you need an eight or a three to complete a straight.

STRAIGHT FLUSH—(N.) Five cards in a row all of the same suit, such as 3♠-4♠-5♠-6♠-7♠ or 8♥-9♥-10♥-J♥-Q♥.

STONE-COLD BLUFF—(V.) To bluff having a very weak hand and no draw at all. "I can't believe that Meng La was on a stone-cold bluff again."

STUD—(N.) Popular term for Seven-Card Stud.

SUCKING WIND—(V.) Refers to times when someone is just plain unlucky. You seem to miss your drawing hands, and your opponents seem to hit theirs.

SUIT—(N.) Symbol appearing next to the number on each card. The lowest suit is clubs, followed by diamonds, hearts, and spades. The letters c-d-h-s, the correct order of suits in breaking a tie, are in alphabetical order, lowest letter equaling lowest card.

SUITED—(ADJ.) In Hold'em, term used when your two hole cards are of the same suit, such as 10♥-K♥. In Stud, term used when your three starting cards are all of the same suit, such as

($7\diamondsuit$-$8\diamondsuit$) $K\diamondsuit$. In Omaha, term used when two of your four cards are of the same suit, such as $7\diamondsuit$-$7\clubsuit$-$9\heartsuit$-$J\diamondsuit$.

SUITED CONNECTORS—(N.) Term used for a suited hand that also runs in sequence, such as ($5\clubsuit$ $6\clubsuit$) $7\clubsuit$, $10\diamondsuit$-$J\diamondsuit$, or $9\clubsuit$-$10\clubsuit$-$K\clubsuit$-$K\heartsuit$.

SUPERTIGHT—(ADV.) Term used when you play only a few select hands. For example, in Hold'em you may decide to play only my "top ten" hands.

SWING—(N.) Roller-coaster ride that your chips may take on any given day when you play poker. "I watched Bobby Baldwin take a $450,000 swing yesterday. He went from $100,000 loser to $350,000 winner."

TABLE IMAGE—(ADJ.) Refers to the way the other players at the table view you. "Dave 'Devilfish' Ulliott had a really fast and loose table image today."

TAKING ONE CARD OFF—(V.) Calling a bet or bets in order to see one more card—it's implied that if the next card doesn't help you, you'll fold.

TAKING TWO CARDS OFF—(V.) Calling a bet or bets with the intent of seeing two more cards.

TEXAS HOLD'EM—(N.) See Hold'em.

THREE-BETTING—(V.) Making it three bets to go—raising when it's already two bets to go. "Hans 'Tuna' Lund kept three-betting me all day long."

THREE-CARD WHEEL—(N.) Having three wheel cards (A-2-3-4-5) in your hand.

THREE OF A KIND—(N.) Three cards of the same rank, such as $2\heartsuit$-$2\spadesuit$-$2\clubsuit$ or $7\heartsuit$-$7\diamondsuit$-$7\clubsuit$. Commonly referred to as "trips."

TIGHT—(ADV.) Poker strategy in which you are very selective in choosing hands to play; this causes you to play very few hands. "John Inashima plays so tight that I knew he had my hand beat."

TILT—(V.) Term used when someone is playing far too many hands because he's emotionally unbalanced. "In the 1993 World Championships, I tilted off my last $100,000."

TOOTHPICK PRINCIPLE—(N.) Idea that you can start with a tiny amount of money in a poker game and end up with a small fortune. "Surrindar Sunar started with a toothpick and ended up with a lumberyard!"

TOP KICKER—(N.) Best possible high card that goes with your pair. For example, with a board of 5-6-A, having A-K in the hole would yield top pair (aces) and top kicker (the king).

TOP PAIR—(N.) Pair of the highest community cards on the board. If the board is J-6-2, a pair of jacks would be top pair. "I had top pair, but I lost to Stu Ungar, who had top pair with an ace kicker."

"TOP TEN" HANDS—(N.) My top ten Hold'em hands: A-A, K-K, Q-Q, A-K, J-J, 10-10, 9-9, 8-8, 7-7, and A-Q.

TRAP (SET A TRAP)—(V.) To try to trick an opponent into thinking you have a weak hand when in fact you have a powerful hand. To cleverly disguise your hand, causing your opponent to call you. "John Bonetti really trapped him on that hand."

TREYS—(N.) Pocket threes.

TRICKY—(ADJ.) Playing hands in unorthodox ways to confuse your opponents. "Toto Leonidas is so tricky that I never know what he has!"

TRIPS—(N.) Common term for three of a kind.

TURN (THE TURN)—(N., V.) In Hold'em and Omaha, the fourth card and the action after the fourth card is turned up.

"Simon 'Aces' Trumper always seems to catch the perfect card on the turn against me!" "I bet on the turn every pot, but no one ever called me."

TURNED IT—(V.) Made a hand on the fourth card. "Tony Dee turned a full house and won a big pot."

UNDERPAIR—(N.) Pair underneath the board. For example, you have 5-5 in your hand and the board is J-8-7.

UNDER THE GUN—(N.) Position of the player directly to the left of the big blind.

UP CARD—(N.) In Stud games, card that you're dealt faceup.

VALUE BETTING—(V.) Making a bet in the belief that you'll win money with slightly more than you'll lose money with. A bet that you may well lose, but you believe the chances are you will win.

WHEEL—(N.) Common term for the best possible low hand, 5-4-3-2-A.

WILD CARD—(N.) Card that you may change to any other card in the deck.

WORLD SERIES OF POKER (WSOP)—(N.) Roughly 33 poker tournaments, the last of which is a $10,000 buy-in event called the World Championships of Poker. The WSOP is the biggest and most prestigious series of poker tournaments in the world.

WRAP—(N.) In Omaha, four consecutive cards in your starting hand, such as 10-J-Q-K. In Omaha, a wrap straight draw.

WRAP STRAIGHT DRAW—(N.) Straight draw in which at least three different cards make your straight. For example, with a hand of 8-10-J-K and a flop of 7-9-Q, you would be able to make a straight if a six, eight, ten, jack, or king came up—this example shows one of the biggest wrap straight draws possible.

WSOP—(N.) World Series of Poker.

ZONE—(N.) Almost mythical place where you're reading players perfectly and making all the right moves. "Phil was in the zone when he won at the World Series of Poker."

Index

table image, 85, 102, 383
table stakes, 132
Taj Mahal (Atlantic City), 5, 75, 108–9, 155,
    264, 267, 283
"taking one card off," 326
Texas Hold'em, see Hold'em
three bet theory, 77–79, 81–82, 87–88, 383
three-wheel-card theory, 218–20, 383
tight, 28, 383–84
tilt, 48, 105, 124, 384
Tomko, Dewey, 135
toothpick principle, 231–32, 384
Top Ten Hands, 29, 30–32, 31, 46–48,
    384
    A-K situation in, 50–55
    basic premise in playing, 35
    examples, 44–55, 60–64
    extending play beyond, 72–73
    folding and, 46–48, 58–59, 60, 68–70
    in fourth street, 56–62
    in NLH, 138, 140–41
    in online poker, 344
    and playing the flop, 40–43
    pocket aces in, 38–39
    pocket jacks in, 39–40
    pot odds and, 62–63
    protecting your hand and, 56–58, 61–62
    raising with, 35–36
    river and, 62–70
    in small blind, 36–37
    in tournament play, 167, 174–75
    vs. jackal, 37–38
    vs. mouse, 38
tournament strategy, 162–75
    aggressive play, 165–66
    money-cutoff line in, 168–69
    psychological advantage in, 174
    satellite events and, 172–73
    smooth-calling, 171–72
    stealing the blinds in, 167–69, 174
    surviving and, 169–70, 174–75
    tight play, 166–67
    Top Ten Hands only, 167, 174–75
    trapping in, 171–72
    WSOP and, 163–64
trapping, 73, 115, 150, 205, 384
    before the flop, 127–28
    on the flop, 129
    in NLH, 140–41
    in Razz, 300–304
    in Seven-Card Stud Eight or Better, 323–24,
        333
    in tournament play, 171–72

Travel Channel, 135, 163, 357
trips (three of a kind), 68, 105, 286, 354, 384
Trumper, Simon "Aces," 385
turn, 16, 384–85
    see also fourth street
two-handed (heads-up), theory, 346–48
two pair, 354
Tyler, Wayne, 373

Ulliott, Dave "Devilfish," 159–60, 383
UltimateBet.com (UB), 37, 44, 338, 339–40, 350
Ultimate Poker Classic, 360
up card, 260, 269, 284–85, 385
    in Razz, 294–95, 296, 298
    see also door card
U.S. Poker Championships, 360
    of 1997, 283–84
    of 2001, 108–9
U.S. Poker Open of, 1997, 75–76

Vahedi, Amir, 159
value bet, 66, 130, 385
Varkonyi, Robert, 162

Wall of Champions, 163
wheel, 192, 290, 315, 333, 385
Wight, David "Porkchop," 339
Wisconsin, University of, 26–28
World Championships of 2001, 24, 200
World Poker Finals, 42, 360
World Poker Open Events, 359
World Poker Tour (WPT), 357, 359
World Series of Poker (WSOP), ix, 6–7, 51,
    291–92, 356, 357, 361–64, 385, 386
    of 1989, 135, 147
    of 1991, 75, 173
    of 1994, 93–95
    of 1996, 127–28, 223
    of 1999, 338
    of 2000, 231, 338
    of 2001, 134–35, 148–52, 156–57, 200, 231,
        338–39
    of 2002, 162–63, 303
    events in, 358–59
    final table in, 363
    live Internet broadcasts of, 338
    origins of, 163–64
    playing in, 361–63
    slogan of, 363
    tournament strategy for, 163–64
wrap straight draw, 238, 385

Zewin, Don "Zulu," 335

**Phil having a good time at the
2001 World Series of Poker**

Phil Hellmuth, Jr., voted the "Best Poker Tournament Player in the World" in 1997 by his peers, has won seven world championship poker titles, four Hall of Fame titles (including the championship event), and numerous other poker titles worldwide. Phil has been featured in *Sports Illustrated, Time,* and *Esquire* and has appeared on the Discovery Channel, E!, ESPN, Fox Sports, and ABCNews.com. In addition to writing for many poker websites, Phil also contributes to *Gambling Times Magazine* and *Card Player.* He lives with his family in Palo Alto, California.

You can find out more about Phil at www.philhellmuth.com.